BECAUSE WE'RE QUEERS

to all my militant lesbian and gay friends may I say,
on behalf of the world,
thank heavens for you all.

SIMON SHEPHERD

BECAUSE WE'RE QUEERS

The Life and Crimes of
Kenneth Halliwell and Joe Orton

First published January 1989 by
GMP Publishers Ltd.
PO Box 247, London N17 9QR.
Second impression March 1989

Distributed in North America by
Alyson Publications Inc.,
40 Plympton St, Boston, MA 02118, USA

British Library Cataloguing in Publication Data

Shepherd, Simon
  Because we're queers.
  1. Drama in English. Orton, Joe,
  1933-1967. Critical studies
  I. Title
  822'.914

ISBN 0-85449-090-6

Printed and bound in the European Community by
Nørhaven A/S, Viborg, Denmark

Contents

Acknowledgements

Thanks to the staff of Islington Central Library for their helpfulness; and in particular to Eric Willats, now retired, who had the foresight to establish and maintain an Orton archive before Orton became an industry, and who took pleasure in showing this material to readers. No such gratitude is due, unfortunately, to Orton's theatrical agent, whose manner did a disservice to her late client and whose obstructiveness did a disservice to researchers.

May I thank, with my love, those who helped in different ways at different times: Keith Cavanagh, Richard Dyer, Elaine Hobby, Mick Wallis, Chris White; and thanks to my editors at GMP: David Fernbach and Martin Humphries.

Apologies

Because of its subject, this book substantially ignores lesbians and lesbian history. It addresses itself to the topic of male homosexuality throughout. We desperately need a lesbian history of the '50s and '60s, and I look forward to its appearance. Much of my work will have to be re-done when that history emerges. This book is only part of a story. We can only go forward in unity.

Introduction

I ought to apologise for not having an 'Ortonesque' title. I have tried. I have toyed with 'cock', 'prick', 'willy', even 'thing', 'twig', and 'bokky'; 'penis' was intractable to jokes; and 'dangler', I'm afraid, was a non-starter.

So the title is based on Orton's own words. And that's a guide to what I want to do with the book. I would prefer to quote Orton than try to be flashly 'Ortonesque' myself. Rather than attempt, uncritically, to join the Orton industry I've tried to write something which is *neither* a journalistic account of Orton's adventures *nor* a critical study of a 'modern English dramatist'. The Orton industry makes its money out of sauciness. Orton's plays are often revived because they are comedies with sex jokes. The journalistic interest in Orton comes from his being a 'fascinating personality', which effectively means he was a queer who didn't pretend to be anything else. It is hard not to think that the outrageousness flogged by the Orton industry is a reinforcement of the idea that queers are weird, shocking, even comical.

Orton became a juicy subject for exploitation as soon as he died a gruesome death. Shocking deaths are commercially sound anyway, but shocking deaths of queers have the advantage of acquiring moral status. They demonstrate that deviancy leads to doom. The death has been a stock-in-trade of the Orton industry from the original newspaper reports onwards: 'Joe Orton, the bed-sitter playwright who became obsessed by death and made a fortune writing about it, died violently yesterday.' 'Award-winning playwright, Joe Orton, 34, was battered to death in a "frenzy" of hammer blows by his flatmate, who had been taking "large quantities of hashish".' The 'official' biography by John Lahr is besotted with it; it figures centrally in two plays written about Orton and his lover: *Cock-ups* and *Black and Blue*; it recurs in most biographical notes; the film of *Prick Up Your Ears* begins with it. That death, though, is all too rarely related to the society in which Orton lived, which was (and is) deeply hostile to homosexuality, and through hostility creates misery and deaths of homosexuals.

You may notice that so far I have omitted a name: Kenneth Halliwell. For the Orton industry his status is that of lover – and murderer. Conveniently enough for a society that hates homosexuals the two roles go together. 'Bent sex will end in tears: told you so.' Halliwell is cast in the part of neurotic queen, the jealous burden on his brilliant young lover. This labelling began as soon as Orton's work was taken up by the professional theatre world. When his first stage play, *Entertaining Mr Sloane*, was in rehearsal, Orton went along with Halliwell. The director, Patrick Dromgoole, became annoyed when Halliwell made suggestions about the production. At the time he was brutally dismissed as 'that goddamn refugee from a second-hand clothes shop'; well after the event Dromgoole was still accusing 'that little prick' Halliwell of causing all the production difficulties. The combination of snooty wealth (seen in the put-down of Halliwell's clothes) and aggressive sexism (Halliwell being called a little prick) came to mark the attitudes of many in that world. Rather more simply, the stage-hands referred to Halliwell as 'Mrs Orton' (Lahr, 1978: 198). (Maybe, in hindsight, Dromgoole should have listened to Halliwell because he went on to make – in Orton's opinion – such a mess of his production of *Sloane* that Orton satirised him in *Up Against It* as Patricia Dromgoole.)

Lahr's account is in part based on conversations with those who knew the pair, but in this account there is not much questioning of, nor much problem about, the extent to which his interviewees were already prejudiced against Halliwell. As I shall try to show, statements are written down as 'evidence' about Halliwell's character, without it being explicitly asked how much of that 'evidence' came from a sexist or homophobic bias. And Lahr's biographical version is now endlessly repeated.

My anger about the Orton industry, and my desire to dissociate myself from it, are based on an anger about the prejudice which thinks of queers as weird, says queer love is doomed to destruction and gets embarrassed about the queer lovers of famous men. In writing about Orton at all I am, of course, contributing to the Orton industry. That can't be helped. But I should like the reader always to be aware that the author at the centre of this book, his lover, and his artworks have been for some years presented to us by cultural institutions which are filled with, indeed built on, sexual and political prejudice. Hence I have finished off the book with remarks, some of them personal, about the Orton industry.

Again, I inevitably end up writing a study of a 'modern English dramatist'. And as such I hope this book might be useful to anyone working on Orton. But I don't think such a study can be separated from consideration of Orton's sexuality and the social circumstances in which he wrote. Mine is a study of a 'modern homosexual dramatist'.

My overall aim is to make a reappraisal of 'Orton' from a radical gay position. This involves rescuing him, Halliwell and the plays from the Orton industry. Most importantly it will mean seeing Orton as a homosexual writer within his historical context. This should bring out the elements in Orton's work that challenged contemporary thinking, but it will also show how Orton's thought was limited by contemporary ideas and by his own situation. (Having made the claim to a 'radical gay position', I should here note that I am using the word 'queer' quite consciously in the book: I mean to denote, historically, a *pre-gay* homosexual identity and culture; but I also think that, in principle, the fact of being queer, bent, different, should be celebrated as a positive alternative to the exploitation and brutality that underlie the notions of 'normal' and 'straight' in this world. Gay Liberation surely taught us that.)

As soon as we think about Orton as homosexual we have to look at his relationship with Halliwell. Now while there's seemingly too little evidence to redraft the life story of Halliwell, it is possible to reinterpret the information we do have. This will show how Halliwell *has been made into a villain*; and that this 'demonising' is part of a prejudice against homosexual relationships. I believe that homosexual relationships, and indeed the self-image of homosexuals, are always shaped by contemporary ideas – and legislation – about homosexuality. Therefore I've included large chunks which are quite general in nature, rather than being narrowly focussed on Halliwell and Orton. So too, in order to explain the force and shape of their ideas, there needs to be the information about homosexual history in the chapters where it seems most relevant.

A description of the shape of the book may help to clarify my aims: there are three parts, together with a conclusion. In Part One I attempt to study the homosexual relationship (and please note here that I am discussing throughout only *male* homosexuality). An account of Halliwell and Orton's life together which concentrated narrowly on them would omit mention of all the pressure exerted on that relationship by received ideas about homosexual 'marriage' and homosexual role-play. So I have included a section on 'The Scene', which is fairly brief and abstract but is based on a reading of a number of 'queer novels', as well as some contemporary sociology and sexology books. This material is too extensive to be presented in full here, but it serves to give some indication of the sorts of ideas about homosexuals that were being continually repeated – and, from some accounts, were indeed thought by homosexuals themselves. Halliwell and Orton were living together in a society which generally oppressed homosexuals, and which loudly announced its own non-homosexual definitions of what a 'good' homosexual was and what a proper homosexual 'marriage' was. Before Gay Liberation there were no other *public* alternative homosexual role models, a situation to which Section 28 of the Local Government Act (1988) seeks to return us.

My introduction of Halliwell and Orton in the book's first chapter is an account of their first publicised appearance together, on trial for defacing library books. I am interested in the reporting, which made no mention of sex or their relationship. The second chapter is an account of the relationship as described and interpreted by Orton's biographer, and an attempt to construct an alternative interpretation. The biography, I shall claim, tends to reflect modern society's hostility towards homosexuals. This hostility had a direct destructive effect on the Halliwell-Orton relationship while they lived, and lasts into the modern view of them. From silence to destruction: the course of homosexual love. This is the *context* for Orton and Halliwell's life and creative work.

Part Two focusses on Orton himself, as homosexual as much as writer. My attempt is to describe Orton's sense of himself as homosexual in a world which he found oppressive. He was independent enough to insist on his homosexual image and his homosexual pleasures, but he was also oppressed enough to seek some way of escape. This avenue of escape was offered by the career of writer, a career which could provide social success apparently combined with 'freedom'. Far from being solved, the problems for Orton developed further since, as a writer, he had to associate with the professional theatre world which was run by a social class he distrusted and despised. That class was also aggressively anti-homosexual and seems to have done its best to separate him from Halliwell. The chapters in this part look at the three roles which were embraced by Orton as he defined himself: as homosexual, as young man, as writer.

The second of those roles needs more explanation. A recognisable youth culture developed in the 1950s. It opposed itself to the 'traditional' values of the older generation and created an image of rebelliousness and energy. An association with youth culture apparently offered Orton allies against the rest of society and marked the difference between himself and the established theatre world. All of the self-definitions, with their insistence on ideas of freedom, were beset by difficulties. The freedom was only a pose. Real power and oppression always remained in the hands of a straight, anti-homosexual middle class. Orton's bids for freedom were always eventually trapped.

Part Three moves from Orton the person to his works. Much will have been said already in describing Orton's ideas. Some of this will have sounded negative in Part Two, since to analyse Orton from a radical gay position will necessarily mean speaking of his mistaken understanding about homophobia and his own uninspected masculinity. Thus after Part One's angry remarks about what straight society does to homosexual relationships and Part Two's cynicism about what straights do to a homosexual's identity, Part Three discovers some positives. I would like to make a gay celebration of Orton's artworks as attacks on a homosexual-hating society. But there are major difficulties, particularly with attitudes to women, so I have spent some time thinking about the roots of misogyny within homoculture. The misogyny can be seen to be learnt from hetero masculinity, and inevitably Orton's position is contradictory and difficult. The other two chapters are more straightforward: in one, the plays are seen as distinctly *homosexual* artworks, with homosexual images and desires. The final chapter here looks at Orton's mockery of patriotism and nationalism, but it puts his views in the context of ideas about homosexuals as traitors and contributors to national degeneracy. Many homosexuals were so insecure that they justified themselves within the terms set by their oppressors, declaring themselves good patriots. Orton attacked patriotism, laughed at Winston Churchill's willy.

Finally, there's the conclusion, returning us to the Orton industry. This is what controls how Orton's works are seen and received in our culture, so we have to end with it. We have also to get angry with it because, while our anger cannot resurrect Halliwell and Orton, it can do battle with the heterosexual accounts of their lives and reproductions of their works.

Before I finish I should explain the title. I mean that the 'crimes' associated with Halliwell and Orton should be ambiguous. They were technically criminals because they defaced public library book dust-jackets. In a more major sense they were criminals because they were queer. The punishment for this crime was death. As far as I am concerned, however, being queer is no crime. The real crime is homophobia, an anti-homosexual passion that is eventually murderous. The book begins with an account of a trial for one crime, involving library books. It ends with the charge that another crime has been committed, against queers. That has to remain only a charge. As yet there has been neither trial nor punishment.

PART ONE: PARTNERS

Chapter 1:
The Men and the Scene

1: The Men

Kenneth Halliwell and Joe Orton first came to public attention one day in May 1962. They were in court on a charge of stealing and defacing library books. The magistrate wanted to 'make it abundantly clear that those who think they may be clever enough to write criticisms in other people's books – public library books – or to deface them or to ruin them in this way are made to understand very clearly that it is disastrous' (*Hackney Gazette*, 18 May 1962). The case had apparently 'caused enormous concern and anxiety to the Islington Council'.

The 'most extraordinary damage' done to the dust-jackets is by now as notorious as many murder trials. The *North London Press* (18 May 1962) reported two examples of damage, the first being Collins' *Guide to Roses*: 'On the frontispiece a picture of a monkey's head had been pasted in the middle of a rose. Referring to a book entitled *Discovery of Art*, Mr Hemming {counsel for the prosecution} said: "On the front, where there should be pictures of eminent persons, there are the faces of cats and a bird has been pasted where the face of an eminent person should be".' The damage consisted of an attack on the beauty of 'nature' and a displayed irreverence towards 'eminent' persons. But Mr Hemming had a third example, decorously omitted from the *North London Press* report: 'In a book on the life of Dame Sybil Thorndike there was a photograph of her sitting on a chair in a room, but the picture of a man's torso had been pasted in front of her face to show her looking at the man' (*Hackney Gazette*). A glance at the dust-jacket shows that she's not looking generally at the man but specifically at male genitals. This is the most openly sexual example, and the most typical one. Counsel's language exhibits the decorum that the dust-jackets were arranged to mock.

Neither the reporters nor the court were interested in the tasteful alterations to the dust-jackets of the Arden Shakespeare texts. This seems to indicate that the offence which worried the court was not mere damage to public property, but that damage's implications. The defacings managed to combine irreverence to Art, irreverence to eminent persons and the presence of sex. The crime involved disrespect for social and cultural authority.

The court reports were silent about sex. There is no hint that Orton and Halliwell might be lovers. Instead both were depicted as unstable character types. In the words of the senior probation officer, 'both defendants were frustrated actors and frustrated authors'. The crime was described as 'childish...prompted by feelings that are unusual'. The prosecutor pointed out that Halliwell had been employed as an actor and that Orton had attended RADA. Enough was known about them to know they had lived together for some time. But there's no mention of homosexuality, only descriptions of childishness, bohemians, people without proper jobs. Also failures. These are categories which can suitably replace the mention of homosexuality.

In their separate ways the two defendants were quite clear about what was going on. The press summarised Halliwell's argument against the estimate of their damage: 'As many as 30 or 60 art plates had been taken from the same book. An Oldbourne book cost 30s { £1.50}. One could get a dozen or more pictures from it and it was still only 30s. worth of damage if one took every picture out.' The argument attempts to prove the fuss about public property was illogical, and was motivated really by a desire to punish weirdness. Orton did not speak publicly. But his explanation for the harshness of the six-month prison sentence was clear – it was 'because we were queers'. In his eyes the precise detail never mentioned by the court was central to the court's behaviour.

The trial shows how 'law and order' cope with what they can't understand. No one explained the defacings as an intelligible attack on arty pretensions and sexual propriety. The explanation was 'discovered' to lie instead in the characters of the defendants, in their so-called immaturity and instability. The process of identifying Halliwell and Orton as social misfits enabled the court to pigeon-hole the criminals even if it could not understand the crime. To have understood the crime would, of course, have meant an unthinkable questioning of the court's own ideas and values.

Although homosexuality was not mentioned, Halliwell and Orton were dealt with in the same way as straight society traditionally handled homosexuals. The 'crime' of homosexuality potentially questioned all sorts of assumptions about social and sexual 'norms', unless the homosexual was himself seen as sick, unstable or problematic. Its image of homosexuality, alongside its legislation, forms part of the method by which straight society deals with homosexuality. The continually repeated ideas about homosexuality are learnt by homosexuals themselves and therefore contribute to the attitudes of homosexuals to themselves and society. For this reason the next section looks at the historical context within which Halliwell and Orton lived.

2: *The Scene*

Any discussion of the lives of homosexuals in the '60s must take account of the social pressures on their sexuality and identity. The male homosexual's sense of himself as a person is inevitably affected by social attitudes and police activity against homosexuality. In the '60s we are dealing with a period when homosexuality was an 'issue' discussed by those who wanted to reform the law that made it illegal in all circumstances. Liberals treated homosexuality as a sort of medical condition: sufferers from it needed tolerance. There were very few public homosexual organisations, pressure groups, newspapers; very few positive homosexual role models. Nobody campaigned under the slogan 'Gay is Good'.

Illegality, isolation and pity all had their effects on the way individual homosexuals regarded themselves. A young homosexual man would have to work hard not to learn that his sexuality was unnatural and sick. Homosexuals who were regularly told that their sexuality was anti-social, dangerous and criminal would be inclined to develop a sense of guilt. Pushed into furtive sex and vulnerable to blackmail, the homosexual learnt to connect his sexuality with insecurity. And always underlying these attitudes and ideas were the very real activities of a police force that hounded and exposed homosexuals.

In looking at Halliwell and Orton we have to remember that very real need for security, privacy and safety from torment. We have to take seriously the force of that ever-present suspicion that one is sick, unnatural, guilty. And that one's sexuality can lead to the betrayal or embarrassment of friends. If these needs and worries are evidence of psychological weirdness in homosexuals, we have to state repeatedly that it is straight society which constructed that weirdness. And having constructed it, straight society blames it.

In the light of this argument, it seems proper to include some quotations and a sketch of anti-queer attitudes before we carry on with the individual lives of Halliwell and Orton:

Button-two dark blue suit, plain navy tie, spotless white shirt and dark brown suede shoes. He was not sure about the shoes. They gave something – he was not sure what – away.

(Martyn Goff, The Youngest Director, 1961)

A preponderantly homosexual drive in an adult and association only with members of the same sex therefore represents some immaturity of development which may be due to a variety of causes.

(British Medical Association, Homosexuality and Prostitution, 1955)

The real music-hall type of pansies are not attractive to anyone. Their behaviour is not meant to arouse sexual desire; it's more like hitting people in the face. It invites antagonism and that's what these people are seeking.

(Gordon Westwood, A Minority, 1960)

'Three times I have been arrested by the same policeman. He told me whenever he sees me, he'll arrest me. Once he dragged me out of a car to arrest me. Another time I was waiting for my affair at a street corner.'

'A detective arrived at the hospital and took me out to the police car although the doctor protested. He said he knew all about me and if I told him everything he'd make it easy for me. If I didn't he said he'd have to tell my mother.'

'...they used my job as a lever to persuade me to make a statement.'

'At the police station I was shown letters I had written to this man. They were quite harmless, although a few phrases could be interpreted to mean that we'd had sex. The policeman told me that they did not want me and it was in my own interests to tell them about the other man. They would move heaven and earth to see that I didn't get into trouble. So after a lot of persuasion and some strong arm methods, I signed a statement admitting sex three times' (7 months imprisonment).

'The police said if I came down to the station, I'd soon be back and it wouldn't interfere with the work next day... I was there for eight hours, never alone for a moment. Eventually I was persuaded to make a statement. It was only then that I realised that they hadn't the faintest idea who the other man was. They asked questions and made up a statement from it, bit by bit. I was a fool to sign it. I told my defending counsel about this but he never mentioned it in Court' (Buggery. 4 years).

'We sucked each other off and then the next thing I know he was trying to choke me. I went out for the count... I was in a terrible mess. My jaw was smashed. I think he must have stamped on my face. I was in hospital for two months. I had to have an operation on my face. The police kept coming to see me, asking who'd done it. They even came to the rest-home where I went next. Just about then another man was caught and at the police station he admitted having sex with me. I gave in then and told them everything' (Buggery. 4 years).

These quotations about the police are all real, taken from Schofield, 1965 and Westwood, 1960. They need bearing in mind when we read stories about queer gossip, queer guilt, queer paranoia. Here is a last one from West, 1955:

When nine men and two youths of seventeen were brought before Evesham Magistrates Court in April 1956 on charges of indecency, a defending solicitor commented that three others who might have been before the Court were facing a higher tribunal. Following questioning one man had gassed himself and another, a married man with three children, lay down on a railway line and was killed. Of those actually summoned one old man of eighty-one was taken to hospital with cerebral haemorrhage before a verdict could be given.

The only good homosexual was one who kept quiet about his sexuality and preferably did not practise it. Practising homosexuality was really only tolerated (by liberals) if it was conducted on the model of heterosexual monogamous marriage. This model governed more than sex, in that a safer existence was only possible if the 'married' homos kept themselves away from queer bars and away from those queers who made an obvious display of their sexuality. The lifestyle of privacy was, of course, more readily available to middle-class rather than working-class men.

The good queer was, in short, one who not only accepted the rules of hetero society but who distanced himself from the activities and meeting-places of other queers. Homosexuals were taught that public displays of sexual identity were unacceptable to straights, and treacherous to other queers: 'the behaviour and appearance of homosexuals congregating blatantly in public houses, streets, and restaurants are an outrage to public decency. Effeminate men wearing make-up and using scent are objectionable to everyone' (British Medical Asssociation, 1955: 16). The homosexual narrator of *Winger's Landfall* (Lauder, 1962: 155) observes: 'much more was at stake, other emotions involved – affection and tenderness as well as desire. Screamers had no such problems. On their superficial plane, their guiding passions were malice, jealousy, and callous, greedy promiscuity'. And the hero of *The Charioteer* observes that camp queers 'had identified themselves with their limitations; they were making a career of them' (Renault, 1953/1977: 131). Consistently, queer novels engage their readers' sympathies with 'masculine' homos who distance themselves from 'obvious' queers.

The repeated narratives in fiction echo attitudes in real life, for those who were campaigning to reform the law against homosexuality said that homosexuals could behave like good responsible citizens, could follow proper careers and exhibit a form of manly self-restraint. Such models of homosexuality were said to be 'well-adjusted', which is to say, adjusted to the values of a dominant heterosexist society. 'Unmasculine' queers who 'flaunted' their sexuality were said to be 'maladjusted', which is to say that their implicit critique of non-homosexual society's norms is not recognised. It is viewed only as a psychological problem of the misfit, not of the dominant straight. Clearly such arguments drive homosexuals into all the quiescence and obedience of the so-called 'masculine' role, and teach them to be horrified by overt expressions of sexuality.

There are a set of negative personality traits associated with the open homosexual; the more open, the more negative. Such a homosexual is seen as a threat to other homosexuals. Furthermore, a declaration of homosexual identity is categorised as effeminate; and effeminacy is connected not only with personal 'limitations' but with a whole set of self-destructive emotions. The queer is taught to be scornful and distrustful of effeminacy, and to be discreet about any expressions of his sexuality. We must remember this set of values when we read that Halliwell was accused of being effeminate, and when we hear of Orton's responses to this 'effeminacy' as it is labelled in his partner.

But it was not just negative traits and effeminacy of which homosexuals were taught to be wary. Any sort of emotionalism or 'lack of control' was associated with homosexuality: 'There are two homosexuals who live on the ground floor. They won't bother you. They sometimes quarrel all night. They are all right except when they are drunk. Then they get noisy' (Wilson, 1960: 35). The vicious trap of this 'emotional' label is that social pressures forced homosexuals into lives which were not emotionally calm or controlled; fear, guilt and insecurity were induced. Yet any expression of these emotions, and any attempt by these means to deal with them, may be taken to be behaviour that had to be avoided, because it declared oneself to be homosexual. So that personal crisis in the lives of homosexuals becomes not just harder to deal with but more intensified, since by being in crisis at all they are revealing themselves to be weak specimens of the mocked stereotype. As we shall see, Halliwell's obvious signs of crisis towards the end produced two effects in Orton: one was a frustration and condemnation of his lover for acting queer; the other was an increased emphasis on his own masculine independence and control.

Homosexuals were taught that when a long-standing partnership was in crisis it was in fact conforming to pattern. There was double-think about homosexual 'marriage'. On the one hand, queers were advised that a 'married' monogamy was the only way in which they would gain a grain of respectability; queer novels are endlessly full of the search for Mr Right. But on the other hand, the marriage was always apparently unstable; it was said to be under threat from jealous queers outside it and from the emotions of the partners themselves: 'The masculine urge for sexual freedom, and the masculine responsiveness to casual sexual approaches, frequently leads to jealousy and quarrels.' In fact, 'something in the *nature* of their perversion militates against lasting love affairs' (West, 1955: 57, 127). So many novels repeat the stories of break-ups; so many homosexuals learnt to believe that partnerships would only ever be transitory 'affairs'. Orton and Halliwell were together for a comparatively long time (for hetero as well as homo partnerships). When their lives became more public, that partnership was pressurised to conform to the pattern of queer break-ups. Orton's sexual adventures were construed as the expected infidelity, to be morally condemned even while they confirmed – satisfyingly – what everyone suspected about homo partnerships.

The real pressure on homosexuals, from police, church, psychiatry, produced a set of mental attitudes that effectively internalised the negative image of the queer. Not only was there guilt, insecurity, paranoia; there was an inability to give a positive identity to one's desires, or even to treat one's sexuality as something nameless. Anti-queer hatred teaches the homosexual to recognise and fear

homosexuals and homosexuality, even in himself. One of the heroes of
a sentimental queer novel has to clarify what his love for another man
is *not*: 'Do you know what homosexuality is? It's wanting to fiddle
with every little boy you see. It's standing on the pier waiting for the
next boatload of sailors to come in. It's giving women an inferiority
complex. It's standing taking peeks in a man's toilet. I'm not like that,
Paul' (Martin, 1957: 128). Comic as this might now seem, it represents
a particular attitude of self-oppression. It's not a million miles away
from those scene queens who muttered angrily that Gay Pride marches
were letting the side down, that homosexuals, one grade lower than
Victorian children, should neither be seen nor heard.

Orton and Halliwell lived their relationship through the decades of
active repression and internalised guilt that I have been describing. To
give proper weight to this historical context is to reject the analysis of
them offered by moralistic heterosexual (and heterosexual-identified)
critics. We need to note that their relationship lasted so long, and to
celebrate that they conducted it in a way which was not modelled on
hetero monogamous marriage. Furthermore, that they were not
secretive about the relationship, nor about their individual sexual
adventures and desires. Moralistic critics condemned the partners
simultaneously for not being monogamous, and for behaving in
public as a pair. This attitude, combined with attacks on Orton's
'promiscuity' and Halliwell's 'effeminacy', seem to repeat the very sort
of language with which dominant hetero society repressed queers.
This analysis of the couple, together with their outlooks as homosexual products of that period, is the subject of the following chapter.

Chapter 2:
Casualty

The popularised version of the Halliwell-Orton story follows closely the pattern of homosexual 'marriage' which is regularly reproduced in queer novels. Their life is made to imitate art: the two male lovers have a mysterious attachment that others cannot comprehend; they do everything together but keep themselves apart from society; they live in a room which is both a refuge and an imprisonment (like Giovanni's room, in James Baldwin's novel); while one makes his career in the world outside, the other becomes prey to jealousy (as in *No End to the Way*); the whole thing ends in a crime of passion, murder and suicide. This is like the moralistic fictional ending which claims that homosexual relationships are always eventually doomed. Only this time it was for real.

This version of the lives of Halliwell and Orton is constructed by the text of the so-called official biography, written by John Lahr. It appeared in 1978 and since then has been constantly reproduced by Lahr and other journalists: the blurb for a touring production of a show based on the Orton diaries describes Halliwell as 'morose and either tonguetied or talking too loudly', with his 'growing paranoid jealousy'. Whoever put together an exhibition of Ortonalia at the National Theatre made sure that the text of Halliwell's *The Protagonist* was opened at a page where one character says: 'we will wreak havoc on one another, you and I,' because it's supposedly significant, fixing Halliwell as murderous, although the script probably dates from around 1950, a year before the lovers met.

It is necessary to speak of a 'version' which is 'constructed' by the biography because the biography is not necessarily the only account which may be made of their lives. It is an interpretation of the facts as Lahr had them, but that does not preclude an alternative interpretation of the same facts. As with any 'history' book, the interpretation of the evidence or the conclusions drawn may be debated and contested. For instance, it can be argued that the biography's attitude to its subjects shows the influences of traditional anti-queer ideas that circulated in discussions about homosexuals in the '50s and '60s.

Halliwell is seen as the jealous monster who destroys the pretty and successful Orton: 'At forty-one, Halliwell was no stranger to horrific death' (Lahr, 1978: 2). Read that quote again...what a truly 'Ortonesque' line, with its grotesque irrelevance about Halliwell's age! It is claimed that Halliwell's effect on Orton was to send him looking for sex in cottages (i.e., for het readers, public lavatories). This is an activity the book finds distasteful and blameworthy: 'Orton died from his shortsighted and indecisive loyalty to a friend' (p.4). (Note that the book can't say 'lover' or 'boyfriend', thus giving a display of something like the 'English prudery' that Orton hated.) The biography openly moralises about queer promiscuity: 'the spectre of death lurked behind his own pursuit of pleasure' (p.33). Tolerance of homos in the '60s was based on the proviso that they didn't flaunt themselves or engage in non-monogamous sex. Non-homosexual writers presented homosex as unstable and self-destructive, which has the effect of policing it (a habit of mind that the AIDS panic nicely fitted into). For the shape of his biography Lahr (and his followers) even use the classic device of the flashback (which was, incidentally, particularly favoured in queer novels). This ensures that you read the whole story in the knowledge of its murderous end, which gives an appropriate effect of doom. Indeed the biography was originally going to be entitled: *Joe Orton: A Revenger's Tragedy*, which 'wittily' (to the 'credit' of the author) fixes Orton into a tragic mould and totally excludes Halliwell's name.

The biography was largely based on Orton's then unpublished diary. This covers the last eight months of his life, and it should be said straightaway that the suggestion of a diary seems to have come from his agent, Margaret (Peggy) Ramsay, as a project for possible publication. Clearly anything written in this way has a very different status from something which is very definitely private. This fact should influence how far we can read the diary as 'sincere' and 'personal'. By contrast, the biography does not seem to recognise that there might be this sort of problem about using the diary as evidence; indeed, the problem of the status of the diary text was worse in the years around publication of the biography because it was then inaccessible to the public. Now that the *Diaries* have eventually been published it is possible to learn more about the version of Orton and Halliwell that is constructed by Lahr's biography. A major feature of the Orton-Halliwell mythology as it is set down in the biography is the (unnecessary and unfair) attack on Halliwell. What might be the consequences of this attack?

A crucial effect of the biography is its reinforcing of the dominant attitude to authors and homosexuals. There's always a tendency in our society to see authors as sole creators of their artworks, as fascinating *individuals*. The partner who helped, discussed, contributed, or simply cuddled, is pushed to the sidelines. (In a small exhibition about Orton at the Haymarket Theatre, Leicester in spring 1988 there were two big photos of Orton, nothing of Halliwell; a reproduction of one of the defaced dust-jackets used in a programme for *Timon of Athens* was attributed to Orton, not to Halliwell and Orton – or even Halliwell alone.) This process becomes especially noticeable in the case of those authors whose sexuality offends non-homosexual society. If a lover can be obscured from view, an author's clear homosexuality can be blurred into an indeterminate 'bachelorhood'/'spinsterhood', about which no questions need be asked. With Orton, of course, we are dealing with a figure like Wilde: an author whose (homo)sexuality is one of the most famous things about them. Indeed, the downgrading of the partner could make Orton conform more to the model of Wilde, where the sexuality is almost acceptable as a personal eccentricity accompanying the wit and charm.

But the problem for those writing about Orton is that Halliwell can't be tucked away, since he insisted on reinstating himself in Orton's history in a way that no one could ignore, by killing him. Thus the writing about Orton-and-Halliwell, which always really wants to be writing about Orton-the-writer, does not so much obscure Halliwell as make him a villain. The effect of this sort of narrative is to transfer the reader's anti-homosexual hatred away from Orton, an unsuitable target since a witty celebrity, and towards the intrusive Halliwell, who thereby becomes a necessary hate-object. Instead of hiding the partner and seeing Orton the writer simply as a bachelor, the partner is labelled as a danger to the writer, and Orton is presented as someone whose sexuality led him into making a fatally wrong choice. Thus he conforms to the tragic queer stereotype, where the deviant sexuality itself is responsible for undermining potential success and causing disaster. In perpetuating this stereotype, the 'official' biography of Orton tells dominant het society something it wants – and needs – to hear about queers.

In his introduction to *The Orton Diaries* (1986), Lahr deals with these points about artists' partners. Possibly he has learnt something from the attacks on the biography that were made by gays and socialists. The author of the screenplay based on the biography, Alan Bennett, had himself raised these issues in the *London Review of Books* (summer 1985). Lahr's declared change of mind about the status of Halliwell is welcome. But despite his declarations, his editing of the *Diaries* still effectively perpetuates the myth about Halliwell which he played a major part in constructing. Before his reevaluation of Halliwell, he tells us Halliwell 'never found himself' (p.12). Then, in the process of 'reevaluation', he quotes Peter Willes: the problem with this is that some of the most aggressive anti-Halliwell opinion quoted in the biography comes from Willes, although Willes' name was deleted – for some reason – from the diary extracts quoted in the biography. Yet the text of *The Orton Diaries* very strongly suggests, several times, that Willes was extremely, almost irrationally, jealous of Halliwell. This apparent jealousy, together with the suppression of his name from the quotes in the biography, should have been presented as a *context* for his remarks, rather than accepting them as unproblematic evidence. But after quoting Willes, Lahr adds in the same tone that 'Halliwell looked old, and irrelevant' (p.19). Thus the hetero man imitates the manner of the closet queen. And this is the problem: Lahr repeats, rather than analyses, what his sources say. He gives the impression that he was close to Orton and Halliwell and hence can speak the authoritative truth about them. But really he is only a critic and journalist who is as open to the faults of his profession as anyone else. To look afresh, and to look as gays, at Orton and Halliwell, we have to read *against* Lahr.

I shall return to these points in the chapter about the Orton industry. My aim here is to focus on the Orton-Halliwell relationship as we can reconstruct it. Let's begin with a brief version of the picture offered by the biography. Apparently everyone spoke of Orton as the successful talent and Halliwell as the unsuccessful appendage, the clog on the bright boy. Terence Rattigan said Orton 'couldn't have lived with him much longer and kept his sanity' – because Halliwell had bored Laurence Olivier in conversation, and gave an 'appalling impression...of Joe' (Lahr, 1978: 34). So Joe, to further his career, would have to be rid of the embarrassing Halliwell. 'Friends', including Orton's agent Ramsay, scorned Halliwell's literary endeavours while they praised Orton's. The divisive evaluation of the two men was continued in the newspaper reports of their deaths: 'Orton was successful. Halliwell was the failure' (*Daily Sketch*, 10 August 1967). The language used by friends and newspapers derives from a learnt social attitude, which frequently recurs in queer novels: the idea that there is an inevitable conflict between successful career and homosexual marriage. In the plot of *The Youngest Director* the hero loses his business career because he won't give up his boyfriend, and in *No End to the Way* the relationship collapses when the 'husband' loses his job. The attitude was a common piece of anti-homosexual prejudice. It is therefore significant that it reappears here as Lahr's explanation of the murder motive: 'Orton did the writing. There was no way to deny him that, except to kill him' (p.37). Lahr's careful detective work leads him to a discovery of one of the stock clichés of the '50s.

The 'friends' interviewed by Lahr are also at pains to make a sexual distinction between the two men. Rattigan observed that Halliwell 'wore a little bit of "slap" ' (p.33); Peter Willes that he 'behaved very much like a camp young man of the '30s. He was an oddity, an irritant' (p.26). An 'irritant': the reverberations of that word go all the way through the traditions of straight (closeted) homo horror at flaunting queens, and presumably it had its effect on Orton. It may be relevant here to quote a man interviewed by the sociologist Schofield in 1960-61: 'It was months before I realised how effeminate he was. But in the end it got on my nerves the way other people always looked at him, so I told him we couldn't go on' (Schofield, 1965: 114). This horrific quotation shows just how far the always vulnerable homosexual *internalises* straight ideas of what homosexuality is – and learns to see as others want him to see. Halliwell's 'ugliness', which Orton had lived with and loved for at least fifteen years, was suddenly 'noticed', brought into being, we might say, by the smart theatre folk. So too his 'lack of talent' and 'effeminacy' were likewise noticed/invented, and said to be an embarrassment.

From the biography I felt I learnt all too little about the people who gave Lahr these opinions: it would have been good to know precisely how these associates were connected with Orton and Halliwell, what their interests were, why they spoke in the language they did. The diary, which Lahr had read, actually gives us much more, and very necessary information. There we find sufficient evidence to make us extremely sceptical about the opinions of Orton and Halliwell's associates. Orton's full-length portraits of such associates as Peter Willes and Kenneth Williams are written with a deal of scorn. The text presents both as classic types of closet queen. Orton is sharp about Williams' self-oppression: 'Sexually he really is a horrible mess. He mentions "guilt" a lot in conversation. "Well, of course, there's always a certain amount of guilt attached to homosexuality." For him, perhaps, too much' (*Diaries*, p.112). Story after story suggests the jealousy of Willes. In particular Lahr uses an anecdote of the two lovers going to a party given by Willes at which Halliwell – as a joke – wore an old Etonian tie. Orton notes how Willes 'cackled with a sort of eldritch shriek. "You're just pathetic! I mean it's disgraceful wearing that tie" '. When Halliwell says he doesn't care about making people angry, Willes says: 'People dislike you enough already. Why make them more angry? I mean – it's permissible, although silly, as a foible of youth, but you – a middle-aged nonentity – it's sad and pathetic'! (p.248). Lahr tells this anecdote to illustrate Halliwell's gaucheness in society, and that's the version Willes himself presents. But the full text of Orton's account of Willes' hysteria offers a couple of very different insights. Firstly, that with unnerring accuracy Halliwell had hit on and sent up the snotty class-aspirations of queens (such as Willes is presented as being); throughout the diary we can see Orton and Halliwell being critical of middle- and upper-class people . Secondly, here as elsewhere, the violence of Willes' responses to those around Orton – and to Orton himself, when he refused Willes' company – would appear to indicate that Willes desired Orton. His possessiveness seems to be expressed in the jealous fits directed at Orton's partner.

A third point needs making here: the diary shows how much Orton values Halliwell above such people as Willes. He later notes that Halliwell 'was still smarting from the "middle-aged nonentity" line. And quite right too. Kenneth has more talent, although it's hidden, than P. Willes can flash if he had the reflector from Mount Palomar to do it with' (p.249). We may overlook this detail, since Lahr – unlike Orton – uses the story to denigrate Halliwell. And once Orton was dead, Willes could get away with affirming that Halliwell was an 'irritant'. But now we can ask, an irritant to what? — to Willes' desire for Orton? This questioning of the authority of Willes' views only becomes possible with the publication of the diary, because in the biography Willes' name is cancelled from the anecdote about the party. Editing, with its control of textual evidence, has a lot of power. Even when he prints the story in the diary, Lahr inserts a footnote quoting Terence Rattigan: 'I'd have liked to go on seeing Joe, but if I was going to have to see Halliwell, too, no, that was too much' (p.248). You may think this footnote entirely irrelevant, but it's inserted to support the Willes analysis. (And finally, a last bit of my 'scholarly' pedantry: when Lahr quotes the Eton tie story in his introduction, he writes 'Old Etonian tie' while the diary transcript has Orton saying 'old Etonian tie'. By foisting a capital letter on Orton, Lahr is displaying a proper correctness about being 'Old Etonian', a correctness that I'd imagine Willes – but not Orton – would admire. Pedantry has its jokes.)

All this said, I can't help feeling that some of Halliwell and Orton's associates have supplied us with a new, more appropriate, name for the biography: *The Revenge of the Closet Queens*. When interviewed by Lahr, they took the opportunity to put down Halliwell and to condemn as doomed the whole relationship. In their statements we can hear the voices of all those frightened queers of the '50s and '60s who felt themselves threatened by the outward display not just of homosexuality but of a homosexual partnership. It was only when the diary was published, with some (though not all!) of the correct names reinserted into the text, that we could see Orton's opinion of some of these people. Lahr's biography not only allowed the closet queens to get away with their vengeful condemnations, it also aided and abetted the secret desire for Orton that so clearly underlies the jealousy against

Halliwell. Lahr suggests that the break-up was caused by Orton's success: thus, 'with a new sense of his worth' Orton could not allow himself to 'interpret' his lover's tears and rages. Where had that sense of 'worth' come from? — from a social world that approved of Orton because he was pretty but not a queen, and was successful at his profitable career: deemed of worth by masculinity and commercialism. Lahr prevents you seeing that Halliwell's problems might be caused by anyone else, because he relates them, in pseudo-medical fashion, to Halliwell's 'nature'. He portrays Halliwell as a confirmed neurotic. And as reader you are taught to despise this neurosis, this 'yapping misery' (p.12).

Despite all the moralising about Orton's promiscuity (and Lahr moralises as much as he accuses the 'loony' Halliwell of doing), the book invites us to enjoy Orton as a sexual being. His prettiness is always noted. By contrast Halliwell is said to be ugly, and in particular BALD. Never has baldness borne reponsibility for so many horrors. The book could even have been titled *The Sorry Saga of Halliwell's Hair*. The insistent and unreasonable criticism of Halliwell's ugliness reads like a symptom of something deeper in the text. The passages describing Orton could be said to contain homoerotic excitement, but this (presumably unconscious) interest is covered up, or deflected, by the rage at Halliwell. The nature of this interest is given away, I think, by the physical, sexual, focus of the attack on Halliwell. As a consequence of these descriptions, the reader's sympathies become involved in the contrasts of pretty and ugly. We are led to fancy Orton and to find it extraordinary that he should want to stay with baldy old Halliwell (the book is also fixated on age). The unspoken model by which the lovers are assessed derives from hetero romance with its ideals of matching partners; the model is not appropriate to real homosexual (or indeed heterosexual) desire. But its function within this narrative is to make the reader almost want the relationship to end.

The biography therefore not only gives importance to, but leads the reader to share, the bitchy analysis provided by the theatre queens. By contrast, a glance at the diary shows plainly what Orton and Halliwell thought of these people and their theatre. ' "Olivier collects young actors like butterflies" someone once said. He doesn't give them parts, though. He has them playing the set' (*Diaries*, p.80). The pointlessly conspicuous expenditure and exploitation that the pair mocked in theatre was of a piece with their hatred of the behaviour of upper- and middle-class people (though in the case of the latter they particularly hated the morality). 'Extraordinary how rude these upper classes can be. Fancy crying out in a rather grand restaurant, "This young man has got £100,000's worth of loot! Tee-hee-hee!"' (p.139). The diary is regularly alert to social class. When Orton is getting angry about the man who is unsuccessfully looking out for a flat for them in Tangier, he reports: 'I said I thought class entered into it somewhere. "The Hon. 'Reg' Allen had no difficulty in letting flats to his own kind" ' (p.120).

There are a number of places in the diary that suggest that Orton and Halliwell worked as a team in their mockery of class pretensions. When Peter Willes showed them a pair of nutcrackers shaped like a human head, they had to guess who it represented: 'Kenneth thought it was Owen Nares { matinee idol, died 1943}. I suggested Dr Goebbels' (p.131). The suggestions can't be innocent: the switch between matinee idol and Nazi characterises what the pair saw as English taste; more precisely it indicates their response to the taste – and attitudes? – of Willes. (On this occasion Halliwell privately described him as 'dotty'; which contrasts nicely with Willes' responses to Halliwell.) I shall be returning to, and enlarging on, these points. I note them here, however, to indicate that the relationship between the lovers and the theatre world was both tense and cynical. Willes claimed: 'I was the only gent Joe ever met... Joe had refinement by nature' (p.131). The remark is both snobbish and wilfully blind to 'Joe's' own attitude to snobbery. Orton did not 'by nature' transcend class barriers; he thought about them, and they bugged him, obsessively. When the theatre queens speak about the lovers, they talk of sex and neurosis but not of class. Yet class was very much the key element in Orton and Halliwell's relationship to that world. Those they despised had the power to offer Orton rewards and Halliwell a cold shoulder.

A further myth that the diary enables us to reject is the notion that Halliwell was always jealous of Orton's sexual escapades. In fact it records his witty responses to Orton's accounts of his adventures. And for Orton the good joke or good phrase had its own almost sexual delight. He rounds off his description of the famous Holloway Road orgy with one of Halliwell's epigrams: 'I told Kenneth who said, "It sounds as though eightpence and a bus down the Holloway Road was more interesting than £200 and a plane to Tripoli" ' (p.106). Of course the place of Halliwell's wit in relation to Orton's sex has been obscured by a myth that wishes to present Halliwell as jealous. So too is obscured Halliwell's enjoyment of sex in Tangier, and indeed Orton's own temperamental reactions to that: ' "Tell your stupid whore to leave me alone," I said, sulking, to Kenneth. "I don't want boys brought to me when I am lying naked and distraught" ' (p.206). Here the joke of Orton's prose is surely against himself, and there are elsewhere straightforward descriptions of his own sulks and irritability. The diary is quite clear that it was not only Halliwell who was temperamental. In recording both the jokes and the author's own bad temper the diary was presumably made to play its own part in contributing, not to the domestic unrest, but to the domestic harmony of the pair. It has its scenes of intimacy, enjoying breakfast or a cup of tea together. But of course most of the prose is taken up with describing an outside world: there's little *narrative* excitement for Orton (or Halliwell) in repeating the familiar details of their private life. And that they were lovers, physically, is often forgotten by the myth. The diary records enjoyable sex between them. What is grim is that these moments tend only to happen after they've taken valium. They needed to relax to enjoy each other. What was making them tense was also destroying their love.

Later on, Orton's promiscuity was a cause of rows. The morning after an unsuccessful evening with two gay friends, Halliwell railed at them and added that 'Homosexuals disgust me!' (p.148). This moment of hatred of his own sexuality is part of a process of alienation which was marked by his calling himself Orton's secretary and wearing an apron about the house. But there is, perhaps, another way of viewing this: Halliwell's calling himself 'secretary' could well have been a joke of the same sort as the Old Etonian tie. Orton's agent suggested he claim Halliwell as his 'personal assistant' against tax; by becoming 'secretary' Halliwell not only highlights the fiddling done by the class they despised, but also how the money arrangements of that class penetrate, disrupt and exploit personal relationships. Of course both things could be going on: consciousness of alienation doesn't stop someone feeling alienated.

Alongside the narrative of Halliwell's 'neurosis' we might place Orton's rage against the snobbish attitudes of Henry Budgen, who was looking for a flat for them in Tangier. ' "It's not the working classes who're likely to misbehave in a flat," I spat angrily at K.H. wishing he were Budgen' (p.124). The two incidents belong together. Halliwell felt the sexual animosity coming from those who wanted, for whatever reason, to destroy the homosexual partnership: for him homosexuality could appear to be the cause of his problems, and he turned his rage against both it and those he couldn't hurt onto the man that he could. For Orton, becoming successful, the problem was how to remain secure among the wealthy whom he yet despised: the powerlessness against them was compensated for by raging against the man they disliked. Both stories show the two lovers responding to and internalising the difficulties of their existence in the world they had entered.

That world was an extremely close one. In the main it consisted of a circle of reactionary queers whose attitudes were sexist and racist: Kenneth Williams described a black singer: 'you should've heard the dizzy cow. Moaning away "bout mah chains" ' (p.85). Such attitudes are accompanied by, and often built on, self-hatred. When Halliwell said in Tangier how he had to discipline their cleaner, he is told: 'How right you are, dear, it takes a woman to deal with a woman' (p.223). That circle imposed its roles, and transferred its own self-hatred, onto the pair. From their friends Orton received confirmations and celebrations of his success, which he needed. But the admiration also served the fantasy of the admirers, by shaping Orton into the pretty star and Halliwell into the ugly failure. In a similar way the pair were shaped by their other small social circle, the cast of *Loot*. But here the relationship of dependence was more obvious: Orton was the author, but it was the actors who made the play live. The actors' employment depended on the success of Orton's play, and Halliwell had no institutional place at all.

There is an overwhelming sense of the smallness of these worlds in the diary, but more than this is the sense of the pair's alienation. However personal the relationship with the *Loot* cast became, the connection always had an institutional aspect (derived from the theatre). So too amongst homosexuals there was a sense of being trapped into a social identity which is alien because created by an oppressive and dominant heterosexual culture. Orton observed that 'Western society pushes people queer who wouldn't be so in the East. There are pressures to conform to the image of the "queer" ' (p.223). Orton wanted to be homosexual without being queer, and he resented the closed worlds which cast him in the roles of queer and success story. The two friends who so angered Halliwell had spent the evening fawning over Orton: 'Their simpering over me was all you can expect from people like that. I saw through it. You saw through it' (p.148). But the ability of both of them to see through this world, and to play games with it, did not mean they could actually escape it. Orton records the advice of his accountants: 'They almost advised me to find a wife and children. Makes tax easier. Solves a lot of problems' (p.115). The world of public success, the world of money, privileges heterosexuality. Orton encountered the pressure at what he regarded as one of his triumphs, the Evening Standard Drama Award. Halliwell (with cynical foresight perhaps) did not want to go to the lunch and encouraged Orton to take his agent. 'On the board it said "Mr and Mrs Orton". Peggy laughed. "I'll be your wife for the afternoon," she said. All I could think of was how embarrassing if, as I'd originally planned, I'd taken Kenneth.' Orton learns to be embarrassed about his sexuality. Furthermore he sees it publicly marginalised: on the television, 'When Frank Marcus announced me as award winner, the sound was off. I appeared briefly with the sound still off and the captions and credits coming over my face. Then the sound came on for the other winners' (pp.57, 59).

Orton was bound into the theatre world economically; furthermore both of them shared many of its ideas (however much they might have hated it), in that neither was a homosexual or political radical, neither sought an 'alternative' or 'radical' gay culture. It was not that such things did not exist (yet), but that they were not part of their dreams. In the diary it is clear that they were as racist, misogynist and deeply conservative as the rest. They were ideologically and economically the inhabitants of a world that simultaneously alienated them. Even in Tangier, Orton noted, everybody 'behaves in a very "Fuck you" sort of way' (p.187).

As we shall see later, Orton's way of preserving his sense of independence in the face of this world was to emphasise his sexuality. Partly this was deliberate shock: 'I read out a line from the judge's summing up {in a rape trial}, "This man was highly-sexed and perverted." I folded up the paper. "It sounds like me," I said' (p.247). But the identification with a rapist expresses something deeper. 'I find lust an emotion indistinguishable from anger. Or, at least, anger predominates when I see something I can't have. I feel I may run mad one day and commit rape' (p.260). These sorts of sentiments come from the closing pages of the diary. It's a tale of frustration that matches Halliwell's neurosis, but is implicitly more violent. The shape this frustration takes derives from Orton's sense of and pride in his own masculinity. A couple of months earlier, in better mood, he notes: 'It was nice to think that before *Loot* and the £100,000, I wouldn't have been such a desirable personage. The Pergola {a homosexual venue in Tangier} had always slightly frightened me. A large bank balance in a gathering of queers is as popular as a large prick' (p.173). His theatrical success gives him social and sexual power; his self-esteem is built on sexual power. It seems that, in writing the diary, he was using his prose to exercise this sexual power, by being witty or mocking of other people's sexual pretensions, including Halliwell's. He could dismiss an 'erotic novel' as 'Not very well-written and so, for me, not sexually exciting' (p.212). There are many moments in which the diary manufactures a clever sentence in order to reaffirm Orton's power over what he is describing.

This use of his own writing becomes competitive and destructive. It is masculinity, as it's socially constructed, rather than promiscuity which is damaging to people. Halliwell was enraged by, and clear about, this masculinity and its writing. The diary records a quarrel in which Halliwell knocks Orton's pen from his hand; Orton reports his accusations: 'I was selfish, I couldn't bear not to be the centre of attention, I was continually sneering at him for only wishing to be masturbated while I was "virile" in fucking boys' (p.222). Halliwell attacks pen and penis; the argument about sex is also an argument about art and social roles. Halliwell was not alone in his criticism, although the myth may have forgotten this. One man, described by Orton as 'a bit effeminate', said to Kenneth Williams that Orton was 'so boring – always talking about himself' (p.235). And Peter Wood recalls: 'I was struck by Halliwell's unselfishness' (p.237). The quarrel about virility took place about a week before they were to leave Tangier. They were perhaps tense, as so often seen in the diary, about returning to the world which was constructing its version of Orton the masculine writer, and which was ignoring or maligning the 'unselfish' Halliwell.

They may have been able to grasp, but they were certainly unable to act upon, the contradiction in their social situation. So they ended up explaining their bewilderment in personal terms, blaming the only targets that were vulnerable – themselves and each other. Thus Halliwell blamed homosexuality itself for the alienation he experienced when the very man he fancied conspicuously simpered over Orton's success. And when Orton experienced rage, but powerlessness, against *real* upper-class figures, he transferred his aggression onto Halliwell. When one attacks the other's promiscuity, when one censures the other's effeminacy, both have learnt to despise the characteristics that straight society ascribed to, and blamed in, queers. Halliwell's apron-wearing was a mocking acceptance of the role thrust upon him by those who admired Orton. But in a real sense, like a wife, he was offered no place outside the private domestic sphere.

Orton as writer was told Halliwell was an embarrassment; Orton as queer was told, by straight society, that effeminacy was a mark of social inadequacy. He learnt, in his rages, to blame Halliwell. 'I found myself saying, "Pull yourself together! There's no need to behave badly" ' (p.99). Thus the 'shocking' Orton learnt to obey the clichés of homophobic social codes, and to apply them to his partner.

Halliwell as writer's partner saw Orton taken away from him; Halliwell as queer was told that promiscuity is a homosexual weakness which disrupts relationships. So Halliwell learnt hatred of Orton's desires.

Before finishing this chapter, it is appropriate to put alongside the remarks of the theatre folk a statement of the contemporary reaction of a young lesbian to the news of the lovers' deaths:

> In one of the quiet, gentrified, residential streets a crowd had gathered at an open door. There was an ambulance, and a sense of urgency as policemen hurried in and out. For a moment I joined the salaciously disapproving crowd, but it was only later, after listening to the news on

the radio, that I realised that the house with the open door had been the scene of Joe Orton's murder by his lover, who'd then killed himself. I telephoned Hazel. I was in tears, maudlin. She seemed angry: 'That's what love's all about' (Wilson, 1982: 148).

In private correspondence with me, Elizabeth Wilson has enlarged on her reaction:

I think I felt an empathy with Halliwell the 'failure'. (I was then trying to write, without success.) The coupling of his failure with Orton's dazzling success does seem to have almost a sinister, parasitical side (I mean, parasitical on Orton's side), almost as if Orton's success depended on his lover's increasingly abject state. It's interesting if Orton's diary covers only the last few months of his life... If he kept this erotic diary *only* during those last few months, then that must be significant – almost as if it were written *at* Halliwell. I just don't think you can read it as an unproblematic text. But I also feel that at the time I mapped the Orton tragedy onto my own situation so that both conformed to the romantic, doomed homosexual affair, whereas perhaps the bitter words of my lover were intended to pierce through that sentimental stereotype.

To this I would only add that most of the commentators on Halliwell and Orton are not only heterosexual (or closeted) but also men. Halliwell was and is treated as a failure at masculinity and commercial artistry; and he learnt to be a casualty. Bless him.

PART TWO:
THE PROFESSIONAL HOMOSEXUAL

Chapter 3:
Orton's Sexuality

This is the first of three chapters that look at aspects of Orton's personal identity. I have chosen to begin with sexuality since this is simultaneously most notorious and most in need of investigation. In particular it is necessary to know how homosexuality was defined – morally, socially, sexually – to appreciate Orton's own outlook and behaviour, and I have spent considerable time on this. The length of this general history will I hope be justified not only for its immediate bearing on Orton but for its contribution to our own understanding of attitudes to sexuality. This is in part why I have fleshed out the points I put down in sketchy form in Chapter 1.

My specific project of investigating Orton's sexuality arises out of a desire to test and question certain assumptions made by Orton's biographer and others. The major area of difficulty is promiscuity. Of this, Lahr says: 'Orton's compulsive promiscuity...showed a need to confirm his maleness' (1978: 147). This sentence has two effects and an analysis of these will serve as a preface to what I want to argue in the whole chapter.

First, the sentence presents Orton as a typical queer – in the grip of psychological and sexual forces that he cannot control. This does a disservice to Orton's consciousness of queer stereotypes. In that he disliked effeminacy (and Halliwell's apron) he was himself the masculine homo. But he rejected the masculine homo's traditional sobriety and 'self-discipline'. For Orton masculinity was an explicit sexual turn-on: he told people he was a body-builder, dressed as a 'working lad' to have casual sexual adventures, did not conceal his sexual encounters. He was angered by the portrayal of queer stereotypes on the stage, particularly in producers' handling of his own work, and hoped that this would change after the 1967 'legalisation' (a very proper, but unrewarded, optimism). Above all, perhaps, he was angered by the naff (hetero) voyeurism of the habits of queers. Once in Morocco he spoke loudly of the physical details of homosex precisely to scare off eavesdropping tourists at another table: 'I want nothing to do with the civilisation they {the American tourists} made. Fuck them! They'll sit and listen to buggers' talk from me and drink their coffee and piss off' (*Diaries*, p.187). (It is, by the way, an apposite irony here that the reprinting of large chunks from the diary in Lahr's biography, and then the publication of the thing itself, enabled straight readers to experience the same thrill at 'buggers' talk' without having Orton's angry voice telling them to piss off.) To conclude this first point then: I want to look at the definition of the homosexual and attempt to explain why Orton may have felt so trapped and angered by it.

Second, the sentence above from Lahr simplifies the reasons for the promiscuity. Maleness, or masculinity as I'd prefer to call it (since we're talking about something culturally defined and constructed, rather than biology) was not seen by Orton as something either natural or unproblematic. His promiscuity was quite conscious and it played its part in defining for Orton his sense of himself as separate both from a world of straights and from the available queer stereotypes. If Orton had always been promiscuous, we have to ask why it only became a problem in the last years. And if he hadn't always been promiscuous, we have to ask why he became so.

The chapter, then, falls into two sections. The *first* surveys 'official' and 'scientific' definitions of homosexuality, its status as medical illness and social deviation. It will also look at definitions of homosexual sex and homosexual love. The section then ends with Orton's challenge to the accepted notions. This leads into the *second* section which tackles promiscuity. Orton's attitude can be related to contemporary portrayals of male sexual revolt, which saw sex as rebellion but always thought of this sex as masculine and penis-centred. Promiscuity can be shown to link with a philosophy of freedom but the freedom only ever seems available to one gender. Orton's position therefore is seen to be both complicated and compromised.

1. The Definition of a Homosexual

Illness

Homosexuality was most frequently described as a 'condition'. It was something like alcoholism or kleptomania. The Kinsey report of 1948 in America had shown that many men engaged in casual homosexual acts. This unpleasant revelation produced a sociological reaction which warned that too many casual homosexual acts might prove habit-forming and thus develop the dabbler into a 'true' homosexual. Homosexuality was hence spoken of as an addiction: 'I want to marry, if I can lick this thing' (Westwood, 1960: 104). The 'true' homosexual was supposedly different in essence from other people; he was moulded entirely and unchangeably by his unusual sexual nature. This is how the liberal Bryan Magee saw homosexuals in the book based on his television programmes, *One in Twenty* (1966, revised 1968). He talks sympathetically of how 'they' *revealed* themselves to him – as if there were some hidden 'thing' to be shown. And later he says that 'in his heart' the homosexual feels alone – as if there is such a thing as a particular 'homosexual heart', an essence shaped specifically by sexuality rather than social environment, upbringing, politics.

To see homosexuality as a clinical case solved a potential difficulty for a society which prided itself on its belief in individual freedom (unlike 'totalitarian' Russians) and yet felt the need to suppress homosexuality. You could thus allow someone to be homosexual, but everyone was meant to know that the condition itself was unhealthy. Similarly, although liberal opinion might have rejected the definition of homosexuality as a *crime*, it was still undeniably recognised as a *sin*. Such arguments appeared on a large scale in the mid 1950s – as soon as the Wolfenden committee was set up to investigate the case for homosexual law reform. Thus, *before* the committee reported, its liberal outlook was subverted by arguments that worked to remove the 'problem' of homosexuality from the jurisdiction of man-made laws and to view it instead as something beyond human legislation, as a natural or metaphysical sickness. The authors of these arguments were judges, churchmen and doctors. The intention, as Lord Hailsham put it, was one of 'shaping the public conscience which is obtained by stigmatising as inherently unlawful an activity which it is of serious consequence to society to discourage and prevent where possible' (Rees, 1955: 31). Similarly the British Medical Association said: 'A public opinion against homosexual practices is a greater safeguard'; the BMA defended the law against homosexuality on the ground that it 'instils in the public mind the idea that homosexual practices are reprehensible and harmful' (1955: 10, 38). Public opinion is not seen here as the *naturally* expressed views of the person in the street (although that person may think of them as natural), but as something to be artificially shaped by the use of authoritative pronouncements and legal sanctions. You invent the person in the street's views for them.

It was urgent to shape public opinion because (in the words of the Study Secretary of the Church of England Moral Welfare Council): 'Men and women do not always appear to possess an intuitive conviction that homosexual acts are immoral' (Rees, 1955: 54). The BMA argued that 'Recognition of the undesirability...of this barren way of life is of major importance, for the adolescent may be pushed one way or another by external suggestion, as well as by an inward drive' (1955: 49). Middle-class liberalism based itself on a belief that 'intuition' and 'inward drive' were natural and private functions in any individual; but moral and medical authorities argued there was a need artificially to shape such 'inner' feelings. And it worked, for by the mid 1960s 93% of the population thought of homosexuality as an illness. (The horrible heritage of that is still with us: the appearance and *publicity* of AIDS have conveniently side-stepped the '70s rhetoric about gay pride, and returned us to the view of an essential homosexual sickness – a view shared even by some homosexuals. AIDS is described in much the same way as Hailsham described homosexuality itself: 'Homosexual practices are both contagious, incurable, and self-perpetuating, and therefore not without their social consequences' (Rees, 1955: 24).

Deviation

Alongside the conception of homosexuality as an illness, which makes it vaguely sympathetic, there was a more culpable image: homosexual practices were 'dangerously antisocial' (Rees, 1955: 58). This has two elements – firstly, indiscipline: 'People who are mainly concerned with themselves and their sensations associate together and obtain from each other the physical and emotional experiences they desire. Personal discipline and unselfishness have little place in their thoughts' (BMA, 1955: 10). Secondly, the homosexual conspiracy – what Hailsham called a 'secret society of addicts' (Rees, 1955: 27). As he develops this point: 'the jealousies and favouritism which any form of homosexuality engenders is ultimately intolerable, and unless homosexuality is thoroughly discouraged these jealousies and favouritisms undermine and disintegrate the whole fabric of social cooperation' (p.31). Homosexuals must therefore not be given democratic rights because their selfish and unfair practices are a threat to the ideals of a democratic society.

In order to be recognised as a good citizen a homosexual must demonstrate his 'unselfishness', which means disciplining his sexual desires to conform to the dominant marriage-based codes of sexual behaviour, or not having sex at all. To repeat what I quoted earlier: 'the behaviour and appearance of homosexuals congregating blatantly in public houses, streets, and restaurants are an outrage to public decency. Effeminate men wearing make-up and using scent are objectionable to everyone' (BMA, 1955: 16). D. J. West (1955) describes how the atmosphere in bars and clubs can 'deteriorate' when they become 'too popular among clients who like to make a public exhibition of themselves', such as 'screaming bitches' and those 'draped from head to toe in black leather' (it's interesting – and useful – to see the leather man categorised with, rather than against, the screaming queen as an obvious queer type, which is very unlike the distinction made today). West concludes that these developments scare off those homosexuals 'who like to keep up some semblance of propriety', and 'give the public a strange idea of what homosexuals are like' (p.106). There at the end is 'public opinion' (this *constructed* entity) being used to control homosexual behaviour, sorting out the proper from the improper. This split between outrageous and sober was used vilely by Masters (1964) to oppose the campaign for a Homosexual Bill of Rights in the United States: he opined that 'interested heterosexual citizens, along with the responsible homosexuals, might wish that the leadership of the homophile movement were in more mature and intelligent hands' (p.114). Behold the liberal trick: homosexuals will be welcomed by the heterosexual community once they prove themselves reponsible, which means opposing all other homosexuals who get angry, outrageous or proud.

The political aim of most of this commentary was to create 'responsible' homosexuals – by training queers to *want* to be what they were told to be, without having to be disciplined by others; in short, to get them to internalise straight society's ideas. When Peter Wildeblood wrote his angry account of his trial for homosexuality in *Against the Law* (1955) he still began by demonstrating his 'responsibility' about his sexuality: 'I know that it cannot ever be entirely accepted by the rest of the community, and I do not ask that it should. It is up to me to come to terms, first with my own condition, and secondly with other people whose lives quite rightly centre upon the relationship between a man and a woman' (p.8). In another equally angry book putting the case for homosexual law reform, *Queer People* (1963), Douglas Plummer (pseudonym) argues that 'the majority of us suppress or control our feelings' (p.26); he speaks of those who come for help to the Homosexual Law Reform Society: 'men who have made no serious attempt to control their lives or to channel their feelings rationally; men who have been weak' (p.100). This is repeated often in the pages of queer novels, particularly those that aim to present the homosexual case sympathetically. Martyn Goff's campaigning novel *The Youngest Director* has his masculine hero preach at length in an attempt to educate his working-class boyfriend: 'Leonard wanted so much to explain that everything he had said was meaningless if they failed to master their own desires' (1961: 62). The greatest enemy in the book – in the eyes of Leonard and the author – is Dave, an evil queer with hints of sadism. We are warned off the flat he lives in: 'The cheap "camp" set-up was typical of many in the seedier districts of London; the disordered sexual lives spilled into even more disordered daily ones' (p.53).

Sexual disorder is not automatically a bad thing, nor need it link with social disorder. But for homos in the '50s and '60s morality, sexuality and disorder were all linked in the very real phenomenon of blackmail, where a mischosen sex act may eventually destroy one's social place. The status of blackmail as a homosexual nightmare came not only from its practical damage. It also gave force to the notion that homosexual desire is always in tension with, always threatening to subvert, one's moral and social status. In Mary Renault's *The Charioteer* Alec speaks about blackmail: 'I'm not prepared to accept a standard which puts the whole of my emotional life on the plane of immorality ... I'm not prepared to let myself be classified with dope-peddlars and prostitutes' (1953/1977: 199) – as if it's all in his own hands to do the classifying! This takes us back again to Wildeblood: 'homosexuals must evolve some form of moral code if they were ever to be tolerated by society' (1956: 19).

The self-imposed discipline or moral code is called 'adjustment': the well-adjusted homosexual will be tolerated by society. Clearly tolerance is a very repressive concept, and it was to be attacked by Gay Liberationists. The homosexual is, for instance, meant to police himself in a way that the heterosexual doesn't. Furthermore, he learns that in him there is this special thing which has to be policed, that homosexuality is bad until he manages to discipline it. The masculine homo learnt to think of the world in terms of those who had self-control against those who didn't, not in terms of homosexual against heterosexual. Moral arguments managed to lump together homosexuality with 'undisciplined' heterosex such as prostitution, rape or paederasty. So the masculine homo saved a lot of his anger for the irresponsible flaunting queens. Thus the concept of adjustment divided homosexuals for as long as 'tolerance' could be bought by the service of policing one's fellows. It's a terrible price to pay, but it's still being paid today ('No effems or limp-wristed types,' say the ads, 'discretion assured').

Love

Once the homo learnt to be well-adjusted, he could be rewarded not merely with tolerance but with the experience of true pleasure. He simply had to learn to recognise what sexual pleasure was. First he learnt that sexual desire other than the heterosexual was unlikely to produce pleasure. Thus Plummer apologises that 'a small minority of us is obsessed with sexual desire which they know to be forbidden by law' (1963: 45). Not merely illegal, homosexual desire usually leads to unhappiness. Everyone said that homosexual relationships were temporary, that it was rare for an 'association' 'to persist longer than three or four years' (Rees, 1955: 26). In his television programmes Bryan Magee said that an all-male relationship lacked the 'anchor' provided by a woman. And the law, apparently basing itself on biology, repeated it: Hailsham said that homos' 'bodily organs' were 'physically unsuited':

> The unsatisfactory physical basis for a homosexual rela-
> tionship...cannot form the basis of a lasting relationship
> physical or spiritual, and this is the end of true love. Its
> necessarily sterile outcome from the point of view of the
> procreation of children also deprives it of the basis of
> lasting comradeship which in natural parenthood often
> succeeds the passionate romance of earlier days.
>   (Rees, 1955: 26)

There are two parts to this view of homosexual relationships: one, that they are impermanent; two, that impermanence is a bad thing. The second does not follow from the first, and if we disconnect them we can open up new ways of thinking about casual sex. But conservative thought in the 1950s doomed homosexuals to a guilty impermanence because they could never produce the evidence of a permanent relationship, namely children.

A more liberal approach conceded that homosexuals could adopt a form of marriage, but it saw the guarantee of permanence as something much more nebulous than children – love. Homosexuals could express their love in a relationship, but, not having all the usual impedimenta of matrimony, they were always – supposedly – open to the temptation of promiscuity. Many people in fact thought the act of homosex was incapable of expressing love and indeed threatened it. A North American homosexual quoted by Leznoff and Westley speaks for many: 'I think if you have sex with a friend it will destroy the friendship' (Gagnon and Simon, 1967: 187). The suspicion by homosexuals of their own sexual acts is learnt from heterosexuals: 'although no one would deny the existence of romantic affections of a homosexual kind, I would myself be prepared to assert that their continuance is only really possible when they do not develop into acts of physical intimacy, in other words, if they remain morally innocent' (Hailsham in Rees, 1955: 27). What speaks loudly in this passage is a heterosexual's defensive, self-repressing, fear of – specifically – the physical act of homosex.

The way to make homosex allowable was to define its context. The BMA provided a helpful vocabulary: 'Many essential homosexuals are discreet and indulge in homosexual practices as an expression of their attachment to a member of the same sex. Some, however, exploit their condition, employing homosexual practices professionally for material gain' (1955: 13). Discreet homosex directed towards one another is good; homosex without a fixed partner, as in prostitution, is bad (note that the BMA can only conceive of casual sex as prostitution). Expression is good, exploitation is bad. Creeping in here is the language of the egalitarian welfare state ideal: to express love for a partner is to treat them as equal; to exploit someone sexually is to create inequalities. For those who have conceptual difficulties (as I do) in distinguishing a merry fuck on the marriage couch from a merry fuck down a back alley, the distinction lies clearly in the context rather than the act itself. It's not that beds are cleaner or squeakier than alleys, but that sex in marriage is part of, and symbolic of, a commitment to a structure which is (supposedly) permanent, secure and above all *productive* – in the 1950s that was important, making children, the labour force of the new Britain. Sex in an alley usually tries not to make anything; therefore it has to be seen not just as *unproductive* but also *unfulfilling* for the people involved (however many that may be). In strict logic the second doesn't follow from the first unless you have been taught that bearing children signifies that you really love someone.

The social structure comes before the sex: 'the family is not rooted in marriage, but marriage is an institution rooted in the family' (Fletcher, 1962: 22). The family functions as an educational institution, but its values are not ' "learned" in any straightforward or altogether rational way; they are actually embodied in people and behaviour' (p.27). This mode of teaching is very powerful because it conceals the fact that it *is* teaching (a lesson that is consciously learned is a lesson that can be rejected). It claims to teach things that are 'natural' and 'common-sense'. It 'provides an "introduction", as it were, to the wider structure of society' (p.28). The family is therefore central in teaching kids that the family-based organisation of society is good, natural and unchangeable, and that kids should perpetuate it by having families of their own: 'the family is one of the most important agencies making for the *continuity of the social tradition*' (p.33). The family, in Fletcher's words, functions like a small model of the welfare state and it brings up new members of that state to believe in and perpetuate its organisation:

> entered into and maintained on a completely voluntary basis by partners of equal status, and therefore entailing a marital relationship based upon mutuality of consider-ation...democratically managed, in that husband and wife (and frequently children) discuss family affairs together when decisions have to be taken, and...centrally concer-ned with the care and upbringing of children – to such an extent that it is frequently called 'child-centred' (p.128)

(where children are the equivalent of the gross national product).

Sex within marriage is good because it is an expression of commitment to this miniature model of the state. This expressive sex is called 'love', defined by Fletcher as involving 'equality and mutuality of consideration' (p.130). The 'modern' marriage relationship 'depends entirely upon free choice and personal responsibility' (ibid). 'Freedom and responsibility': the slogan of a supposedly democratic society. A citizen can have personal freedom in a civilised society, but s/he has to know what the limits to that freedom are, so responsibility has to be learnt. Any freedom which threatens society or deviates from the dominant values may be said to be an irresponsible freedom and rejected. What 'love' means changes from one historical period to another, but it usually retains the sense of a natural and personal emotion. When it is defined in the early '60s as Fletcher defines it, it is seen to validate the notion of freedom and responsibility, and to make that contradictory concept into something 'natural' and personally felt.

Homosexuals could demonstrate their 'adjustment' to society by expressing their love for one another. But this 'love' was firmly placed within a theory of the modern family and the whole social organisation. It offers the prospect of pleasure for as long as certain rules are obeyed. Peter Wildeblood quotes a Church of England report:

> It should be recognised that homosexual love is not always at a genital level. The homosexual is capable of a virtuous love as clean, as decent and as beautiful as one who is normally {!} sexed (1955: 93).

For Wildeblood this is important because it indicates the emotional equality of the homosexual. Nevertheless that 'virtuous' love is tinged with repression. To be beautiful it must be like the love which makes families (which oppress homosexuals); and its beauty is measured by contrast with the implied ugliness of genital sex. In other words this elevation of love simultaneously devalues casual homosex. Thus Bryan Magee points out that it is up to homosexuals to demonstrate to a sceptical hetero world that homosex is an expression of feeling and concern and not a 'dirty act done for kicks' (1966/1968: 14).

Orton Against Love

Queer literature, perhaps not surprisingly, is full of cynicism about this 'love'. To admit love for another man is to identify oneself as queer: the law reformers stoutly declared their capacity as queers to love. But not to declare love does not automatically mean that someone is conservative and cowardly, for a suspicion of love can indicate a suspicion of the whole repressive social set-up that one might commit oneself to by declaring love. So Nicholas in Mitchell's *Imaginary Toys* (1961/1964: 31) says: 'Sex has become a burden because we cannot believe that we are happy until we have experienced Romantic Love.' This can become a torment to the 'sensitive' young queer: 'I was scared of him... Because I was in love with him' says Ian, fiercely condemning Jimmy's reference to 'an easy lay' in Hampton's *When Did You Last See My Mother?* (1967: 10). Homosex is supposed to be both unfulfilling and tainted with physicality; and 'love' is never guaranteed to be real: 'Two people don't just fall in love, and that's the end of it. There are duties to their families to be considered, and their duty to their vocation. And besides, very few people are enough in love to spend the rest of their lives together. That only happens in books and films' (Martin, 1957: 110). Gary, the fictional character who speaks here, has fully absorbed the official line on love between queers: without a family structure it's neither permanent nor real.

Orton made his position on the matter of 'love' plain. In his smashing little television play *The Good and Faithful Servant* he deals with the institutional control over people's lives. The 'firm's personnel lady' Mrs Vealfoy manages the births, deaths and marriages of the employees. The political satire is typically Orton, typically 1960s – an anger about 'public' control of 'private' lives. In one scene Mrs Vealfoy interviews Ray, a casual unemployed 'youth of today', who has got his girlfriend Debbie pregnant. Debbie is a secretary with the 'firm', so Mrs Vealfoy sorts out the problem by getting Ray to marry Debbie and by offering him a job; so he becomes institutionalised and controllable. Mrs Vealfoy tells Ray:

> 'I think what you have done *is* wrong. Not for any religious reason (I'm an agnostic myself), but simply because love-making should be kept for one's marriage partner alone. Outside marriage the act may seem the same, but I have my doubts as to whether anyone derives any real and lasting satisfaction from it. There is no finer sight than two married people making love' (p.80).

Compare this with a clergyman speaking in all sincerity in Hauser's *The Homosexual Society* (1962: 87):

> 'It is not wrong to love one another, whether man or woman. What is wrong, terribly wrong, is to perform a sacred act without reverence and true feeling for the other person. This is why God will see an illicit sexual affair as the misuse of a sacred gift. If people really loved each other they would be content to wait until they were married. If a man loves another man truly that can be no

sin. The physical act is a mere detail.'

Orton mocks the concept of marital sex and 'true' love, and he makes the reason for the mockery explicit. Mrs Vealfoy's advocacy of true love cannot be separated from her institutional power over people's lives. And the life that we note Mrs Vealfoy particularly imposes upon is that of the *young man*. The play forgets about – or isn't interested in – Debbie and her pregnancy. The central interest is in Ray who is sexually attractive because he is irresponsible and vulnerable. The enemy of his sexuality is the older, married, woman.

Despite the play's heterosexual setting, it seems largely aimed at demolishing a habit of thought common among homosexual law reformers. For example, the hero of *The Youngest Director* loses a successful job because of prejudice against his sexuality. This prejudice is shown to be ridiculous not only because Leonard is good at what he does, but also because his homosexual love is firmly disciplined, is true and marital: 'sex could be beautiful, could be a way of expressing love, could provide the most complete intimacy with one other, treasured person' (Goff, 1961: 138). He has learnt the language of the dominant non-homosexual order. Orton puts that language back into the mouth of the dominant order to remind us where it really belongs – Mrs Vealfoy: 'Love-making is a beautiful thing. And we must treat it with the respect it deserves. Physical love is one of the finest ways a man can express his feelings for a woman' (*Servant*, p.80). She speaks to her silent victim Ray. All her philosophising is of a piece with her use of files, intercoms, microphones – devices to impose her and the firm's voice and opinions on people's lives. Sentiment about expressive love is seen to suit the outlook of someone who believes in controlling and institutionalising the individual. For Mrs Vealfoy, 'a regular wage packet', 'a steady job' and marriage all inevitably connect. *The Youngest Director*, as a law-reforming queer novel, argued for the place of homosexual love alongside ideals of business success and family life. Orton's play, by contrast, rejects a society based on the values of business and founded on controls passed off as 'love'.

2: Promiscuity

As Politics
What *The Good and Faithful Servant* doesn't say, but could imply, is that if Ray were homosexual he could not be fitted into the marriage and job structure. Casual homosexual sex rejects expressive love. Orton's attitude may be clarified by looking at what I think is the similar position of Thom Gunn (1962: 24):

> Why pretend
> Love must accompany erection?
> This is a momentary affection,
> A curiosity bound to end

Orton's diary records that Halliwell accused him of being interested only in physical sex, not love. Many people called him heartless.

I want to suggest that this rejection of love was a rejection of a sexual prescription and the social organisation that enforced, and depended on, it. Clearly Orton felt deeply about Halliwell – the problem was what one called that feeling. Finding a name for the homosexual partner still remains problematic within homosexual culture because the words carry overtones derived from non-homosexual culture. To use the word 'affair' is to imply transitoriness, while 'my other half' implies monogamous marriage: neither can appropriately describe the homosexual model. And 'lover' is all too often a non-homosexual word for an illicit adulterous partner.

Orton carried out his commitment to casual homosex by cottaging (looking for sex in public lavatories). His biographer moralises grandiosely about promiscuity as a 'flirtation with death' (which is precisely the sort of moralism Orton opposed), and how cottaging encounters 'confirmed his sense of human suffering and outrageousness' (Lahr, 1978: 32-33). For my part, the tragedy of human suffering has always seemed somewhat inadequately figured forth by a few lads messing about in urinals.

But Lahr's inapposite moralising apart, the debate among gays over promiscuity and cottaging is serious. On the one hand, they are seen as forms of sexual behaviour that reinforce the images of homosex as outcast and criminal. The (supposed) treating of sexual partners as anonymous objects rather than people, and the choice of secret and illegal places for sex acts, are both taken to imply an inability to think of homosex as something dignified, public and innocent. On the other hand, promiscuity and cottaging are advocated as a refusal of the patterns of sex prescribed by non-homosexual society. Instead of accepting the idea that their homosexual desires are the dark impulses which prevent queers from being properly integrated, the operation of these dark desires is celebrated. The clear separation from the norms of non-homosexual society is seen to be pleasurable. This second viewpoint has as one of its most eloquent spokesmen John Rechy, for whom, in a society where sexual norms are maintained by the operations of a brutal police force and prejudiced judiciary, the 'promiscuous homosexual is a sexual revolutionary' (1978: 28). Although Rechy is writing at a later date than Orton, as both writer and sexual 'outlaw' his twin roles illuminate some of Orton's thinking.

For Orton promiscuity was justified by its social and 'political' effects. He suggested that complete sexual licence was the only way to 'smash the wretched civilisation'; he resolved to hot up *What the Butler Saw*: 'Sex is the only way to infuriate them. Much more fucking and they'll be screaming hysterics in next to no time' (*Diaries*, p.125). His play *The Erpingham Camp* shows how the 'forces of impulse' erupt with catastrophic effect when anyone tries to repress them. Orton's views here are, as Jonathan Dollimore (1983) has pointed out, very much in line with 1960s sexual radicalism, which derived in part from the writings of Wilhelm Reich and Herbert Marcuse. Reich saw the patriarchal family as necessary to the structure of social exploitation, which is guaranteed by suppressing sexuality in children and thereby making them incapable of rebellion. Thus to insist on being sexual was to be rebellious. These ideas were taken up by US homosexual underground writers such as William Burroughs and Allen Ginsberg. They were expressed thus in England by Jeff Nuttall (1968: 164): 'The perfect orgasm as studied and preached by Wilhelm Reich, was seen simultaneously as a holy union with the cosmos and a cure for the squares, who, it is assumed, are largely so suicidal because they never get a good fuck.' The queer in *Imaginary Toys* feels that 'civilisation is against the quick blast of joy' and resolves to adopt a 'responsible hedonism' (Mitchell, 1961: 30, 41). Such ideas were in turn taken up by the Gay Liberation Front, with Dennis Altman arguing in 1971 that homosexuality 'represents an assertion of sexuality as an expression of hedonism and love free of any utilitarian social ends.' He quotes Marcuse: 'Against a society which employs sexuality as a means for a useful end, the perversions uphold sexuality as an end in itself' (which is the argument of *The Good and Faithful Servant*); this idea then strikes at the very organisation of capitalism – hence the hostility with which homosexuality is regarded (p.80). Orton said that 'if you have the kind of sexual freedom Lawrence advocated, the kind of corrupted industrial society he detested would automatically be smashed' (*Plays and Players*, 1965).

History has demonstrated Orton to be wrong. Numbers of homosexuals have felt able to be more open in their sexuality, more free in their lifestyle, without capitalism crumbling (although it is true to say that right-wing political opinion has become more obsessed with homosexuals and more explicitly repressive towards them: one *could* argue that attempts to shut them up reveal, among other things, a sort of panic). Up until recent times, in gay clubs, gay businesses, gay bars, capitalism has found an easy new source for its necessary profits; that ease is made more difficult, however, by the extent to which gay commerce is obliged to mobilise against anti-homosexual repression. (But for many lesbians and gay men the capitalist ghetto will remain oppressive in the ways that it organises their sexuality.) Orton was wrong because he was muddled, as were others, about the sexual revolution. Two contradictory ideas are evident in the quotations in the preceding paragraph.

On the one hand, the individual can choose hedonism, adopt a sexuality that defies squares. This is the strategy of 'personal revolution'. It is based on the belief in the freedom of individuals to do their own thing. As such it is merely a version of the competitive individualism that characterises bourgeois capitalist society. Its so-called radicalism is prepared to leave intact the whole structure so long as space is found for the individual to behave as s/he wants. There is no question about what the individual *is* nor why s/he wants what s/he does.

On the other hand, an analysis of how sexuality can be incorporated into the *structure* of capitalism has a very different thrust. Something which is supposedly as 'personally private' as sexuality is seen to be shaped and used by a 'public' economic structure. The personal, far from being separate and individual, is shown to have indissoluble links with the public and political. This analysis speaks of the 'politics of the personal'. It is genuinely radical in that it shows that what 'personal revolution' takes for granted, namely definitions of individuals and individuals' senses of themselves, are all constructed by society. Once we know that these definitions and senses are not so much natural as constructed, then they are seen to be open to change: nature is nature, but construction can be dismantled. For Orton, as for the others, the full radicalism contained in a 'politics of the personal' was limited by the confusion of 'personal revolution'.

Orton knew how he was defined and labelled as a homosexual by society and he hated the repressive attitude of that society. His way of expressing his hatred, however, adopted the strategy of 'personal revolution' rather than a 'politics of the personal'. He attempted to use sex to infuriate his enemies. Thus *What the Butler Saw* ends with a false penis held in the air. The comic plotting has been handled in such a way that the traditional theatrical devices for returning madness to sanity and disorder to order develop instead into further disorder. The scene of rediscovery of kinship and familial relations in comedy usually promises a happy end. Here, in Orton's version of the ending of a late Shakespearean comedy, and in a specific parody of *The Importance of Being Earnest*, the discovery scene confirms that sexual liaisons have in reality been incestuous. Another traditional device for ending a comedy is the finding of the object that was lost. This time it produces before the audience's eyes something they would rather not see – the hitherto missing penis of the statue of the national hero Winston Churchill. The revelation of the penis as it is held aloft marks the climax of the transgression of taboos and the collapse of traditional proprieties. It is the triumphant expression of homosexual rage at heterosexual civilisation.

There is more to Churchill's penis than meets the eye. The combination of homosexual rage and comic penis is not unique to Orton. It can be traced in the culture of the 1960s. As we trace it we shall learn more of the effects of the 'personal revolution', and thus have a deeper understanding of Orton's promiscuity. I shall return to this promiscuity after the small cultural survey which follows.

The Triumph of the Willy

Late in the 1960s there appeared books that used comedy to align the reader with homosexual – or simply anti-naff – feelings against the dominant moral order. For example, Michael Campbell's *Lord Dismiss Us* (1967) is the story of the attempts of the new headmaster of a boys' public (so-called) school to restore 'public school spirit' and clean up 'corruption' – specifically homosexuality – amongst the boys. It's a parody of those latent or sentimentalised homosexual stories of schoolboy life (most famously, Roger Peyrefitte's mawkish *Special Friendships*, 1958), though it is not itself free of the usual guilt, neurosis and death. Nevertheless, the main thrust, as it were, of the comedy is the mockery of the moral horror of the headmaster. His wife, Mrs Crabtree, is comically humiliated by having her fall devotedly for the excessively camp chaplain (who only likes grubby boys). The humour lies in the head's inability to prevent the boys' homosexual adventures. The climax of comic horror comes with a performance of the traditional school musical, which involves boys taking girls' parts – received with randy mirth by the male audience. This conclusion celebrates the joy of the sex-minded boys in the face of moral repression. But it also incorporates – significantly – a joke at boys wearing girls' clothes. Such a joke is basically conservative; and it coexists with the randy anarchy.

Randiness and cross-dressing are seen again in Gore Vidal's *Myra Breckinridge* (1968). Myra, self-styled 'Woman Triumphant', wages her campaign against ageing macho star-cum-businessman, Buck Loner, and also successfully humiliates (and converts to homosexuality) the most handsome straight all-American boy out of those that she teaches. (She fucks him with a dildo.) Myra's whole comic campaign aims to make fools of straight masculine men – 'what excited me was his profound embarrassment, for he has the American male's horror of smelling bad' (p.137). The campaign is conceived as vengeance for her homosexual husband Myron.

Part of the appeal of the book is that it offers the reader a sexual wish-fulfilment, a pleasurable fantasy revenge on a non-homosexual world. By the time it is revealed late in the book, many readers guess that Myra is the sex-changed Myron. The joke is good because you guess the quicker depending on how ready your mind is to entertain ideas of 'deviant' sexuality: if you're very straight you don't guess at all. The book, like Orton's plays, ends with a parodically rosy picture of a macabre reintegration into the straight world – a send-up of the dream of law reformers.

To these two examples of triumphant 'deviant' sexuality, let me add a more esoteric third: Kyle Onstott and Lance Horner's *Child of the Sun* (1966; they are also authors of the Ortonesque-sounding *The Tattooed Rood*). The book consciously tries to reclaim the historical reputation of the Roman emperor Marcus Aurelius Antoninus. Rome is said to benefit from his rule, and his love for his partner Hierocles is heroic and selfless. There are scenes of homosexual utopia when the two sneak off from Rome to a farmhouse they've bought (like popping off to the wilds of Epsom). These scenes are meant to be more sympathetic than the nasty politicking of non-homosexual Rome. But despite its homo pride the book is also shaped like the old-style queer novels. In his youth Antoninus (then called Varius – what a name for a bent hero!) is an effeminate camp queen with a voracious appetite for legionaries. Under Hierocles' influence he learns to be more manly, dresses more simply and becomes better looking – and develops into a more capable ruler, of course. The return of his old promiscuous desires is seen as a threat to his partnership and indirectly causes his death. So there's still the old policing narrative: the only good queer is a manly queer, promiscuity causes destruction, a queer's main problems are with his desires.

Where the book most nearly comes close to the real world of the 1960s, its more militant sexuality resurfaces. For example, Antoninus wants to popularise in Rome his religion of sun worship, a male religion. He plans to affiliate his god with the ancient religion of Rome, the worship of the goddess Vesta. As a symbol, he as high priest will marry the chief vestal or Virgin Maxima. His visit to her is a comic scene, with the laughter working against the chaste woman who is secretly sexually frustrated. She herself clearly fancies Hierocles: 'One glimpse of him, especially the muscled thighs which showed beneath the hem of his tunic and his thigh-bound sandals was enough to disrupt any virgin's thought' (p.195). Antoninus, and the narrative, elaborate on the attractions of Hierocles; the virgin warms to the idea of a marriage which she no longer wants to be merely spiritual. This prepares for the comic climax when Antoninus presents her with his proxy in marriage:

> Antoninus pointed to the youth who strode across the *peristylium*, his thin silk robe moulded to his body as he walked. He was indeed all that Antoninus had

painted – sloe-eyes, sinuous as a leopard, virilely handsome, exuding maleness.

Aquilia took one look at him and fell back in her chair.

Antoninus looked down at the crumpled figure. 'This
time she has really fainted. Aegenax was too much for her'
(p.200).

The reader is invited to identify with the sexy males; the frustrated
woman can't handle the sorts of desire that the reader enjoys. The
physical presence of sexy masculinity has created disorder in and
humiliation of the representative of traditional order (as also happens
in Orton's work).

This book is also close to the 1960s in its description of the state of
religion in Rome: 'What little religiosity still existed in Rome was in
the province of Rome's female population' (p.180). Common in the
'60s was a stereotype of the moralistic woman, seen as a repressive and
conservative force. She was associated with moral control – Aunt
Edna, Mrs Grundy – and specifically with the backlash against
permissiveness – as in Mary Whitehouse's Clean-Up TV campaign or
Vicky's cartoons of Tory ladies. This is the stereotype behind the
Virgin Maxima, and of course behind Orton's Mrs Vealfoy. Now, in
the stories of triumphant randiness, what we might call stories of the
penis rampant, the scheme is to celebrate sexy youth against repressive
order, to pose sexual potency against sexual frustration. But simultaneously the scheme places the male on the side of potency and the
female on the side of the repressive.

There is no representation of potent, rebellious, sexy female desire.
Orton's Debbie in *Good and Faithful Servant* is a weepy typist and Gore
Vidal's Myra is of course not a woman at all. This misrepresentation of
the woman is not so much to do with the authors' sexuality as with the
the particular notion of sexual revolt which is at work here. A brief
glance at a heterosexual version of the same theme shows that
although the young woman is now the central figure, her supposed
attractiveness is formed precisely out of her lack of potency.

In *Candy* (1958, US only) the jokes always work against the
characters who try to discipline their sexuality. The randy Aunt Livia
talks endlessly and openly of her desire for the penis, comically
embarrassing those who are more decorous. Dr Dunlap finds his
attempt to behave authoritatively undermined by the uncontrollable
sex drives of the woman he is lecturing. The book is obsessed with the
penis: its sexual object is the innocent Candy whose altruism always
ends up (supposedly hilariously) in sexual encounters. Candy does not
have active desires of her own, but a vulnerable innocence which is
always exploited. It is neither altruism nor propriety but sex which is

the ultimate reality; and it reappears in comic disorder wherever it is repressed. The book ends in a Tibetan temple which is struck by lightning, so the Buddha's statue collapses and pushes Candy up against a dirt-covered holy man. While the Buddha's nose slips up her arse, the holy man's cock is embedded in her cunt. When the rain washes his dirt off, she discovers the holy man is her father. The tableau, with its shocking relationship of sex and taboo, is very like the end of *What the Butler Saw*.

The difference between the two tableaux is that whereas Orton attempts to undermine masculine authority, *Candy*'s picture of father-daughter incest keeps that authority in place. Indeed the picture revoltingly helps reinforce that power by making a joke out of a form of sexual abuse which seriously threatens and damages many young women. Candy's father may be a silly character, but the heterosexual male reader is offered the pleasure of a final double, and involuntary, penetration of the female sex object. Candy is always seen as the object of masculine desire, and the power and 'naturalness' of that desire are reinforced throughout the book. The penis rampant in *Candy* throws into disorder moral repression, but it *reaffirms* the power of another source of repression, namely masculinity.

Homosexual authors were therefore dealing with something highly ambiguous when they celebrated the penis rampant. The problem can be illustrated from *Myra Breckinridge*. Myra's ultimate weapon against the male is a false penis. When she uses it to bugger her all-American boy victim, she apparently turns against men the symbol of potent male sexuality. The buggery scene works as a specific homosexual fantasy in the sense that it reverses contemporary notions of homosexual 'unmanliness' and effeminacy, and it reverses the mockery of homosexuality. Through the comedy, non-homosexual society's distaste for and disapproval of homosexuals are converted into the hilarious shock evinced by one who is the butt of a joke (or whose butt is the butt). Yet non-homosexual readers find *Myra* funny too. The reason for this is possibly that even while Myra is humiliating men, she is affirming the power of the penis. There is *no* challenge to men from what, classically, men find it hard to cope with, namely the potent desiring female as independent force – most often fantasised by men as the consuming vagina.

The idea of the rebellion represented by the penis rampant is, then, a highly confused one, precisely because of the association of the penis with masculinity. The rebellion is also a reaffirmation of something which is repressive.

We may be able to get a clearer picture of this confusion and its consequences if I say a little about the *philosophy* of sexual rebellion. Popular psychology spoke of sex 'drive' or 'impulse' which was part of a person's (especially a male's) *biological* make-up. By contrast, morality and discipline were concepts learnt from *society*. Of the 'drive', Benjamin Morse (1964: 54) said: 'The strongest need, for the majority of teenage males, is that of being a man, or proving one's manhood both to one's self and to others. This drive, fundamentally sexual at root, may express itself in a variety of ways.' The drive is something that can express 'itself', a biological thing that precedes all social rules. The comedies of sexual disorder suggest that male impulse can never be kept down. Impulse is living, morality abstract: Jeff Nuttall spoke of youth culture and 'the reaffirmation of life by orgy and violence' (1968: 9).

The release of impulse was often connected with the search for 'freedom' in the face of socially imposed codes. This search is related to sex in a rather nasty novel by the 'existentialist' Colin Wilson, *Ritual in the Dark* (1960). The non-homosexual hero Sorme is disgusted by the idea of his own non-existence (!) and has a violent longing for 'far more freedom than we possess' (p.209), which leads him to dissatisfy-ing sexual encounters. The villain, Nunne, is a queer with a history of interest in sadism, a 'lone wolf' type who hates women. He, it is hinted, is the Jack-the-Ripper figure being hunted through the novel. The reason why the book creates a 'thinking', 'existentialist' hero is that he, as a 'normal' man, understands the murderer's 'revolt' against society. He knows the urge to let something out of oneself, the problem of freeing one's impulses (it sounds like potty training): murder apparently promises a sort of freedom as does sex. Loony as this sounds, we might compare the sexologist Benjamin Morse's explana-tion of the adolescent girl who 'desires to assert herself as an individual, to prove herself by an existentialist act akin to the murder committed by the protagonist of Camus's *Stranger*' (1964: 109). (*The Stranger* was the classic existentialist novel.) Or compare it with the sentiments of another novel, John Rechy's *City of Night*, where the hero's 'masculine restlessness' achieves a form of freedom in hustling and where the ever-present loneliness is only fought off in momentary orgasm: 'Life is lived on the brink of panic on the streets, intensifying the immediate experience – the realness of Today, of This Moment' (1964/1984: 147).

Sorme, in Ritual in the Dark, argues that men are different from women. He quotes 'an old Army saying: A standing tool has no conscience'; for men, he thinks, sex is 'a raw physical appetite...as well as a way of expressing love... Whereas, for a woman, sexual intercourse is a climax of lovemaking, an expression of tenderness, not an end in itself' (Wilson, 1960: 3). In a society that spoke of the male being tamed within the family and of sex as the expression of a commitment to marital values, here is a restatement of the male's sexual difference, of his 'drive' seeking its own self-expression and threatening to develop murderous forms if repressed. This is a darker, and more pretentious, version of the comic penis rampant. This is a penis demanding its freedom (whatever that is) from a repressive society. It is a masculine backlash against the caring sharing welfare-state sexuality, the free enterprise penis. Thus all that's best about the West was available to the Russian agent Tatiana in the company of the adventuring masculine hero Bond, the 'wonderful sense of freedom being alone with a man like this' (Fleming, 1957: 1). In the figure of Bond, on his solo adventures, the combination of masculinity and individual enterprise guarantees freedom (as understood by Western capitalists).

To the image of the penis rampant we have been able to add a philosophy of freedom and enterprise. In order to complete this survey, I want to end with some rather more abstract thoughts about the penis as a symbol. These thoughts are necessary because my survey has landed us in an apparent contradiction. In queer novels, particularly law-reforming ones, masculinity was associated with disciplined social behaviour, propriety, success in business, stable relationships. Yet in the last few paragraphs I have spoken of the masculine 'drive' as something connected with disorder, instability, impropriety or murder. How can it be both?

For my explanation I need to use some elementary concepts from that influential science of the inner person, psychoanalysis. It tells us that the link between masculinity and order, authority and propriety is first made by the appearance of the Father in a small child's life. The Father is not so much the biological possessor of a penis as the presence who instructs the child both in the requirements of social order and in the regulation of sexual desire (on a heterosexual model). This masculine ordering presence may be summarised in the symbol of the phallus (in order to distinguish it from the merely anatomical penis). The queer novels' opposition of masculinity to effeminacy and flaunting operates as a reinforcement of the value and power of the phallus.

In stories of the penis rampant, however, the phallus – the image of authoritarian masculinity – is often seen as the enemy. For example, Myra is hostile to Buck Loner; and the emperor Antoninus is hated by one of the very masculine Praetorian guards, who is a member of a fanatically chaste Christian sect. The headmaster in *Lord Dismiss Us*, Candy's father, and the new-found grandfather of Ray in Orton's *Good and Faithful Servant* are all both comic and potentially repressive in that they are seen to be guardians of law and order in the school and family. Against them works the comedy of an anarchic sexual desire, the penis against the phallus.

This conflict is clear in the opposition of Antoninus to his guards or Ray to his grandfather, but what of the 'women' – Myra and Candy? Myra, as I have said, uses a false penis to carry out her revenge: although she no longer possesses one biologically, it is still seen as the most potent weapon. Candy is more difficult: she is portrayed not as an agent of chaos but of innocence and passivity. It is the comic narrative of the book which invites its reader to take pleasure in the operation of the penis upon Candy; she acts as a catalyst who turns masculine figures of order and authority into men filled with rampant desire. This process works even on her father at the end of the book, so that the archetypal figure of phallic authority breaks a supreme taboo (though catering for a fairly common fantasy) by inserting his erect penis into his daughter.

Candy aims to produce in its readers a sense of pleasure in the operations of the penis and a sense of potency in masculine heterosexuality. This pleasure is common to all the stories we have looked at and it tells us why the opposition of penis and phallus is rarely disquieting, if not actively enjoyable, to masculine men. The opposition continually suggests that the penis is something potent and that those who do not have this potency are silly. Furthermore, it insists that the only 'real' form of sex is genital. Pleasure in the operations of the penis rampant is based on fantasy about owning such a powerful weapon and, by contrast, fear of lacking one. To think of sexuality solely in terms of owning or lacking a penis is the lesson that the Father – the figure of phallic authority – teaches the young child. Such a lesson excludes the female genitals as well as all forms of non-genital sexuality. So we can say that the opposition of the penis to the phallus is only an apparent opposition, in that it reinforces rather than questions the lesson taught by phallic authority – namely, that the penis is a source of social potency, and that it is most important to own one.

With these thoughts in mind we can return to Orton's work, to appreciate further its radicalism and its problems. A scene in his only published novel, *Head to Toe*, plays with the relationship of penis and phallus. All the action of the book takes place on the body of a dying giant, and the drifting narrative moves all over the body. At one point some tourists arrive to inspect, as sightseers, the erect penis of the giant (pp.86-87). The scene is more than a random prod at prudish readers. It has the effect of parodying the obsession with the penis in so many contemporary hetero novels: for example, 'Bond hated someone else touching his gun. He felt naked without it' (Fleming, 1957: 187). Orton's sightseers don't gaze at a symbol of the penis but instead look upon the anatomical thing itself. This calls into question the authority traditionally allocated to the penis. The tourists are not admiring an instrument of social control or a weapon for social competition but are marvelling at the thing's size as a biological phenomenon. It is pleasurable not because it promises social potency but because it offers an awful lot of penis. It is not viewed as the emblem of the whole man's power to impose his will on society but, because the tourists live on the giant and therefore cannot see him as a whole man, the penis is seen as an attraction in its own right. The reader who takes pleasure in Bond's gun takes pleasure in the social power of masculinity. The tourists who enjoy the giant penis enjoy it not as symbol but as anatomy. The latter, we might suggest, is the homosexual pleasure.

At the end of *What the Butler Saw* there is the intention of shocking the audience by showing them the replica Churchill penis (the hilarious implication behind this is the existence of a statue of the naked Churchill). Quite apart from the mockery of a 'national hero', the specific sexual taboo that Orton breaks here relates to the display of an erect penis. The mystique of the penis in British society is preserved by the way it is concealed. We are permitted to see the penis symbolised in many devices of social control and images of power – the aspects of phallic authority – but we rarely see it as the anatomical thing in itself. Held aloft at the end of *Butler* it is seen as ridiculous, because it is an inanimate replica of something highly improbable in the first place (the naked statue). The characters' awe when it is produced parodies the reverence for the authoritative phallic control. The penis becomes proportionally sillier the more closely it is connected with the importance and status of Churchill. Orton's joke here is directed at phallic authority. Up to now, most of the pleasure of the play came from the sexual anarchy. Masculine desires led to chaos and confusion. The implication is that the activities of the penis do not produce order and propriety but the subversion of norms.

Promiscuity's Promise

Orton's joking with the penis and the phallus shows him opposing authority but remaining basically committed to masculine sexuality. The literary image of the penis rampant combined male sexual revolt with an existentialist search for freedom. And, for Orton, the image was not merely literary. Promiscuity, for him, promised freedom in that it was the reverse of the trapped homosexual marriage, with its commitment to a social order that he hated.

Halliwell's attempts to claim his fidelity led to more demands for freedom by Orton. The tension at work here can, I think, be likened to a process described later by John Rechy: 'The pressures produce the sexual outlaw, create his defiance. Knowing that each second his freedom may be ripped away arbitrarily, he lives fully at the brink'

(1978: 31). Orton invented false roles for himself when he picked someone up for sex – he pretended to be a working lad. The diary revels in the distinction between the false role – the bit of rough – and the reality – the West End playwright. For John Rechy, who plays a similar game, the split of roles which hustling permits is precisely its attraction: 'On the streets I disguise my feelings, I play distant, tough, a role...as defensive, I suppose, as it is arrogant. I keep my two "selves" apart – the writer and the sexhunter' (p.67). When hustling, because he is paid, he gets a 'feeling of emotional detachment as freedom' (p.153). Presumably Orton, as he created roles for himself, experienced a similar 'freedom'.

I want to suggest that the 'freedom' was not simply a freedom from the demands of Halliwell, but freedom from the smart theatre world he had recently joined. It is typical that he left early from the first-night party of *Crimes of Passion* in order to go cottaging on the way home. He describes the sex he had as being more enjoyable than the party. The sex and the theatre were as closely connected with each other as they seemed distant. For Orton found himself in a contradictory situation. He hated the prudery of middle-class society (and I presume this extended to all those closeted theatre-queers), yet it was that very society which was going to put on his plays, which would give him a public voice and make his career. The problem that he could not resolve socially or economically could be *temporarily* solved in sex. He could act the working-class lad and indulge in a form of sex distasteful (supposedly) to the smart world, yet also keep intact his other 'self', the playwright. Thus the promiscuity offered illusions of 'freedom' from a social problem.

It became a domestic and sexual problem when Halliwell, forced by Orton's new career and friends into *his* role of wife-at-home, started moralistically trying to limit that 'freedom'. (And it should be said that in responding moralistically Halliwell was only using the language society made available to him – sex was consigned to a private, moral space, not spoken of as social and political. Had it been spoken of politically, Halliwell's response would presumably have been different; he was a desperate man, but not silly.)

Cottaging thus gave Orton a temporary solution to a particular problem arising from his career. In saying this, I have to avoid sounding clinical or moral, for that would do an injustice to Orton's attitude to sex. The language I want to guard against is fully present in the 'official' biography, where Orton is shown as 'hounded' by passion, compulsively promiscuous, seeking 'release' in casual sex. Behind such phrases is a conception of sex as something expressive of the inner self, with drives that need release. Orton himself was in no such panic about sex. His diary is not tinged with guilt. His sexual practice shows that he was intellectually free of the ideals of one-to-one intimacy and of 'expressive' sex (as indeed was Halliwell, except when threatened). Orton's account of sex in a cottage with eight other men speaks of enjoyment. He delighted both in his own fictional role *and* in the role adopted by a partner (for example, his account of a scene with a man who takes an explicitly masochistic role). When Orton remarked that the problem with sex in foreign countries was that shared language could play no part, he was not thinking of sex as an 'expressive' outpouring of the real innermost being. For him the pleasure of sex lay in roles and games; he had no single self he wished to 'express' but a series of selves. This is perhaps his real-life equivalent of the casualness about sex shown by the youths in his plays, which we'll come on to later.

It's an attitude that radically questions in many respects the sexual ideals of his own day (and indeed the instant moralism that appeared in some quarters after the advent of AIDS). The problem was not, as his biographer has it, this attitude, but what his new social life and contacts were doing to his lover and their relationship. It was the new society with its attitudes and pressures, not the promiscuity, which tore them apart.

Chapter 4:
Boys, Freud and Fathers

As Orton became more successful, his life became more difficult. On the surface, he was achieving what he had been after for years. At a deeper level there were tensions and contradictions. In particular these were clustered around two aspects of Orton's identity, his social class and his sexuality. When he achieved fame as a theatrical writer he received it from the hands of a middle class that he had spent years despising. With that fame, as a homosexual he entered a world that was either anti-homosexual or closeted about its sexuality (they amount to the same thing).

In the previous chapter I tried to show how Orton's 'promiscuity' was a challenge to some dominant ideas about homosexuality and personal relationships, and specifically how the promiscuity insisted on his difference from the new world around him. This chapter looks at a second aspect of Orton's identity, a second way in which he insisted on his difference. The key idea here is 'youth'. Its importance for Orton lay in its social and cultural significance, for by aligning himself with youth culture at this period he was associating with those who were seen to be in revolt against the values of a dominant order. The youth of the '60s was both sex object and rebel. It was a pose which could allow Orton to be both successful and different, and hence to escape the contradictions in which he found himself.

Just as in the last chapter I thought it necessary to describe at length how homosexuality was defined, so here I shall again take considerable time in exploring the associations of the word 'youth'. All this history-writing has bearing on Orton in that he was a product of a specific historical period. He died over twenty years ago: if we treat him as a modern writer we shall not be able to explain his ideas properly.

A few words in advance about my exploration of 'youth' will, I hope, indicate its bearing on Orton's ideas and, incidentally, explain the title of this chapter. I shall look first at what youth culture represented, and in particular at its masculinity – youth meant boy. Then we can see what youth culture appeared to offer homosexuals, its attractions and indeed its associations. Ideas about 'youth' in the '60s cannot be discussed for long without mentioning the popular theories of Freudians, which were as influential on attitudes towards youth as towards sexuality. Here again we shall discover Orton making a radical challenge to the thought of his own day, and it shows us an Orton who was very much more intellectually astute and aware than he is popularly presented as being. To finish, we have to return to politics and look at what the youth rebellion was directed at, what sort of enemies it identified as targets. For Orton, after all, the attraction of youth culture was not simply the attraction of sexy masculinity but the attraction of rebellion.

Before the wider exploration begins, let's note how Orton himself fostered his association with youth culture. His image-making then affects us now, for writers about him constantly speak of his 'boyish' good looks – although the looks were in fact those of a successful man in his early thirties.

When Orton first met Rattigan the playwright it was at a posh restaurant, the sort of place that has dress codes involving neckties: Orton wore a black leather jacket. The clothing is a social label. In his plays the sex objects are young men, all of them vaguely criminal in some way but more vulnerable than the adults around them. Orton's role cultivated the same blend: he was an unrepentant ex-prisoner, but in theatrical gatherings he appeared as the youthful apprentice willing to be 'advised'. (Fortunately he was in reality too much of a craftsman to take up Rattigan's silly suggestions for *Sloane*; but the chaos of different advice he got for *Loot* made it a right mess.)

Orton's plays exploited the current moral panic about the state of the 'youth of today', the supposedly too-affluent kids who hung around in coffee bars 'looking for kicks'. 'Kicks?' says Ray's grandfather, 'they're very much in the news at the moment, aren't they?' (*Servant*, p.66). When Mr Sloane kicks Kemp to death (a different sort of kick), he is wearing black leather. Theoretically in the play this is the uniform given him by his employer, but its associations are closer to the fetishised gear of the rockers, the classic young hooligan group of the mid '50s onwards. At Easter 1964 mods and rockers at Clacton had the first of what was to be a series of spectacular, and arrogant, pitched battles in seaside resorts. In the original production of *Loot* by Marowitz, Hal and Dennis had mod haircuts and suits.

Orton's use of the youth or 'hooligan' image was not merely provocative, however. Youth culture was seen to offer social possibilities and an outlook relevant to other 'outsiders' in society. The homosexual in *Imaginary Toys* longingly contemplates a society in which for those under twenty-five 'everything would be as free as nature allows' (Mitchell, 1961/1964: 32). A feature of the fictional youth culture created by the older homosexual novelist Colin MacInnes in *Absolute Beginners* (1959) is its acceptance and assumption of sexual variety (a feature somewhat played down by the recent awful film musical based on the book). When youth culture saw itself repressed by parents and family it took up a position familiar to homosexuals. But whereas homosexuals were taught to feel guilt, youth was defiant – and furthermore it was deliberately hedonistic in the face of those who would oppress it. Thus it acquired its atmosphere of 'freedom', which so appealed – often sentimentally – to the homosexual. To examine these ideas more fully, let's begin the exploration of youth culture.

1: *Youth Culture*

The 21-year-old Ray Gosling, a youth leader in Leicester, described the 'youth of today' in 1960:

> The boy stands up in his sexual and phallic dress, a rebel against a sexless world of fear, and from his own he has made gods. In his dress, his walk, in his whole way of life he makes a private drama for the world that failed him to take note of. 'Look at me, look at me and those I, with my money, have defied.' ...The boy stands in the age of the contraceptive as a potent hope. He stands in an age of frustration as a dream lover, a sub-American idol.
>
> The subject is male, in his late teens and early twenties. He was born either in, or just before the last War. His family and his background are working-class. His education was paid for by the State... He is talked about in the posh monthlies. He is mentioned in the family journals. He is headlined in the popular press, and he is analysed in the educated magazines. He has done something. He has moved it... He stands on a stage spotlit in blue, on a street corner in sodium orange, asking for real, for love in an artificial age. He is your son, the nation's hope, the child of the emancipated common man, the idol of a moneyed age, the hope in a world full of fear.
>
> (*Dream Boy*: 30)

The boy is also, we might add, the object of sexual desire. He inhabits a fantasy in which masculinity provides the answers to a frustrated society. The youth culture is separate from and, in consequence, necessary to a sexless world. The figure of the boy is fetishised by the adult media. His new spending power is part of his rebellion and his masculinity. It is defiant, yet full of promise – the sexless adult world waits to be spent upon by the youth.

The new spending teenager was the subject of a tv documentary broadcast in March 1960, *Living for Kicks*. Young people were, in general, seen to consume while their parents invested their earnings in family and home. They conspicuously spent on leisure items and thus apparently refused their place within the disciplined world of work and family. They occupied a new world outside the home and workplace...at least, they refused the *ideals* of the home: many could afford to spend simply because they lived at home. This separateness was called rebellion, even though the rebels were notoriously inarticulate: 'The boy does not understand his new power. All he knows is that they are wooing him. It is the feeding of the line that he is most afraid of. For centuries his people have slaved for them, but he is the boss now. The Labour Exchange wants his labour. He does not have to plead for a job. He has the money. He has the power' (Gosling, 1960: 31).

There is no place for Gosling's youth either in the dreams of old empire or in the socialist promise of a new world. In another article Gosling rejects the reports on youth provision of both the Labour party and Lady Albermarle's committee. 'Club organisers and leaders do not seem to have cottoned on to the mental attitude of young people in a booming Britain' (Gosling, 1961: 3). Youth was said to be 'unclubbable' – it wanted to live outside the institutions provided for it. Thus it was seen as a threat to a society which, as it became more comfortable, simultaneously became more distanced from its young. Horror at the new youth is sensationalised in that reactionary novel by Anthony Burgess, *A Clockwork Orange* (1962) which describes a city terrorised by youth gangs. While at night the older 'middle-aged middle-class' generation is in its blocks of flats watching tv, frustrated youths roam the abandoned streets. This vision is an indictment of a welfare state that can make no provision for its hooligans. A similar horror story is told in the less well-known, but more clearly moralistic *Teddy Boy Ahoy* (1963). The central figure becomes a teddy boy in reaction to his upbringing:

When he walked down the street he imagined the
passers-by staring at him because of the patched clothes
upon his back. Seeing the clusters of teddy boys on the
street corners, he longed to be like them. They were all
smartly dressed. To his young eyes they were like idols,
clean and smart-cut, standing out sharply against the
grubby little back streets that he had known all his life
(p.9).

His hooligan life lands him in a remand home which only has the
effect of hardening him: 'He hated them all. All those who talked with
their snotty-nosed accents. He wanted to kill them. Kill. Clear all the
English countryside of them' (p.46). This arguably laudable sentiment
is meant to be a symptom of a decline from petty crimes and sex to – of
course – murder. The hooligan's reaction to a society which praises
family and social cooperation is to become individualist: 'He wanted
to take his own revenge without getting help from any quarter' (p.73).

The separateness of youth culture was seen particularly, and to
some attractively, in the cult figure of the rocker. The motorbike
which he rides is a promise of freedom, its speed symbolically rejecting
the constraints of a slow-moving everyday life (and in reality it was an
accessible form of transport for those who couldn't afford cars). It is
also potentially an engine of death (given the blindness of most car
drivers) with which the bike-boy flirts to obtain his 'freedom' in an act
of existential 'self-assertion'. The poems of Thom Gunn celebrate this
separateness – 'In goggles, donned impersonality', 'Concocting selves
for their impervious kit' – and also the rocker's sense of purpose in a
world of grey and familiar sameness – 'One joins the movement in a
valueless world.'

At worst, one is in motion; and at best,
Reaching no absolute, in which to rest,
One is always nearer by not keeping still.
                    (Gunn, 'On the Move', 1957: 11)

Eliot George (Gillian Freeman)'s somewhat sentimental novel *The
Leather Boys* (1961) has its two male lovers celebrate their freedom
from their gang by riding out together. At the end, it is his possession
of Dick's bike that enables Reggie to get over his lover's death (as a
result of a gang fight). The novel's final vision describes new worlds of
masculine competition and attraction: when Dick comes up alongside
another leather-clad biker, 'He revved his engine while waiting for the
lights to change. Neither he nor Dick looked at each other but kept
their eyes on the stop light, each accepting the unspoken challenge'

(p.126). The freedom to compete – for many that's what the youth rebellion amounted to. It's a romantic individualism little different from a Tory backlash against the concept of state planning and provision.

The real revolt threatened by youth culture was said to be sexual. In 1969 Gareth Stedman Jones traced the roots of the major, left-wing, student rebellion to the lifestyles of the young working class, who had apparently rejected traditional British puritanism. This analysis seems in fact highly unlikely – and sentimental in the extreme – but it is characteristic of the '60s fantasy of youth's potential. Jones' essay fails to demonstrate where the non-puritan rebellious working-class youth were; it also fails to note that the 'new' sexuality of youth was not so much a questioning of gender roles or a statement of feminism, as a concentration on the male, on young masculine sexuality.

Gosling's dream boy in his 'sexual and phallic dress', the fetishised image of the leather-clad biker at the end of *The Leather Boys*, the obsessive loathing descriptions of young male clothes in *A Clockwork Orange* – 'the wanted boy, the sex crucified boy and the cuddly kid. The girls moved down the hit parade, and in came the Boom for Boys' (Gosling, 1961: 3) – the male body was an object on general display. Jeff Nuttall said that Elvis was the queer boy's pin-up, to which might be added James Dean among others. I distantly remember my grandmother pointing out to me two (rather late-in-the-day) teddy boys with the words 'Look at those pansies.' For her, the displayed male was the equivalent of that other disruption of traditional masculinity, homosexuality. But there's a crucial difference, which we shall return to: the man who is nothing but a sex object is vulnerable to the desiring looks from others, whereas the displayed male is in a position of control. An example: the Dave Clark Five on *Ready Steady Go*; behind them, screens with silhouettes of dancing girls; off-screen, the screaming girls – the real young men on display between silhouetted and disembodied females; at one moment the harmonica player looks across at the guitarist with a look that acknowledges the screams and their role in causing them, but it's not, I think, a look of desire.

The new displayed male is, carefully, not effeminate. In his account of the dream boy Gosling says the boy has robbed an old lady, hit a policeman, had knife fights with his friends. The leather gear of the rocker announces the distance of his toughness from 'ordinary' society. While husbands were supposedly learning to stop being hunters and to express their love 'naturally' within marriage, youth culture was a set of anti-natural poses – as Thom Gunn says in his poem about Elvis:

Whether he poses or is real, no cat
Bothers to say: the pose held is a stance,
Which ... may be posture for combat.
    (1957: 31)

The pose of toughness and separateness apparently questions the authority of the dominant order. Jeff Nuttall, anarchist and exact contemporary of Orton, celebrates youth for showing society its violence: he speaks of 'a biological reflex compelling the leftist element in the young middle class to join with the delinquent element in the young working class for the reaffirmation of life by orgy and violence' (1968: 9). The violent pose replaced political alignment. 'We despise the masses, the Labour Party and the working class,' says Gosling in 1961, while in 1959 MacInnes has the hero of *Absolute Beginners* say: 'Your pinko pals did what they wanted to when they got power, and why should we nippers thank them for doing their bounden duty?' (p.37). The official left had little to offer to youth and its views on 'personal' politics were often highly conservative. Once in office, the cynical behaviour of the Labour party leadership smashed apart any dreams of utopian socialism.

For Nuttall, what lies beneath leftist politics is a 'biological reflex'. In the essay of Gareth Stedman Jones referred to earlier, the explicit leftism of students is seen as a version of gut anti-puritanism. Drives, instinct, sex – all are portrayed as more 'real' than politics. Youth culture seemed to celebrate a separateness or freedom which was 'real' in that it was based on sexual expression, especially on affirmations of masculinity. With these ideas in mind we need now to return to Orton to see their relevance to his life and work.

2: *Orton, Youth and Homosexuality*

In an interview Orton agreed that he was not only 'out of tune with the existing social set-up' but 'with the political alternatives that are usually offered' (*Plays and Players*, 1965). In his notebook he transcribed a quotation from Albert Camus' book *The Rebel*: the quotation comes from a section in which Camus examines Soviet socialism and argues that the search for freedom can turn into a despotism, that rebellion can beome political cynicism. For Orton an alignment with youth enabled him to express his anger about the dominant order without leading him into adopting discredited political positions (such as those of Wilson's Labour party) and without losing his sense of individual 'freedom'. These points should become clearer as this chapter progresses. I want to focus in more detail here on a third advantage coming from alignment with youth – sex.

Youth culture offered a version of male sexuality which was not 'straight' in adult terms, but neither did it reproduce the images of flaunting queen or law-abiding masculine homo which were both circulated in homosexual culture – and which Orton rejected. The tough but sexy dream boy was a fellow outsider. He was the fantasy of a genuinely erotic male sexuality. He was neither the oppressive boring norm nor one of the stereotypes which were so discredited (and therefore desexualised). Some of the most widespread and popular homoerotic images of the '50s and '60s were those in the wonderful collections of rockers, sportsmen and cowboys photographed in the US by the Athletic Model Guild: here the emphasis was not just on the body of the youth, disconnected from social group as in physique magazines, but on aspects of clothing that signified elements of youth culture and on group shots that invoked a world of youth gangs or changing-room horseplay. The great thing about the Athletic Model Guild photos is that they are celebratory; the novels by contrast are often full of dissatisfied longing: when the young homosexual hero of the novel *Aubade* visits an amusement arcade, he 'wished that he were wearing the kind of clothes that would help him fit with these people of his own age. He wished that he could jive' (1957: 109).

Youth culture seemed to offer the prospect of fellow-feeling or even solidarity to the lonely homosexual, for here was another minority pushed around by the nameless 'them' of the dominant order. The sociologist could claim that 'a close relationship between juvenile delinquency and male homosexuality exists at the present time' (Morse, 1964: 128); or, put more erotically, 'young person 1960. Dreaming of being a Boy-God, or being in love with a Boy-God' (Gosling, 1961: 3). 'Dreaming' is the important word. Much of the homosexual attitude to youth culture was a fantasy identification with desired sex objects. The first issue of *Timm* combined queer magazine images with youth pop culture icons: physique and 'art' shots (i.e. with Greek column) of men in posing pouches; boys in leather jackets; a feature on Dave Dee, Dozy, Beaky, Mick and Titch. The first issue of *Jeremy* in 1969 combined play reviews, a gay guide and an article headed 'Barry Gibb Undressed – A Bee-Gee's Wardrobe'. Its editorial is a disguised plea for homosexual toleration under cover of defending ideals of private choice. At the same time it promotes a picture of youthful sexual ambiguity and youthful disregard for stuffy mores, as if youth is naturally tolerant: '*Jeremy* is for people who simply don't care about sex – one way or the other...human nature cannot be regimented and not everybody's need is alike... Morality concerns us all but private morality is the concern of the individual.'

The picture of a liberated youth promoted by *Jeremy* fits with Peter

Burton's autobiographical descriptions of homosexual commercial youth clubs in Soho in the '60s. He says they had more in common with straight mod clubs than with the sober and exclusive male-dominated clubs of the adult homosexual scene. But we can't be too romantic about this picture, for the behaviour of youth in central London may be a special case. Against Peter Burton's story may be placed Mick Wallis' verbal account of petty-bourgeois mods in Cheshunt in the late '60s, who were violently homophobic. The important thing here is not so much the *reality* as the image, the repeated suggestions of homosexuality in connection with youth. It may be seen in the explicit moralism of *Teddy Boy Ahoy*, where the hero responds with disgust to the practices of the approved school: 'One of the boys was getting into another boy's bed. He listened hard, discovering that the same thing was happening all around the dormitory, as if at a given signal. The place was alive with queers. They were practising homosexualism' (Harper, 1963: 75). Or it may be implicit and unlabelled: there's tv film of Jerry Lee Lewis in studio performance with the audience gathered around the piano; included for much of the time on camera is a youth with his left hand resting firmly on the shoulder of his male companion while they move in response to the music; the 'innocent' closeness is definitely physical and has the atmosphere of 'boys together', while girls are really only noticeable in a different shot, often dancing on their own. The scenario may have been set up by a director; but even if not, someone had directed the cameraman to keep that image in focus.

The point about the fantasy identification with youth culture was that it did not depend on a real liberalism. One of the major attractions of the fantasy was that youth was sexy but firmly outside homosexual stereotypes. Its very aggression (including its homophobia) constituted its notional 'freedom'. In this way, I have suggested, Orton the homosexual might have wanted to identify with youth culture because of the role it offered him. But it needs saying that this interest was not simply that of passive identification. He also had a more active, more homosexually campaigning interest.

In Orton's plays, most of the young men are apparently living for kicks. They take a casual attitude to right and wrong and are prepared to be criminal. Now the contemporary moral hysteria about mods and rockers *blamed* the pointlessness of their lives, their living for kicks. Indeed, in 1967 Pamela Hansford Johnson argued that the real cause of the horrific Moors murders (which involved torture of children) was an atmosphere of 'affectlessness'. This was her word for a casualness produced by the attitudes of 'swinging London' and general hooligan irresponsibility. She went on to blame playwrights for contributing to the violence of society, listing among others works by Orton and Edward Bond. Earlier, in 1965, she had parodied the plot of *Sloane* in her novel *Cork Street, Next to the Hatters*. In Orton's play, however, although Sloane is a murderer, he is – like all the other youths – eventually vulnerable to corrupt representatives of adult society (who happily blackmail him). In other words, we can discover that Orton reversed the terms of the moral panic by attacking the repressive society rather than its victims.

In particular, Orton's young men are casual about sex. This is not in itself a new feature of fictional young men of the '50s and '60s. Reviewing *Look Back in Anger* Kenneth Tynan spoke of the hero Jimmy Porter's 'casual promiscuity'. He was presenting the play as something new, a voice for the times. But in fact Jimmy Porter's attitude is far from casual and he has a crisis precisely around his sexual relations. The play shows him not to be screwing around but approaching a 'mature' monogamy. While Jimmy enters the adult world, Orton's lads remain lads and they drift beyond heterosexuality: 'He says you spend your time thieving from slot machines and deflowering the daughters of better men than yourself {as angry young men classically did}... And even the sex you were born into isn't safe from your marauding' {which is where angry young men drew the line} (*Loot*, pp. 11-12). At the opening of *Ruffian on the Stair* Mike tells Joyce, whom he lives with, 'I'm to be at King's Cross station at eleven. I'm meeting a man in the toilet' (p.13).

The inability to recognise the 'sacred' line dividing homo- and heterosex is part of the lads' criminality. Such an attitude threatens society, because it questions the organisation of gender roles which help to make capitalism work: women servicing the men who compete for wealth. So in the early '70s, to threaten a society that needed changing, the gay radicals took up the chant: 'Hey hey! straight or gay – try it once the other way.' In the theory of Herbert Marcuse, which was influential at this period, the only way of resisting the transformation of the person into an 'instrument of labour' was to resexualise the body: 'The perversions...express rebellion against the subjugation of sexuality under the order of procreation, and against the institutions which guarantee this order' (Robinson, 1970: 156). Orton's lads are battling with institutions which impose order upon them.

This portrayal of youth rejects traditional attitudes in queer writing. In the queer novel youth is seen as a state of innocence; the time up to the first sex act is an Eden which can never be regained, so queers spend their lives searching for a lost innocence. At the first sex act most youths are shown to acquire guilt. Such repeated stories act as warnings against the so-called *acquired* homosexuality. Casual sex, we remember, was said to be dangerous because it might be habit-forming, and proselytising homosexuals were always on the prowl for a vulnerable youth to convert... It was against such beliefs that Peter Wildeblood spoke of the seriousness of homosexual relationships: 'A chance homosexual act, induced by the absence of women, does not make a man into a homosexual for the rest of his life. What may do so is a deep emotional attachment...with another man' (1955: 109). The problem with Wildeblood's argument, however, is that it does not challenge the central idea, that while heterosexuality was supposedly flexible and could be temporarily *deviated* from, homosexual identity, once acquired, was fixed – a man became *a* homosexual and as such was clearly and definitely labelled as a casualty. In this context the characterisation of Orton's lads is important, because it refutes ideas both of guilt and of single sexual identity. They are given shady pasts. Orton wanted them to be played with a sense of sexual knowingness – he thought the Hal and Dennis of the Manchester production of *Loot* were too innocent (and when they were casting for *Loot* he wrote: 'Not Bolam. He's good but oh, dear, he's as clean as a whistle sexually'). There's no Eden for these youths. They are always already corrupt. And their sexual encounters appear never to fix them in a sexual identity. Orton rejected the homosexual stereotyping that might be imposed on the relationship of Hal and Dennis: his note for a US production says: 'Americans see homosexuality in terms of fag and drag... They must be perfectly ordinary boys who happen to be fucking each other' (in Lahr, 1978: 248).

Insofar as his plays create pictures of sexually ambiguous young men, we can say that Orton shared the homosexual fantasy about youth culture. It has indeed been one of the major points of this chapter that Orton was attracted to the image of youth because that image offered him a specific way of defining his own identity. Where Orton differed from a number of homosexuals was that his identification with youth was as much to do with social anger as with sex. It is when we speak of Orton's anger that we have to move from an analysis that simply sees him as a trapped man looking for identity.

We have to speak of an aggressively campaigning Orton. So, in this context, we have to note how his lads depart from and question stereotypes. I mentioned above how the tradition of youthful innocence in queer writing is subverted, but there's a more influential stereotype that is undercut here. This is society's stereotype of criminal youth, whose 'undisciplined' sexuality is a symptom of a general disrespect for social and moral rules. The image is succinctly described by Simon Raven in an article on male prostitution published in *Encounter* in November 1960. Among the categories of prostitute is 'the classical type of "lay-about", who has somehow got it into his head that the only money worth making is to be made from shady enterprises of whatever kind.' Male prostitution is seen as a way of making 'easy money', of dodging out of proper hard graft. And most prostitutes, hence, can't handle money properly. In Simon Raven's image of this 'lay-about' whom he calls Micky, the economic instability is always accompanied by, and reflects, a sexual instability. 'Micky's trouble is that as soon as he gets a little money he suspends any attempt to make more while he either drinks, frolics, or gambles the lot away. (When well off, Micky spends a lot on female prostitutes, though his sexual flexibility is such that he has been known to produce a very young "fancy boy" of his own.)' (p.21). Orton's creation of Hal in *Loot* seems a precise development of this stereotype, except that Hal is also made compulsively truthful. The play is put together in such a way that the audience almost *desires* Hal to be less innocently virtuous since it is precisely this characteristic that makes him vulnerable to those who are more corrupt than he is. Hal and his mate are sexually ambiguous, criminal, and handle hopelessly their stolen loot; but against them, Orton places Nurse Fay and Inspector Truscott who are adult, violent, and very good at corruptly handling money. Whereas Raven's essay on prostitutes tends to blame or mock the boys for wanting a quick route to an easy life, Orton's plays show us those who really have it easy. These people are the businessmen, the managers, the corrupt policemen, those who have it easy because they have social power. Alongside these the youthful hooligans are in reality vulnerable; their sexual ambiguity is simply an irrelevance. Sloane ends up blackmailed into spending his life between Kath and Ed; Hal and Dennis end up paying off Fay and Truscott. In one case money is involved, in the other simply sex. But the two endings relate together in that they portray an adult society which exploits the youth it has sexual fantasies about.

Orton's reworking of the stereotype of hooligan youth makes him, I think, a more useful commentator on this '60s 'problem' than self-proclaimed moralists such as Pamela Hansford Johnson. His own fantasy identification with youth goes hand in hand with an anger about the hypocrisy and prejudices of contemporary moral debate. But Orton's interests here took him beyond moral debate. He started to ask questions about the theories which were commonly used to explain human psychology, sexuality and behaviour. These theories were loosely derived from Freud, and it is to Orton's dealings with Freudianism that the final section of this chapter is given.

3: Orton's Challenge to Freudianism

It is revealing that theatre directors and actors had a specific problem
over how to play the sexuality of Orton's boys. Its 'flexibility'
apparently defies stereotyping and labelling. When the critics began
writing about Orton, however, they managed to find a descriptive
label for the boys, whom they called 'polymorphously perverse'. This
term is pinched from the theories of Freud, who used it to describe the
undiscriminating sexual desires which he thought characteristic of the
very young child. These boys are seen to be childishly undiscriminating. The effect of labelling them in this way is to make them *safer* as
characterisations. The sexual casualness which originally functioned
to undermine stereotyping is now, through this terminology, seen as a
symptom of a 'clinical' or 'psychological' condition; it is fixed in a
compartment marked 'weird' or 'not normal'. Once again, the lads are
seen as the problem. They are the ones who appear to be oddly
immature, unlike the disciplined adults.

A 'Freudian' term is employed to 'explain', and in effect cover up,
Orton's subversiveness. I am therefore unhappy about accepting this
terminology. If we accept uncritically the 'Freudianism', we accept
something of which Orton himself was suspicious.

Orton's plays certainly make mention of Freud, but those references
are jokey and subversive. For example, Hal and Dennis hide their
stolen money in Hal's mother's coffin, which means disposing of its
former occupant. Hal reacts: 'Bury her naked? My own mum? *He goes
to the mirror and combs his hair.* It's a Freudian nightmare' (*Loot*, p.21).
The stage direction to go to the mirror is not incidental. The gesture
invokes the 'narcissism' which so many heroes of queer novels
supposedly exhibit, and with it we recall the famous attachments of so
many homosexuals to their mothers... But here the prospect of what
might happen to his mother has no traumatic impact on Hal, since he is
already established as queer and criminal. It may be a Freudian
nightmare, but it's no nightmare for Hal. The gesture of hair-combing
belongs not so much to the homosexual 'condition' of narcissism as to
simple youthful casualness.

Another example, from *What the Butler Saw*: the psychiatrist Dr
Rance announces proudly that he sent Freud a picture of his own
family, all wearing straitjackets: 'My foot placed squarely upon my
father's head' (p.86). Rance is established as a violent, somewhat
unbalanced person. The joke of the photograph is that Rance expects
Freud to approve of a straitjacketed family. This, it is implied, is where
Freudian views of the family lead. Freud sends him back 'a charming
postcard'.

Orton's references to Freud show an awareness of this influential figure. His interest runs alongside his views on youth culture, in that Freudianism made pronouncements about young people in their relation to families, sex and desire. But Orton's interest is also sceptical and critical. The reason for the scepticism may be explained by showing what Freudianism *stood for* at this period. After my explanation, I shall return in more detail to Orton's *responses* to Freudianism.

In 1955 D. J. West reported on a survey of 'sexually maladjusted boys': they 'came from parental homes characterised by sexual anxiety and prudishness, maternal authoritarianism, quarrels between parents, and paternal punitiveness' (p.188). Although there may be variants on this pattern, in general 'sexually repressive homes are particularly liable to generate homosexual or "feminised" sons if the father is absent or is a rejecting, aggressive disordered person who forces the child to view masculinity as an unattractive role' (pp.188-89). (It's worth noting that the tacit admission that masculinity has to be sold to the boy accepts that masculinity is neither an inevitable nor a natural role.)

In the late '50s many people were saying that the family was in decline (they should see it in the '80s...). Fletcher quotes some of these charges in the first preface to his book on the family (which aimed to counter ideas of decline), for example George Mack, grammar-school headmaster: 'It seems to me that the father figure has lost much of his awe and all of his majesty'; and an unnamed correspondent: 'The decline in moral standards during the past fifty years has been coincident with the gradual emancipation of our women' (1962: 236-37). The second quotation closely echoes the Morton report of 1956, which blamed the incidence of stress in the home on the emancipation of women.

We should note here that in so many novels about queers, there is a close, if not dominating, relationship with the mother and an absent, or ineffectual, father. The same objects of concern appear in the novels and in the social commentaries: the inadequate father, the domineering mother. Families in which the woman has too much authority apparently produce queers. This is a moral lesson urging husbands and wives to adopt proper sex roles. The interest in 'Freudian' explanations of how queers are made has, I think, less to do with queers than with the effort – in '50s films and social commentaries – to resist changes in gender roles. Thus we are given the scenario: women's emancipation 'undermines' the (male) nation because it 'produces' dominant mothers who then 'produce' queers (and if all that's true, then more strength to their elbows).

Fletcher demonstrates how the 'modern family' may be made a stronger social unit. It works by regulating and integrating an individual's natural instincts: 'The family is that form of association in which both some degree of *fulfilment* of these natural propensities and some necessary degree of *regulation* of them is combined' (p.20). Fletcher's terms are a version of some we've already met – sexual expression and self-discipline. Such a blend of 'regulation' and 'fulfilment' is a model in miniature – at the personal level – of a planned democratic society. It is only in the family that the potentially selfish if not dangerous instincts get their proper regulation and their rewarding fulfilment. In this model we can see how the whole 'Freudian' theory of impulses in need of release has been adopted to justify the structure of the family. Sex outside that structure, we are told, is likely to be neither regulated nor fulfilled. The theory of impulses had the effect of presenting as 'naturally' fulfilling (at the *personal* level) a *social* organisation which was based on the promise of individual freedom held within necessary limits. In these ways at this period 'Freudianism' sustained and 'explained' the status quo.

This repressive and conservative Freudianism had its enemies. Many women resented a theory which argued that a woman's 'natural' role was subordinate and procreative. Many homosexuals felt oppressed by a theory that presented them as 'abnormal'. With the development of the Women's and Gay Liberation movements in the years after 1968 this repressive Freudianism was openly opposed. More importantly, feminists and gay radicals returned to the works of Freud. They discovered there a body of theory that, far from saying that the current model of nuclear family was 'natural', instead suggested that children had sexual desires, that heterosexuality was no more natural than homosexuality and that male and female roles were learnt from society rather than inherited from one's anatomy. Freud's texts could be used to make feminist and gay critiques of gender roles and the family. Freud, we might say, could be used against the conservative so-called Freudians.

Orton was dead before the major gay re-readings of Freud started to appear. His plays, however, seem to indicate that he was already using Freud against the repressive Freudian ideas of his own society. While the incidental references to Freud may be critical jibes, the dramatic action of the plays is, in a bigger way, more akin to the texts of Freud themselves.

Orton's first stage play, *Entertaining Mr Sloane*, is a modern version of the Oedipus story. In an interview Orton claimed that he had used the most famous Oedipus plays, those by the ancient Greek dramatist Sophocles. Although nobody has really believed his claim, *Sloane* does have some close points of contact with the Greek. In Sophocles, Oedipus is lame and his father strikes him with a 'two-pronged goad', while the old man Kemp temporarily lames Sloane by jabbing him with a toasting fork, and Kemp is called Dadda; the relationship of Ed with his father uses lines from *Oedipus at Colonus*; Ed is a comic reworking of Creon.

For most people Oedipus was more closely associated with the name of Freud than with Sophocles. In Freudian theory contemporary with Orton mention of Oedipus would occur in explanations of the formation of homosexuality, where the male homosexual was said to have a 'mother-fixation'. The ancient myth told how Oedipus killed his father and unknowingly married his mother. Freud applied this story, with its rivalry (killing) of the father and its desire for (marrying) the mother, to a stage in the development of all children (but principally boys). The 'Oedipus complex' is a triangular situation involving mother, father and child. The child feels desire for one parent and animosity towards the other, but this desire does not operate heterosexually. The child may desire the parent of the same sex and hate the parent of the opposite sex. The stage of the 'Oedipus complex' is crucial in the development of sexuality and the orientation of desire, in that the child makes a choice of love-object of a particular sex and makes identification with a particular sex. At this stage too there is a focus on the genitals, and identification with the father brings a particular concentration on the phallus. It is the boy's discovery that the mother does not have a phallus that leads him to fear castration.

Although in the Oedipal situation either parent can be the love-object or the object of rivalry, the so-called 'normal' or 'correct' development is for the boy to identify with his father and renounce incestuous fixation on his mother. For to desire the mother leads to the threat of castration by the rival/father; and to desire the father, and thus become like the mother, is to lose the phallus. The fear of castration ties in with the taboo on incestuous relations with either parent. Thus the potential bisexual desires of the child are repressed. The 'successful' graduate of the Oedipal stage takes as his love-objects mother-substitutes – i.e. other women.

The child turns from the Oedipus complex out of fear of losing his own penis. Instead of desiring so dangerously either parent, he identifies with the father. In doing so, the boy himself learns the supposed authority and severity of the father, and thus upholds the father's command against incest. Thus the turning away from the Oedipus complex plays its part in constructing the 'superego' of the boy child. But Freud concedes that the Oedipus complex may not be totally destroyed by the fear of castration. It may only be temporarily repressed. In this case the desires of the Oedipus complex remain in the *unconscious*.

Popular notions of the Oedipus complex forgot or ignored Freud's insistence on the bisexuality of the child's desires, where the child could fix on either or both parents (at different times) as love-objects. So too, Freud's suggestion that the Oedipus complex may only be repressed, not abolished, makes the sexual identity of the adult something more unstable than is usually acknowledged. The popular version of the complex thought that it was only the male homosexual who remained immaturely stuck in the Oedipal stage, a man who had failed to develop. Furthermore, this failure was seen to be character-ised by an 'unnatural' fixation on one parent, in particular the mother. Freud suggests that all children pass through a stage of such fixation and there is nothing unnatural about this. Secondly, while 'successful' Oedipalisation was seen as normal and natural, for Freud there is nothing natural about a process in which the child is influenced by threat and fear, and in which it internalises an already existing cultural taboo. So the texts of Freud can be seen to have many more radical implications than were allowed by '60s 'Freudians'. This discrepancy, together with the clearly repressive notions of the 'Freudians', made the whole influential theory a battle-ground. It was a battle in which Orton's comedies participated.

In *Entertaining Mr Sloane* Orton constructs an Oedipal situation recognisable as such to Freudians, as much as to Greek scholars. The stranger Sloane is picked up by Kath and offered lodgings in her house; her father Kemp knows that Sloane is a murderer and Sloane kills him to shut him up; before this Kath's brother Ed has offered Sloane a job. Both Kath and Ed fancy Sloane, which is the motive for their friendship; at the end of the play they agree to cover up the murder in return for Sloane sharing out the rest of his life between them, as a sex-object. Orton spells out the terms of the Oedipal triangle: Kath hopes that the desired Sloane will 'live with us then as one of the family' (p.165), and when later he accuses her of trying to run his life and of being possessive, she replies that 'A mamma can't be possessive' (p.191). She casts herself into the role of mother in order to allow her to keep Sloane's sexual charms for herself. Her possess-iveness as mother is thus explained as sexual jealousy.

Orton's 'family' was greeted with distaste by audiences. The reason for this is that Orton specifically subverts contemporary sentimentali-sation of the family. He led his audiences initially to expect a menacing or psychological drama about a 'youth of today'. This sort of drama involved a focus on the casualty child at its centre, the narrative gradually revealing his or her real crisis and its deep psychological roots. The discovery of these roots may lead to an indictment of the parents in some respect – as in, say, *Rebel Without a Cause*. But the adult-child relationship is never seen as inhabited by sexual desire. Yet here is Orton's shocking subversion, for both Kath and Ed desire Sloane. Neither of them is really a parent, but Kath calls herself a mother *in order to* cling onto Sloane. Ed offers Sloane a 'proper' masculine model (which involves misogynist scorn for the woman), but this too is a way of getting the boy for himself.

Orton is radically diverging from contemporary 'Freudian' social commentary. In writings on the family the woman who was not properly maternal was seen to be unnatural and to produce a failed child – a homosexual. The father who was not properly masculine and authoritative likewise (apparently) deviated from nature and produced a failure. The *social* role – mother, businessman – is described as a natural role. And these 'natural' roles were seen to produce good families and properly adjusted children. The Orton version, however, suggests that the mothering role and the authoritative role are convenient fictions adopted to aid the pursuit of something much deeper, namely sexual desire. In the Orton family it is only sexual desire which is natural and the operation of this desire involves aggression and competition. Furthermore, this desire knows no cultural taboos. Kath and Ed are sister and brother and their final sharing of their love object Sloane is arguably incestuous. Sloane himself is a murderer, perhaps a psychopath, certainly a hooligan, but this in no way diminishes his status as love object for the other two.

Orton is rather closer to Freud in his 'family' than are the so-called Freudians. The Freudians blurred together social role and 'natural' role, obscuring the function of desire. For Freud, sexual and social identity are constructed in the Oedipal stage in the interplay of desire and prohibition. When the boy is threatened with castration he chooses to preserve his penis and abandon his desires for his parents. Sloane is blackmailed by Kath and Ed. The threat of imprisonment is a version of castration. The only way in which he can preserve himself is by agreeing to their plans. So Sloane's social and sexual roles are produced not by the operation of 'natural' drives (as in the supposed criminal instincts of hooligans) but by threat, fear and taboo: just as in Freud's model.

Let me leave *Sloane* for a moment, to point out another example of Orton using Freud against the 'Freudian' defenders of the family. *What the Butler Saw* ends in a parody of *The Importance of Being Earnest* and all those other plays in which characters suddenly discover they are related. In the plot, Geraldine has been desired by Dr Prentice, and Nick – a hotel page – is said to have raped Mrs Prentice. Both Geraldine and Nick spend some time in each other's clothes (while the clothes are vacant) and to Dr Rance their sexual identities seem the opposite of what they are. By the end of the play Geraldine and Nick are discovered to be sister and brother, and they are the children of Dr and Mrs Prentice (who are married). The conventional discovery scene brings to an end all the misunderstanding of the plot and restores harmony. Orton invites us similarly to celebrate the ending. But the problem is that it is incestuous. The very moment of the return to order is also the moment of profound sexual disorder. Here again the structure of the family is for Orton, as for Freud, no guarantee of harmony and stability. As we've seen, the 'Freudians' used the idea of the family to discipline sexual behaviour and to justify gender roles. Freud's 'family' is the place of power contests and incestuous desires. It is no place of innocence and stability. While bourgeois society claimed to use Freud to justify its repressive, family-centred society, Orton returned to Freud to discover sexual irregularity in the family. His ending to *What the Butler Saw* throws the real Freud family into the faces of the bourgeois audience. He discovers that the structure that had been used to regulate is in fact a nursery of anarchy.

In revealing the operations of sexual desire in the family Orton undercuts ideas about parents and children. The literature of youth culture focusses on the sexuality of the teenager. Older generations and parents are not seen to be sexual. The supposed problem for youth was to tame its sexuality. The usual play about problem youth shows how the youth learns to become a disciplined adult. But, if we return to *Sloane*, the narrative here begins to tell us more about the adults than the youth. He remains mysterious, a catalyst for the sexual desires of the others. He is what they want to make him. They adopt their roles in relation to what they wish to see in him. Kath: 'You've got a delicate skin... Just a motherly kiss. A real mother's kiss' (p.166). Ed: 'Do you wear leather...next to the skin? Leather jeans, say? Without...aah...' or again: 'Too much of this casual bunking up nowadays. Too many lads being ruined by birds' (p.182). In other words, the youth is desired as a sex object by the older generation. His status as a murderer is only shocking until such time as he agrees to the demands of Kath and Ed. His status as a hooligan and his 'untamed' sexuality are powerless when compared with the schemes of Kath and Ed.

In a wonderful Freudian irony, the bid Sloane makes for freedom is precisely what traps him. As a proper child in the Oedipal scheme, Sloane kills the father, Dadda Kemp. He attempts to free himself from the threatened repression in order to fulfil his own desires (for freedom, money, girls). In doing so, he discovers not freedom but repression on a larger scale, namely the law. Sloane – and the audience – have to learn that the world does not consist of individuals in free competition but of institutions which structure the life of the individual. In giving to Kath and Ed the power of law to imprison Sloane into their desires, Orton links a psychoanalytic critique to a social one: Kath and Ed are the parents who construct the individual's identity, and they are also those who use the law to impose on the individual subject.

The social-sexual solution at the end is a business contract. Kath thinks it's a 'lovely idea', because it suits her, whereas Sloane's feelings don't enter into it. This is Orton's picture of how hooligan youth (and implicitly the queer too) are 'integrated' into society. The process was called 'adjustment'. Most of the other plays likewise end with a negotiated settlement that fixes the youths into their place. Ray is made into a husband; Fay separates Hal and Dennis: 'When Dennis and I are married we'd have to move out... We must keep up appearances' (*Loot*, p.87). At the end of *Loot*, the coffin which has been so central has acquired two meanings: the resting-place of the dead mother, the resting-place of stolen money. It is the latter rather than the former which really, in Orton's world, binds together social groupings.

These negotiated endings indicate that the process of settling down into approved social and familial relationships is not so much natural as artificial. Adult society imposes roles on youths, gives them identities. The imposition is enforced by cultivating a sense of guilt and criminality in them. This guilt is then exploited by the adults – Kath, Ed, Fay, Truscott – to obtain their own desires. The moral sensibility of the youths simply makes them more vulnerable in a world which is not at all motivated by morality.

In this way Orton's plays answer a typical view of youth, as exemplified by Professor Carstairs in his 1963 Reith lectures, which consisted of 'a psychoanalytic account of the development of the adolescent, his need for an identity and his need to achieve a mature sexual life within marriage' (Wilson, 1980: 105). Orton's version of psychoanalysis and Freud is one that radically undercuts that of Prof. Carstairs. Orton argues that none of the development of the adolescent is 'natural', and that talk of development, identity, maturity, conceals power struggles. The society into which the hooligan lads are integrated is much more violent than they are. Mike shoots Wilson in the (false) name of marriage: 'He was misbehaving himself with my wife.' To which Joyce replies: 'But I'm not your wife. And he wasn't' (*Ruffian*, p.43). Kenny speaks for the rioting holiday-makers in *The Erpingham Camp*: 'We're doing this thing not for ourselves, but for our wives and loved ones – pregnant now and in the times to come...Have a bash, I say. Have a bash for the pregnant woman next door!' (p.78) – and they go off and loot and set fire to the camp.

These random acts of violence are supposedly rare in adult society, where instead violence is more commonly organised in institutions. It is thus mainly only the deviants of that society – its hooligan teenagers or homosexuals, for instance – who encounter that violence as it compels their 'integration'. Orton's political viewpoint identified targets very similar to those later attacked by the Gay Liberation

Front: the family and religion, police and psychiatrists (whose witch-hunts, interrogations and 'cures' threatened homosexuals). It might seem odd, given what Orton clearly knew about police treatment of homosexuals, that his Inspector Truscott is a comic figure; but he is also, of course, a very violent one. In Truscott Orton is killing off the cosy bourgeois stereotypes of policemen. Truscott's Sherlock Holmes pipe and magnifying glass are juxtaposed with his casual brutality. He is not the chatty moralist of the popular tv series, *Dixon of Dock Green*, not the ordinary bobby on the village street, nor the comic little Norman Wisdom of *On the Beat* (1962). Nor, however, is he the new 'realistically' depicted policeman of *Z Cars*. That series caused controversy when it appeared, but Orton carefully did not package *Loot* as 'problem drama': he did not want his audiences adopting ready-made stances of liberal concern for 'social problems' (and anyway that sort of play would not have been put on in the theatres Orton wanted to reach).

Truscott's comedy is partly based on his outrageous deceitful verbal logic (he passes himself off as a man from the Water Board when he wants to search a house without a warrant). He has a complete lack of moral responsibility: 'Can an accidental death be arranged?' 'Anything can be arranged in prison' (p.86). These dramatic characteristics are entirely relevant to police methods against homosexuals, where rumour and verbal allegation were used to track down 'offenders', where lies were told in order to get pleas of guilty, and where accused men's lives were ruined by police telling their families and employers. The creation of Truscott comes out of a homosexual's clear-eyed view of the police, a view normally only shared by the underprivileged, by socialists and other criminals. To illustrate my point, let me quote Peter Wildeblood who was certainly no political radical. He is describing the police methods used to extract evidence against him, and then says:

> I know how difficult it is for a law-abiding citizen to believe that the police, in England, acquire their evidence in such a manner; two years ago, I should have found it hard to believe, myself. We have all been brought up to believe that crime-detection is carried out by painstaking research and brilliant intuition, *à la* Agatha Christie; the truth is that it relies almost entirely, if this case is typical, on trapping the accused man into making an incriminating statement, or by coercing someone else – often an accomplice – into giving evidence against him.

He goes on to note that 'some hundreds of police officers are themselves convicted each year, usually of breaking and entering, and sometimes of blackmail' (1955: 65). Ah well, at least we can say that the rate of conviction has dropped...

So Truscott the policeman who neatly handles lies is as much nightmare as farce. As soon as Orton gets the audience laughing, he springs the violence upon them; he insists that when Hal is beaten up by Truscott he should scream with pain and have a bleeding nose. The kind of people who angrily walk out of *Loot*, said Orton, are 'the kind of people that are magistrates' (Lahr, 1978: 101). There is no law and order, only power: McLeavy's sentimental belief that the police are 'for the protection of ordinary people' (*Loot*, p.86) is a laugh line. Through all the plays a belief in the benevolence of the police is always a joke. Orton was queer; he should have known.

After Gay Liberation psychiatrists were openly attacked as the civilian police of heterosexual society, the psychonazis. They 'helped' homosexuals to adjust to 'normality'. In *What the Butler Saw* the two psychiatrists, Prentice and Rance, both make claims to be sane, yet each behaves in a way that is crazy. When Rance triumphs it is because he holds a gun. His power depends on a weapon, not upon a superior rationality or correctness about sanity. Any one of the other characters might as well have held the gun, no one is more mad than any one else. There are only power and self-interest, without ideals or morals. The audience can feel comfortable with the play's jibes at mad psychiatrists but by the end they too are constructed into madness: Nick (to Mrs Prentice, nodding to Geraldine): 'She can see me. Doesn't that prove I'm real?' Mrs Prentice: 'No. She's mad.' Nick: 'If you think I'm a phantom of your subconscious you must be mad.' Mrs Prentice (*with a hysterical shriek*): 'I am mad!' (p.84). The audience can see *all* of the characters, so where does that leave them?

Later, Nick says to Rance: 'Look at this wound. That's real.' 'It appears to be.' Nick: 'If the pain is real I must be real' (p.87). Games are played with theatrical convention. The fake wound that an audience is prepared to accept as real – by convention – is said to be *appearance*. Nick's expression of pain is, in the last instance, only performance by an actor. A theatre audience needs and wants to believe in the reality of Nick in order to enjoy the story. But the price paid for a belief in this reality is the belief that we watch and enjoy real pain. Otherwise he has to be accepted as not real. A similar moment arises in *Loot* when Truscott says: 'What has just taken place is perfectly scandalous and had better go no farther than these three walls' (p.83). A character whose reality an audience takes on trust observes there are three walls to a room, as indeed there are on a stage set, the audience sitting where the fourth wall should be. The joke unsettles an audience in that it invites them to perceive that they are watching artifice, even while they are taking as real what they see.

Relevant to the theatrical situations Orton constructs is the radical psychiatrist R. D. Laing's attack on concepts of sanity and madness:

> I am aware that the man who is said to be deluded may be in his delusion telling me the truth, and this in no equivocal or metaphorical sense, but quite literally, and that the cracked mind of the schizophrenic may *let in* light which does not enter the intact minds of many sane people whose minds are closed (1960: 27).

Laing's 'existential' study in sanity and madness attacks thinking about psychosis as 'failure of adjustment, or *mal*-adaptation' – which parallels precisely the language used of queers. I make this reference to Laing to show that Orton in his own way was demolishing the authority of the psychopolice, who claimed to divide reality from madness. For Orton, as a queer, was 'maladjusted' and knew about psychiatric terrorism.

When Rance's gun gives him power, it is more than a weapon: it is a symbol of a penis. The analysis of those who repress youth (and homosexuals) has to finish with those other agents of repression – non-homosexual adult men (Ed's an exception to the non-homosexual bit, but we'll return to him). Truscott is a policeman, Erpingham owns a holiday camp which makes money by organising people's leisure time, Rance is a psychiatrist, Pringle makes money from a crazy religious sect which organises people's 'souls'. These men all have the symbolic authority of the father. They are not necessarily family men but they represent authoritative presences. The father is the one who brings into the Oedipal triangle a sense of legislation and taboo; he is the transmitter of law and prohibition.

Homosexuals were supposedly formed because sons had no proper masculine model with which to identify. Much contemporary thought (based on 'Freudianism') spoke of the need for father-substitutes, the need to find the father in order to become normal. This connects with the suggested solution to teenage rebellion – the stricter enforcement of parental control and harsher punishment. In the outlook of the radical philosopher Marcuse, the father is the capitalist entrepreneur who crushes rebellion and creates a sense of guilt in the rebels. And this is the scenario Orton's plays tend to follow: they are not about rebellion but rather its suppression.

We've seen how the plays end with contracts and deals which establish stability. The final scenes do not represent images of a changed world, but of order restored. *Erpingham Camp* ends, after its rioting, with the lying-in-state of Erpingham; *Good and Faithful Servant* ends with a factory dance and the sound of the voice of Mrs Vealfoy, a manager, amplified through a microphone. Both are images of control, of occasions on which the general public 'knows its place'. *Loot* and *What the Butler Saw* end with characters expressing a need to keep up appearances, to reproduce what is expected. Truscott the policeman carries off his corrupt financial deal unscathed; Ed the businessman satisfies his desires without any loss of control. By contrast, the character who kills the father – Sloane killing Dadda Kemp – ends up most trapped.

In Freud's theory the boy child who fears castration learns to identify with the father. Identification brings security and internalises the father's own severe authority. As with other Freudian ideas, this one reappears in the popular literature of the period. In *The Leather Boys* Reggie remembers to call the prosecuting counsel 'Sir' when testifying against the hooligans who killed Dick; this pleases the prosecutor: 'He reminded Dick of his old headmaster. When you were really in trouble he spoke quietly, like this, asking you to tell the truth. He never shouted or scared you' (George, 1961: 117). To obey the father, help the law, speak the truth, produces security. Reggie the homosexual is taken under the wing of authority, firmly opposed to rebellious hooligans. And the father also, of course, controls that other 'weak' group, women: for James Bond's secretary, 'every day it seemed more difficult to betray by resignation the father-figure which The Service had become' (Fleming, 1955: 8).

In *What the Butler Saw* Orton wrote a comedy around this symbolic father. It was, naturally, Halliwell who spotted what he was up to (and no one else writing about Orton seems to have done so). Halliwell discovered Orton's *Golden Bough* sub-text which included 'the castration of Sir Winston Churchill (the father-figure)'. The play opens with Geraldine Barclay arriving for interview for the post of Dr Prentice's secretary; she places a small box on the table where it remains throughout the rest of the play; in conversation she remarks that her grandmother has been recently killed in a gas explosion which also blew up a statue of Winston Churchill, parts of which embedded themselves in her grandmother. Prentice, following a classic farce pattern, attempts to seduce his new secretary: from here the problems flow. Everybody eventually becomes involved in a sequence of lies and disguises and misunderstandings, until even the truth has no effect or authority. The confusion centres on the loss of sexual identity and the blurring of madness and sanity. When Sergeant Match enters the play he is looking for the missing part of Churchill's statue, as he explains in a hilarious speech full of official and right-wing cliché. He soon loses his uniform, becomes drugged and has a woman's dress put on him. At the end of the play a form of order is restored, at which point the missing part is found in Geraldine's box and held aloft. The part is a penis. Its presence accompanies the return to order; in its absence, while missing, rationality and sexual identity had collapsed. And it has, I suppose, to be Geraldine's box which it came out of. She is never inquisitive enough to open the box, and in the same 'closed' way insists on her virginity throughout the play. The box is only opened after she has experienced a change of sex, as it were, and a variety of humiliations and indignities. Unknown to her, her box all the time has a penis already in it; her virginity, by implication, is not only a false position but one that necessarily engenders chaos. (Although I think this is the argument of the play, I find it sexist and dissociate myself from it.)

The action of the play, as in most good farces, is structured so that whatever is repressed keeps returning when it is not wanted. There's wonderful stage business when Prentice tries to get rid of Geraldine's clothes. He is continually caught out with them in his hands, and his efforts to conceal them lead to increasingly 'mad' behaviour; the objects themselves won't even stay put: Prentice tries to hide Geraldine's underclothes and shoes in a flower vase, but one shoe won't go in. That ends up in the bookcase. Thus the heterosexual scheming male ceases to be able to repress from consciousness what he wants hidden. For the audience, of course, the anarchy of the farce is the pleasurable bit, the absence of the ordering father is enjoyable. Only when it's all over is the penis produced. Yet *this* moment is the most explicit mockery of the masculine, for it breaks a social taboo in putting on display that which is meant always to be decorously hidden. This is a taboo so forceful that the cast of the original production imposed censorship on themselves and changed Orton's text, to avoid display of the penis. The missing penis (we should call it a phallus) is loaded with all sorts of authority: Churchill as male hero, as war victor, as national hero, as nationalist, as Conservative, as substitute monarch. Churchill the Father of the State. But the authority can only be retained as long as the phallus is treated with proper awe, understood as significant symbol rather than shown for what it is. On display, it slides from being the phallus into a simple penis. This triumph of the willy – when seen, all too clearly, *as willy* – offers not security but shock, embarrassment and laughter.

The laughter is directed at the authority of the father because it is that authority which oppresses not just youth, but homosexuals. Orton could seek an identification with youth culture not only on the basis of a dream of freedom (which is where we began) but in an attack on shared enemies. The repressive order of the father can be found in the police and in psychiatry. Where such behaviour stems from, and is most clearly seen, is in the behaviour of parents within the family.

Contemporary ideas of proper parenthood oppressed both homosexuals and youth. Thus Orton took the so-called Freudianism that justified and rationalised the repressive family and set against it ideas more close to those of Freud. So his plays show violence present not only in the demonised youth but in the conduct of respectable adults.

Yet Orton landed himself in a difficulty. For his attack on the forces of repression is not contained in the oppositional or alternative artworks that might be associated with left-wing culture or with the youth ghetto. He chose as his vehicle the very type of play that most commonly reinforces sexual and social norms, the West End adult sex comedy. Thus there is an apparent contradiction between message and vehicle, and it's a contradiction that hampered Orton throughout his working life. The next chapter will look at why he should have made this choice about his artform and how it affected what he was saying.

Chapter 5:

Orton as Writer

This is the third and last of the chapters which aim to look at the ways in which Orton defined his social identity. As with the other two I am trying not simply to describe a consciously selected role, but something to which, I think, Orton felt real emotional commitment. Both his so-called promiscuity and his affiliation to youth culture enabled him to fly in the face of a class and set of proprieties that he disliked, even while he was becoming a member of that class. At the same time, youth culture offered, and promiscuity acted out, a promise of individual freedom from despised constraints. In this chapter I shall suggest how Orton's sense of himself as a writer was again associated with the personal desire to be individual and separate. Simultaneously, on a political level, the writing was another means – perhaps the most articulate – of attacking the values Orton hated.

1: The Value of Detachment

Nowadays Orton's plays are often seen as part of the range of 'adult sex comedies' so frequently performed by desperate reps. They seem simply to be more funny examples of a common and rather non-arty dramatic form. Yet Orton's view of his own writing differed from that of his audience. He insisted on what he called stylistic detachment. He was critical of the loose construction of other people's plays and stressed that his aim, unlike that of most contemporary dramatists, was to pursue a theatre of ideas. It is necessary always to be sceptical of what Orton said in interview, but this notion of detachment remains consistent and has a central position in his life and work.

The detachment implies not only polish and rigour of style, but also hardheadedness, personal toughness. Orton claimed that it was his time in prison that brought detachment to his writing. He spoke deliberately not as a penitent sinner but as a hard new realist. While he admitted his admiration of, and debt to, the style of Oscar Wilde, he was careful to separate Wilde's writing from his personal life, which Orton described (inaccurately) as 'flabby'. This gives us one clue to the desire for detachment: it was a way of escaping the stereotyped queer

image. Emotionalism was so often associated with effeminates and
homosexual casualties; *No End to the Way* dismisses the 'pretty crappy
sort of novels about your kind of life, and they're all so sort of *noble*,
and the characters in the story seldom if ever get to even *touch* each
other... It's always vague and all too pretty-pretty' (Jackson, 1965/
1985: 231). *No End* tries to be different by telling it tough and 'real'.

Orton's 'detachment' can also, I think, be seen as a version of the
contemporary cool style adopted by the new media personalities, of
the likes of Len Deighton, Terence Stamp, Mary Quant. These
so-called new aristocrats had neither inherited wealth nor
'distinguished' class position. Their fame was conspicuously based on
their own abilities (including, presumably, their ability to be famous).
The media image was one of youthful vitality, classlessness, posed
revolt against convention (and because posed, going nowhere). This
was the world apparently available to Orton, who sold a play for
filming and was invited to write a screenplay for the Beatles. So he too
comes on cool while baiting the moral panic about sex and violence: a
few years after the scandalous *Lady Chatterley* obscenity trial (1960), he
remarked that the book failed in its presentation of sex. In the face of
the furore over Edward Bond's play *Saved* (with its celebrated scene of
a baby being stoned in its pram), Orton described it as a 'remarkably
cissy play'. (We can only guess at what motivated Orton's contempt, if
he wasn't just play-acting: possibly he disliked the obvious seriousness
of the play, which was put on at the *arty* Royal Court (later the venue
for Orton's own plays); possibly he thought it too clearly moral and
preaching; perhaps he envied it its furore.) Orton's remarks in
interview often adopt the tone of '60s satire, deadpan, unimpressed,
worldly; this was preeminently the tone of those who could handle
society and make a success of themselves.

Most of the time Orton cultivated a distance from the theatre world,
reminding them that he had come from the gutter. He remained the
'bed-sitter playwright', though apparently thought his area of Islington was becoming too posh: 'Late at night you hear car doors banging
and people singing out "goodnight darling" ' (*Daily Sketch*, 30
November 1966). His diary records this affected mannerism in his
agent, who called him 'darling'. Orton's earliest recorded artworks
poke fun at the values and proprieties of the middle class, but they are
jokes in which very few people shared. When he wrote letters to
newspapers under false names, he selected the more heavyweight
middle-class dailies (or such people as the manager of the Ritz hotel);
but nobody except his closest friends would have been in on the secret.
When he and Halliwell doctored the library books, they used to watch
from a distance how people reacted. It was their game alone.

These jokes had the important function of constructing the

apparent relationship between their perpetrators and an unwitting general public. Because the jokes were private Halliwell and Orton could sense their separateness from those at whom they laughed. Only they were in the know, so they could feel superior. The private jokes worked as much to define the jokers' own individuality as to attack a class they despised. That individuality was always of a double nature: Halliwell and Orton were, on one level, indeed the unknown, vulnerable petty criminals; at the same time, in their own eyes – and possibly in the opinion of later generations – they were unacknowledged but powerful wits.

When he became famous, Orton's life became more public, he had to work with many other people. In the increasingly frequent interviews Orton told lies about himself to the reporters. In a *Plays and Players* interview he said: 'I was married, divorced, operated on for acute appendicitis, photographed in the nude and arrested for larceny. Then came a six-month spell in prison.' Truth and fiction blur, the whole thing stylishly run off. Again, a private joke is at work; only Orton and Halliwell know the discrepancy between life and fiction, and thus Orton's 'real' self seems to be kept separate from the interviewer. In another statement he claimed his parents 'saved like mad to send me to business school at 15 so I could work in a solicitor's office but I spent a year making out with the birds in cupboards.' The slick machismo version of 'Orton' is modelled on contemporary media stars and films (this line could have come from *Alfie*, for instance). The lies work both as a send-up of news media and as a defence of his 'secret' self. The more official the record, the more absurd the detail: in the potted biography on the back cover of the BBC's *New Radio Plays* (1966), we are told 'he was married, divorced, thrown from a moving vehicle, and arrested for larceny' – the aspect of criminality is always included.

Media coverage gave Orton opportunity to invent false selves. As much as with the casual sexual partners and his cottaging expeditions, he was able to be the person that the other person wanted him to be, to create the self that suited the occasion. So it had to be to *Plays and Players* that 'Orton the writer' said: 'Strindberg has been a strong influence, particularly in his later works like the *Ghost Sonata*' (it's difficult to imagine anything further removed from Orton's work than this high-art, expressionist mumbo-jumbo). 'And I've read and been very impressed by all the Ben Travers farces, which I should say are ripe for revival.' (Orton described his work as parody of bad theatre: there's a sense, given Orton's view of the contemporary stage, that he could say Ben Travers *was* (still is?) ripe for revival – it's what the theatre deserved.) Strindberg and Ben Travers, the combination is carefully chosen...and has sent researchers in later years scurrying off to find more of Orton's 'sources'.

When he was invited to meet the successful playwright Terence Rattigan, the conversation displayed 'Orton the boy wonder'. It was a combination of flirtation and piss-take: 'Mr Orton wore heavy boots, blue denims, a white sweat-shirt open at the neck and a black leather jacket. He was perfectly at home and at ease with Mr Rattigan just back from Ischia and correct in blue suit and MCC member's tie ready for the Test match.' Rattigan name-drops in conceited fashion, then Orton asks: 'Do you ever start a play just with one first line, Terry?' The use of the familiar Christian name, the implication about Rattigan's dramatic style – both are deliberately cheeky. Later Orton says that he is not committed in politics or sex: 'The English art of compromise is the thing.' This is said to Rattigan, the dramatist who in 1956 altered the text of *Separate Tables* to obliterate its homosexual concern in order to compromise with the censor. (By contrast, the less established Osborne refused in 1965 to agree to the cuts and alterations imposed on *A Patriot for Me*, a play Orton assumed would be 'serious' – in the best sense – about homosexuality.) So Orton's invented selves were as much attack as defence. We shall see later on what sort of 'thing' he thought the English art of compromise was. But we can note here, lastly, that in *Plays and Players* he attacked dramatists who compromised; and he named Tennessee Williams, another fairly closeted queer.

When Orton and Halliwell entertained the publishers Monteith (of Faber) and Brain (of Hamish Hamilton) they gave them a meal of rice with sardines and then rice with golden syrup. I take it that Halliwell and Orton watched with some amusement how these wealthy well-fed men managed to swallow their meal. The games and subversions sustained a sense of Orton's apparent 'distance' from the rich arty world. When his agent advised him to keep a diary, she can't have had any inkling that what she would get would be not only an 'amusing' record of sexual adventures, but an account so insistently graphic, so venomous, so name-dropping, that it was (until very recently) deemed unpublishable. Ramsay herself, who described Orton as 'very charming, very cute', said in 1984 (in *The Times*) that 'he always spoke the truth which can be very chilling'. She was deceived about this truthfulness: instead, her remark seems to indicate that Orton did his flirtation act with his agent as well (until he got angry with her).

The publishing and theatre people were of the middle class which Orton said he disliked. Yet he had to mix with them. So they – and the press and its readers – were held at a distance through the false selves. This distance, though, was itself an illusion, because Orton depended on their very real money. His fictional games were necessary because they gave him the feeling that he had the freedom to control his own life, to protect his own individuality.

We can now understand the development of Orton's unique dramatic style as an extension of the private jokes and the creation of false selves. That style has become known as 'Ortonesque', which is itself a mark of its success in individualising Orton since it obscures the major part played by Halliwell in forming that style. One of the central features of the style is a declaration of its own stylishness. In developing it Orton distinguished his work from all other types of dramatic writing: he was not making kitchen-sink drama or drawing-room comedy or penthouse expressionism. The style placed Orton's work beyond the available categories, announcing its individuality in the fact that it could only be called 'Ortonesque'. But even while it states individuality the style is doing a second job. It is preventing any concept of the serious and 'real' author behind the artwork. There is no sense of a 'committed' writer – an Osborne or Bond – writing a play to express his view of contemporary social problems, no sense that the writer is politically engaged. And certainly there's no sense of that other, equally relevant author-figure, the campaigning, law-reforming homosexual, aiming to use his writing to tell the truth about the homosexual 'condition'. The very presence of the glittering style prevents us seeing the plays as artworks which patently declare the real concerns of their author. The author is both present and concealed. 'Ortonesque', the creation of Orton the author, is the dominant feature of the plays; but since Orton the author is a producer of self-declared style, there can be no concept of a committed Orton who makes the plays his own political and moral vehicles.

To finish this section I want to suggest that the individuality was more than illusory, it was self-contradictory. Firstly, Orton made a mistake in thinking that the individual self could always be defended and hence have a separate untouched existence. The very procedures Orton used in defence began to influence what was being defended. The Ortonesque style was a pathway to fame and money. It was a sellable commodity precisely because it was the style other people expected from him. After all, it was what he was paid for. I feel this is most apparent in *Loot*, which was revised to other people's demands, and in the screenplay written for the Beatles which was financially the biggest project he ever had. Stylistic individuality can, hence, be seen from two viewpoints: one, that it marks out the uniqueness of the author; the other, that it is the precise commodity which the author has to sell, and is only valuable at such time as it is sold. When Orton produced Ortonesque for the expectations of others, he was in part being shaped by those others. Similarly with the sexual life. Orton's creation of roles to please sexual partners did not only protect the 'real' Orton who lived with Halliwell. It also gave him pleasure. When he took pleasure in being appreciated by others, Orton was shaping himself to suit them, rather than remaining distant. He wanted to feel he was separate, that his adventures were just games, and I think that he used the diary to cultivate the impression, for himself, that it was him who controlled the sex. His role as author (of the diary) gave him power – after the event. But during sex, just as during interviews, he performed to get his pleasure, which came from the responses of others. The 'defence' of the secret Orton was really a shaping (by *others*) of the secret Orton.

My second point about the individualism concerns its political status. Halliwell and Orton's early attacks on the middle class were not affirmations of solidarity with a political party or with the working-class movement. Orton's later dramatic style explicitly severed any links with groupings of 'committed writers'. The private jokes are meant to preserve the individuality of the attacker, not to lose this in an alliance with other oppositional authors. Similarly, the cottaging expeditions gave a sense of sexual freedom because Orton was on his own. It was not the sort of interest in freedom that led him or Halliwell to join other homosexuals in campaigning for rights which might lead to real freedom. The individualism, whether it be that of the writer or that of the adventurer, has much in common with Orton's middle-class 'enemies'. For middle-class capitalist society enshrines ideas of individual competition. Orton's attitudes have much in common with the outlook of middle-class masculinity. In this light, much of his anger looks like the envy of the lower-middle-class man for those above him who have already made it into positions of wealth and power.

Orton's insistence, despite all of his cool pose, was on discipline, hard work, wide reading; he endlessly polished away at his writing. The combination of stresses on hard work and individual effort are in keeping with the petty-bourgeois class in which Orton was placed, despite all his games of 'distancing'. (His venom towards that class is a symptom that he recognised its closeness; and felt this was the closeness he needed to work hardest at destroying.) One story from the days of his new-found success shows us a different – dare we say 'real' – Orton. When he received the Evening Standard Drama Award, and one of the neighbours pointed out how you could see the workmanship, Orton wrote in his diary that it was 'like turning round the Rokeby Venus to see how the frame was made' (*Diaries*, p.59). The cleverness of the choice of analogy goes hand in hand with the contempt for the neighbour. The Rokeby Venus, a painting slashed by a suffragette, has a special place in art history. Orton is in part celebrating his own iconoclasm: he makes art out of slashing art, but his neighbour only looks to see how it's made. For Orton the art, for the neighbour the frame. His remark shows his petty-bourgeois pride in getting the prize that means he's made it (in all senses), even if he's made it in the eyes of a world he most of the time despised.

2: Style and Politics

The style has to be examined more closely. I shall however aim to avoid detailed analysis of the plays, since this is best done in the rehearsal room rather than on the page.

Contemporary reviewers were quick to spot the use of journalese in Orton's plays. Characters were said to speak phrases picked up from newspapers and television. The alertness to this feature of the plays derives from a concern, widespread in the '60s, with the influence of the news media on people's lives. Newspapers, said Graham Martin, offered 'interpretation intended to do the reader's thinking for him in an idiom which for various reasons he finds satisfying' (Thompson, 1964: 84). Some examples here may serve to illustrate both the concern and the attitude of writers to it: in the world of *A Clockwork Orange* television drugs the minds of the flat-dwellers; in Osborne's *Under Plain Cover* (1963) the journalist with his head full of censorious newspaper phrases hounds the happy 'kinky' (but private) couple, Jenny and Tim. Novelists hit back not only by parodying journalese and its social attitudes (as in Michael Frayn's *The Tin Men*, 1966) but also in showing the poor unfortunates whose heads and lives have been filled with second-hand thinking. This concern with the effects of media on people's lives relates to an increasing preoccupation in the '60s with the impact of corporate institutions on the private person. There was a distrust of anything that threatened the status of the individual. But this concern got mixed up with another attitude which was rather less liberal.

The problem of people's heads being filled with second-hand ideas can be seen not as infringement on the individual but instead as the individual having ideas not suited to her/his status. Thus the satirist mocks, rather than pities, those who have pretensions to supposedly educated speech. This mockery is a backlash against the declared 'classlessness' of the '50s, when education and opportunities were meant to be on offer to all. It was notionally possible that the lower-class person could take an interest in the art, culture, political debate which had hitherto been the (supposed) preserve of the upper orders. But the satirist obstructed this possibility by depicting as foolish the lower-class people who tried to acquire an articulateness and discrimination which was not 'theirs' by origin. Thus in the '60s we find a comedy built out of pretensions: the hero of Rodney

Garland's *Sorcerer's Broth* (1966) takes his mum to an art gallery. 'These Flemish masters looked real superb on the walls. "Fancy," Mum would say stopping before one. "Fancy." Then: "Look," she'd say, "just look." But after a time she'd mastered the subject and the period. "There's a man hanging on that gallows in the corner, Don." At the next *tableau*: "This is truly many splendoured," she opined' (p.90). Garland has specially learnt the style (perhaps from Orton?); it's very different from his previous novels. The comedy reinforces a very snotty attitude about what 'art' is and how you should respond to it (personally I think Don's mum got it right). The tension between snottiness and liberalism also characterises Brigid Brophy's *Flesh* (1962), which claims to be liberated about sex. Thus we find: 'Only a few of Marcus's possessions gave him pleasure and pride: his art books, for which he had had a specially deep shelf made – few people he knew possessed both the books and a shelf that would accommodate them' (p.20). Poor Marcus lacks the laid-back well-off bohemianism of the upper orders who are used to living with real art and have the space for the coffee-tables on which to keep their art books. This humour may be liberated about sex; it's definitely not so about class.

The satirical comedy often combines a mockery of the 'common' (the shared = the vulgar) with a harking back to some standard of 'proper' education. Such values underlie the laughter in Orton's writing. But when his plays are working well they make it difficult for an audience to watch with an undisturbed snotty composure. Watchers are *caught* between the comically ridiculous and the morally improper (I developed this analysis in an essay I wrote a few years ago: see Shepherd, 1978). In particular, in *Erpingham Camp* Orton contrasts the obvious 'vulgarity' of the campers with the elevated language and artistic sensibility of Erpingham and his Padre. The play itself is to be staged in the style of the Royal Shakespeare Company combined with the soundtracks of some of the more august state ceremonies. All develops into chaos: Erpingham is ridiculed and killed, and the solemn staging becomes increasingly a joke, a joke which subverts the theatrical taste and decorum of the audience.

If Orton's comedy unsettles its audience, there's a political point to it. The journalese style was often associated with a specific class of speaker, the petty bourgeois. An attack on the pretentious petty bourgeois mainly came from a position that was certain of its own status in the articulate upper middle class. It was a comedy that all too frequently reinforced the security of a theatre-going audience. Orton's work was not free of potentially snobbish class attitudes, but it is interesting and useful to see that he was conscious of this and took measures to deal with it.

When I did some work on the development of Orton's style (work somewhat hampered by the refusal of the latter-day Orton guardians to let me see any of the unpublished stuff), I compared the early radio version of *Ruffian on the Stair* with the later stage version. Orton afterwards refused to let anyone perform the radio version. It doesn't have the control of his developed style and it owes much to Harold Pinter, even while it sends up his work: Joyce is having a Pinteresque conversation with a monosyllabic Mike till she says: 'Why don't you say something? I get no pleasure, you know, sitting here talking to myself!' (p.197). Mike's speech is carefully ungrammatical in the radio script: 'they was horribly injured,' 'shouldn't of let him in,' which is later deleted; Wilson says he's come from Hackney, which is deleted. Thus the conventional markers of class ignorance are dropped. In this way, Orton shifts the class assumptions of Pinter's language. Secondly, he undermines the Pinteresque idea of 'menace'. In Pinter's early work, the source of menace in the action is the stranger, the person from outside brought into the home. Orton reverses this: *Sloane* opens with a 'rough' young man being brought into the house, the dialogue is 'Pinteresque', we can expect him to be violent and he is; but finally he is less powerful than the inhabitants of the house and ends up their prisoner, showing that the 'ordinary' folk are the real threat. So Orton rejects a drama that reinforces middle-class theatre-goers' conceptions of themselves as the normal ones who face threats from outsiders or silliness from their 'inferiors'. This is why Orton wanted his plays initially to look as conventionally 'West End' as possible: he wanted a 'theatre of reassurance' stage-set for *Butler* so he could spring his anarchy on a class that thought it was secure in the theatre as well as outside it.

The language Orton's characters use is not only the language of tabloid newspapers. They also use the language of public institutions, such as the law, the church, the health service, the money market – all of whose utterances claim to be objective and truthful (and as such play a large part in shaping people's ideas about their lives). An example of this language might be this sentence from His Honour Judge Tudor Rees, who edited a book attacking homosexuals called *They Stand Apart* (1955): 'He was a man of good education who had held a very responsible position in the banking world' (p.20). When such phrasing reappears in an Orton play it has lost its objectivity and become comic. Ed tells Kath: 'You've got to realise my position. I can't have my sister keeping a common kip. Some of my associates are men of distinction. They think nothing of tipping a fiver. That sort of person. If they realised how my family carry on I'd be banned from the best places' (*Sloane*, p.177). The Tudor Rees terminology is muddled in with other language: 'common kip', 'fiver', so it becomes pretentious and funny.

Another language spoken by Orton's characters is more nebulous in its origins. It is a language of 'traditional common sense and decency', of public responsibility and propriety – the language of broadcasters, of Movietone newsreels, of addresses to the nation, the war effort and 'pulling together': 'At the outbreak of the Second World War, George was called upon to supervise his department, and to take on a lot of extra responsibilities. He didn't complain, though. He shouldered his share of the burden which we all had in those days.' (George is a doorman; the patronising speech is spoken by the personnel manager, showing that the sense of wartime equality was short-lived.) The employee learns the language of the manager: 'As I stand on the eve of a well-earned rest I have no hesitation in saying that I've worked hard for it' (*Servant*, pp.57-58). This language is often specifically associated with reactionaries and Toryism: the local council, composed by and large of no-nonsense men and women of the "sixties" ', 'with the full support of the Conservative and Unionist Party – the council decided to sue the heirs of Mrs Barclay for those parts of Sir Winston which an army-type medical had proved to be missing' (*Butler*, p.46).

In his celebrated essay published in 1969, 'Components of the National Culture', Perry Anderson said that 'the culture that is immediately central and internal to any politics, is that which provides our fundamental concepts of man and society' (Cockburn and Blackburn, 1969: 216). The provided concepts are most easily learnt and internalised when we don't notice them being provided. When, for example, the Wolfenden report discussed prostitution (and when others discussed flaunting queers), it measured prostitution's (or queers') appearance against the sense of decency of the 'ordinary' citizen 'who should be able to go about his business without the constant affront to his sense of decency which the presence of these women affords' (I have borrowed this point from the National Deviancy Conference, ed. 1980: 10). The reader nods in agreement with what is said about the ordinary citizen, imagines s/he is that citizen and shares that sense of 'decency'. Nothing in Wolfenden's prose makes the reader question what this ordinariness and decency are. Marcuse made the same point about mass communications, entertainments and commodities that 'carry with them prescribed attitudes and habits' (1964: 24). People are controlled by the language and culture they use and live in; they unwittingly learn a whole set of concepts which they think of as natural truths and common sense. To return to Anderson, discussing philosophy: 'The cult of common sense accurately indicates the role of linguistic philosophy in England. It functions as a chloroforming ideology, blotting out the very memory of an alternative order of thought' (Cockburn and Blackburn, 1969: 237). A reading of queer novels indicates how homosexuals learnt to think of themselves in terms of the concepts provided by a repressive non-homosexual society; so they often genuinely thought they were guilty, emotional, unnatural, sick.

In realistic drama (which Orton saw as naturalism and rejected), the dialogue is meant to be a close imitation of everyday speech so the audience concentrates on the person doing the speaking, wants to know about their inner feelings and problems or whatever. In an Orton play the speech is not the expression of each individual character so much as a collection of phrases borrowed from recognisable sources. As we saw with the quotation from Ed in *Sloane*, the various sorts of language are combined together with frequent changes of verbal, and later on performance, style from speech to speech, line to line, or within phrases. Official-sounding language may suddenly be replaced by the texture of a romantic novel. At the opening of *Servant* there's Edith's 'I was crushed up against a wall by a section of the crowd,' and later Buchanan's 'You've a look about you of the only woman I ever loved' (pp.51-52). Linguists would call this variation of language a change in register: it's funny because it produces unexpected effects in what is always recognised as familiar. Orton himself called the style 'collage'. It's the equivalent in words of what he and Halliwell did with the library book dust-jackets (and Halliwell continued this in his own artworks).

The effect of linguistic 'collage' is that an audience notices language. It ceases to be invisible, simply accepted as a means of communication alone, and it becomes marked out through its changes in style. Thus language seems to originate not in the individual 'heart' but in the organs, as it were, of mass media, the giblets of Fleet Street. The person is not a free individual being but something always constructed from outside, full of learnt concepts (if not giblets).

Orton's dramatic language may be said to correct the way we think about the 'fundamental concepts' (Perry Anderson's phrase) of our society. It does so because, first, language is shown to be acquired by people, and more importantly the moral standards and values embedded in language are also acquired. They are not natural or instinctive parts of an individual's make-up. When an Orton character thinks s/he is speaking sincerely or spontaneously, the audience is recognising learnt cliché, hence the laughter. This is one reason why Orton wanted his characters played for real. It is up to the audience to spot that what is sincerely felt is in fact second-hand (you don't get this effect when actors send up the characters; such playing also makes Orton's work easier on the audience). So, concepts such as morality, decency, normality are seen to be *acquired*, not natural.

Second, a major joke about all the moralistic language is that Orton shows it to be misapplied. When an audience shares with the characters a sense of the seriousness of a situation, it treats what is said on stage as normal, appropriate responses to the dramatic situation. The audience, as it were, sees what the characters see and does not question the analysis that characters might make of their own situations (and therefore, for example, hangs about patiently for three and a half hours while Hamlet misunderstands that kings are for killing). In an Orton play the audience sees and values things very differently from the characters. Characters are comic because they are led, by their second-hand morality, to misunderstand and view incorrectly the situation in which they find themselves. So, an acquired set of concepts such as morality, decency, normality, is shown to lead individuals to, as it were, misrecognise their own situations; to see the emperor's new clothes while in fact he is naked.

This use of language is just one part of the politics of Orton's style, and it might be said to contribute to the education of the audience. There's a second element, however, which works more aggressively as an attack on the audience. This element is composed of riot, frenzy and anarchy.

In a conventional farce, after all the disruptions there is a return to order at the end, which an audience finds satisfying. Orton's plays end without a satisfying restoration of order. Some endings are openly cynical compromises by the characters; others are clear parodies of community rituals (the state funeral of Erpingham, the firm's dance at the end of *Servant*). Orton's comedy does not restore its audience to a sense of social harmony after tribulations have passed. The theatrical method uses humour in much the same way as it is defined in a contemporary manifesto of American anarchists: 'the dynamite and guerilla warfare of the mind' (Nuttall, 1968: 63).

Orton's name for his intended effect was 'Dionysiac'. The term comes from the ancient Greek celebration of the god Dionysos, which involved drugged or drunken orgy (which departs somewhat from the p's and q's of present-day Mykonos). The celebration allowed the everyday rules of social behaviour to be suspended in an indulgence to excess of appetites and pleasures. Frenzy may thus be seen as rebellion against repressive decorum. In *The Erpingham Camp*, a play based very loosely on *The Bacchae* by the classical Greek dramatist Euripides, the holiday-makers in a frenzy express their anger at the repressive regime of the owner by looting and burning the camp. (In Orton's first version there was a character called Don who was Dionysos; in the published version, Kenny is Dionysos, naked except for a leopard skin, the god's typical clothing.) Similarly 'Greek' is the ending of *Butler*: the drugged, dazed Sergeant Match appears from an illuminated skylight (the heavens) in a leopard-spotted dress (the Dionysos leopard-skin), no longer the representative of authority but its opposite.

The idea of Dionysiac rebellion fits nicely with youth and anarchist rebellion. Neither works from an articulate position, each creates its effect by indulging desires that the dominant order wishes to curb. Ray Gosling's dream boy 'has become a new Dionysos, and the world sings a paean to his purity; a purity born of a fear created by his father's generation' (Gosling, 1960: 30). And Myra Breckinridge concludes: 'the Dionysian is still a necessity in our lives' (Vidal, 1968: 92). In Orton's plays the plan was to drive the audience wild. In its most successful manifestation, in *Butler*, the action increases in pace, bodies erupt steadily more frequently into what started as a decorous room ornamented with a set of french windows; the bodies become undressed, transformed, smeared with blood; the set itself changes as iron gratings crash down over the windows and a blood-red glare fills the room. Towards its close the play begins on its recognisable happy ending where real identities are discovered and children restored to parents. The audience, like any comedy audience, has awaited the development which will end comic disorder and the play ensures it *recognises* the signs usually associated with a happy ending. Simultaneously the audience discovers how it is trapped, for as we know the happy ending depends on an acceptance of incest. The trick of the text is to show an audience what it agrees to when it relaxes into a happy ending. The audience *sees* itself to be like the characters in expecting an ending to disorder; but discovers that ending to be alien and uncomfortable. Thus trapped the audience is driven wild. The first performances succeeded: people stormed out or barracked the players.

Now, the attraction of the Dionysiac idea itself (as an *idea*) is that it apparently makes cogent and complete a form of rebellion which is, in reality, shot through with contradictions and difficulties. It is a rebellion which reacts against what is dominant; disorders rather than makes new order. You have to have a library book before you can deface it. Thus the particular achievement presented by Orton's work is an endless questioning of morality and sexual identity. All is in flux, values are always undercut. The only reality is a contest over power. *But* the limitation of this Dionysiac rebellion can be noted if we ask where this radical shuffling goes to from here.

3: The Limits of the Writer

Orton had no political practice outside his artworks. He was not a homosexual law reformer or a Gay Liberation activist (even if some of his ideas may seem to have prefigured those of Gay Liberation). While all of his artworks seek to create disorder, they are made in such a way as to guarantee the author's distance from the crime. The main thrill in defacing library books, after doing the job itself, was to *hide* and spy on the borrowers. In the theatre, at the moment the dramatist's text is performed s/he is absent from it. S/he may be a watcher, but not (in Orton's theatre) an actor. This split is crucial. Thus, while Orton's written texts may have had careful schemes to promote disorder, they were reordered, tidied, made acceptable by manager, director, actor – all those over whom Orton had no real control. The early, often disastrous and stupid productions of his plays illustrate how the theatre writer is always fatally compromised for as long as s/he remains simply a *writer*. All of Orton's stress on a theatre of ideas and a rigorous style had no effect if the production company did not share or understand those ideas.

Orton's frustration with the productions of his plays and his realisation of powerlessness were grimly ironic. For his specific theatrical style had to perform the function of keeping him 'free', classless. His plays were too stylish to be realist, too violent to be 'well-made'. He rejected and mocked the class from which he originated, but kept enough loyalty to it to distance himself from the middle class. But the style only offered a fake resolution to his problems of social identification: he was – finally – attached to the middle-class theatre, that's what gave him his career.

The style also promised another 'freedom', an escape from queer stereotyping. The detachment of the writing rejects homosexual emotionalism and confessional intimacy. Orton could adopt the elegant theatre-queer style of Coward or Rattigan, but deny the style its usual function of covering up homosexuality. His style enabled him to flaunt homosex without stereotype and without guilt (more of this later). Yet it's another fake solution to another trap. Precisely that style gave him success as a writer; and as the success grew, the relationship with his lover became more difficult: *because he was reentering a closed heterosexist society* after living almost as a recluse with his lover. Halliwell was treated like dirt by the people who were making Orton's career and exploiting his talent. I have already noted, in the Introduction, the theatre director Dromgoole's despicable treatment of Halliwell. But here should be recalled the grimmest story, that of the moment of achieved success: the Evening Standard awards lunch. Halliwell didn't want to go, so Orton went with Margaret Ramsay. The organisers apparently expected Orton to be married or at least to have a female partner (which might have been a piece of malicious homophobia, for surely someone must have known). Ramsay told Orton that she would be his wife for the afternoon. He was apparently glad he had not gone with Halliwell.

Here, where you might expect Orton to be at his most triumphant and aggressive, he was at his most vulnerable, prepared to be most embarrassed about his sexuality. Why? Because he wanted that award; it meant something to him in terms of career and identity. He valued what he was to be given by the new world that he had entered, so – essentially – he respected that world. If he did not respect it, he would not have taken the award, but he could not afford to refuse it. For all the pose, he was, economically, the inferior. Which all means that, instead of being aggressive towards the institutionalised heterosexism, it created in him guilt and embarrassment. It should be noted that Ramsay was his *agent*, the person who would develop his career in this new world and with whom his relationship was primarily economic. Her gesture of being his 'wife', instead of bolstering Orton's pride in his sexuality and in his lover (when he most needed it), effectively obliterated the 'problem' of Halliwell. It is a symbolic moment: the agent offers a new role that excludes the lover. The long-standing but illicit homosexual love is replaced by the deceitful but face-saving economic partnership. Orton's moment of great triumph was simultaneously a moment of homosexual sell-out.

Orton's promiscuity, his identification with rebellious youth, his role as writer, were all strategies to assure himself of his own personal independence. But they were all full of deep contradictions. Orton was not as much in control of his life as he thought he was. His problem was that his political understanding did not analyse society in terms of economic and social organisation. Like many in the '60s he was cynical about politics and political commitment. So he expressed his opposition as something individualistic: he made gestures of defiance and artworks of provocation. He was, of course, right to feel anger about the society around him because it wanted to destroy his sexual partnership. But his individual anger gave him no control over his circumstances. He and his lover Kenneth Halliwell were indeed destroyed.

They did not have the political links, the shared commitments, the oppositional solidarity with others that would have helped them survive their society. These are the fatal limits to their essentially individualistic challenge to that society.

Orton – and Halliwell – did, however, leave a set of artworks which were produced from that anger. These artworks remain, like their authors, vulnerable to those who hold the real, *economic* power: the theatre managers with their profit motive, the career interests of actors and producers. Nevertheless there exists in the written texts a potentially radical questioning of straight society. It is to that questioning, to that proper legacy of Halliwell and Orton, that we now turn.

Chapter 6:

Sexy Hooligans

The previous three chapters have all ended somewhat negatively, as critiques of the limitations of Orton's outlook. I hope to have shown, however, that these limitations often had their cause in the vulnerability of Orton's position: he had been a struggling isolated homosexual writer and suddenly made it good in a heterosexist society. It is necessary, I think, to remain angry with that society even while acknowledging Orton's mistakes and compromises.

By way of balancing the chapters that focus on Orton's self-identity, we move now to three chapters which look at his artworks and messages. Those messages can be seen in the context of, and as a counter to, the critique of Orton's personal outlook. The analysis of the playtexts shows a subversion of some of the heterosexist assumptions perpetuated in a number of contemporary homosexual artworks, as well as a straightforward anger against non-homosexual society. Therefore the chapters that follow, firstly (in *this* chapter) look at the artworks as specifically and joyously homosexual artworks. Then I tackle the much more difficult subject of Orton's views about women. Finally I shall look at homosexuality and the state. The intention is to broaden the focus, to turn outwards from Orton to see how the particular products of the writer eventually always engage with the large political questions around homosexuality, gender and nation.

Again I must clarify that I'm aware of an increasingly narrow concentration on *Orton*, rather than Halliwell and Orton. Again the reason is the same: lack of information about Halliwell. But I hope throughout to acknowledge that Halliwell contributed to Orton's products and that his contributions were valued by Orton. How much the works that came out under Orton's name were products of their *joint* thinking we can never know, but we must never forget Halliwell's creative influence.

Finally, the analysis of the plays needs to come near the end of the book and to be polemically stated, because we have the plays with us still. Who is 'we'? That, reader, is for you to decide. Currently, heterosexist culture feels free to turn the plays into heterosexist comedies and to forget about their homosexual anger. Happily there are no authors to object to this transformation, since heterosexism had the foresight to destroy them. It seems imperative therefore to reclaim the plays from a radical gay position: to make it clear that, while the plays' politics are not always attractive to a radical gay position, they are still – most definitely – homosexual plays.

1: Presenting Homosex

Orton's biographer says that his 'compulsive promiscuity...showed a need to confirm his maleness' (Lahr, 1978: 147). This remark assumes that queers are not proper men, that this fact panics them, and that they are in the grip of passions they cannot control: age-old anti-queer assumptions. The model can be overturned to suggest that Orton promoted an image of promiscuity to test and provoke assumed heterosexuality: as a conscious project. The problems entailed in this, as we shall see, were caused by the heterosexist society in which he worked.

When Halliwell and Orton chopped up the library book dust-jackets, they frequently constructed the original designs into homosexual images (I take it, by the way, that it was principally Halliwell that did the work since visual collage tended to be his chosen artform while Orton's medium was words). Thus *The Queen's Favourite* came to acquire new meaning with the picture of two men wrestling. *The Steel Cocoon* developed phallic implications with the addition of a naked male torso in jockstrap, and a collage of mainly naked men where the author's photo should be. The cover of the book about Robert Helpmann specifically alludes to what is normally concealed from accounts of his work, his sexuality. The male body has become the object of interest. The famous cover showing Edith Sitwell as Nurse Edith Cavell (which featured in the trial, and has now mysteriously disappeared from Islington Central Library) has the heroic nurse staring not at the blank wall of her prison cell (as in the original), but at the naked male torso of a statue. Similarly, on *Seen any Good Films Lately?* the comic little cartoon man, who previously would indicate that the book was about 'light' entertainment, is now looking at a film screen which includes a half-naked blindfolded man. That man is not young or conventionally sexy. Several of the dust-jackets carry images of older men: John Betjeman with the body of a tattooed man; an almost naked man in front of a Renaissance painting which shows bared limbs, here making clear that what is being tested is the idea of 'acceptable' male nakedness. In addition to their homoerotic images, the dust-jackets are irreverent about the bodies of older men, exposing to the gaze what is normally hidden. The 'maleness' which Lahr assumed to be a simple concept was made by Halliwell and Orton into a problem: What happens when you make a male body the object of society's gaze? When do two men shown together become homoerotic? What happens to male authority when you take its clothes off?

In his plays Orton continually infiltrated the action with images of sexy boys. These images are carefully set up, created in front of us, and thus become fetishistic. Thus several of the young men in the plays spend some time partially clothed: Sloane drops his jeans for Kath to nurse his leg; the husbands in *Erpingham Camp* are parted from their trousers; Nick wanders around in his knickers. So far this action is part of a farce convention: the comedy of men who lose their trousers. But Orton pushes further. The boys are dressed again, but in clothing more overtly associated with homosexual soft porn. The classic case is Sloane who is re-dressed in 'boots, leather trousers and a white T-shirt' – the gear of the homosexual leather bar (yes, there were some in those far-off days), which Orton was somewhat into himself. (As well as having himself photographed nude, he was also photographed in peaked cap and heavy mac.) In *Erpingham Camp* Kenny volunteers to be Tarzan-for-the-week, and thereafter wanders around in underpants and leopard-skin (perhaps like those covers of the Edgar Rice Burroughs paperbacks, with their drawings of Tarzan naked but for animal-skin bikini pants). The most extended piece of re-clothing business comes in *Butler*:

> Sergeant Match takes off his boots. Nick appears in the doorway of the dispensary. Dr Prentice hands him the boots. Nick takes them into the dispensary. Sergeant Match takes off his tunic and hands it to Dr Prentice. Nick, without his shoes and wig {he had been disguised as a woman}, appears in the doorway of the dispensary. Dr Prentice hands him the Sergeant's tunic. Nick turns. Dr Prentice unzips his dress. Nick takes the tunic into the dispensary. Sergeant Match takes off his shirt and tie. Nick wearing only his underpants, appears in the doorway of the dispensary. Dr Prentice hands him the Sergeant's shirt and tie. Nick goes into the dispensary. Sergeant Match drops his trousers. Mrs Prentice enters from the hall (p.64).

The man with his trousers down is no unusual figure in farce, but there is a distinct difference between the two men who undress here. Nick does not fit into the same category as Match. The business has been handled so that it goes beyond a conventional farce scene.

Clothing jokes in farce often reinforce conventions about sex roles: for example, the man with his trousers down is funny because he loses his traditional dignity as he becomes uncovered (whereas the *woman* who is undressed is supposedly sexy); and the man dressed as a woman is again comic because this is supposedly improper for a man (and usually involves a mocking imitation of 'feminine' behaviour). Orton saves the conventional farce joke for the policeman Match, the figure of law and order. He is the one caught with his trousers down when the woman enters.

But Orton pushes the business beyond sex stereotyping. Nick is not so much comic as erotic. The scene would be simpler if it consisted of two men swapping clothes, but there's a third, male, party. While Match undresses *himself*, Nick is aided by the third man, Prentice. The young man's body is fetishised by the action: three times Nick has to appear in the doorway of the dispensary, as if in a frame. This formalises, makes pictorial, his stages of undress. Secondly, Nick is handed clothes by Prentice; but the more clothes he is handed, the more naked he becomes. The clothes cease to function as useful objects. Instead they are emblems of Prentice's attention to Nick's body. Most crucially, Nick's undressing remains a secret between himself, Prentice and the audience that watches. There is no farcical moral horror here. He is not caught out by the woman's appearance. Only when Mrs Prentice gazes in shock at Match is the audience returned to the conventional values of farce, with its trousers-down humour. But they have been earlier gazing at something more unaccustomed, the homoeroticised male body.

Later Nick reappears in underpants and police helmet, just sufficiently overdressed to be fetishistic. There are similar Athletic Model Guild or *Body Beautiful* photos of men naked or in posing pouches wearing construction helmets, cowboy hats, Roman helmets. The gear that Nick wears is apparently necessary within the development of the plot. And here, as elsewhere, the logic of the narrative produces semi-pornographic images. Orton is joking against heterosexual norms: the nominally straight situations in the plays keep on producing, irrepressibly, sexy images of young men; like the dust-jackets they crop up where you don't expect them.

But besides joking against non-homosexuals, Orton is doing battle with contemporary versions of homosexual soft porn. This took two forms, both of which are infected by a sense of homosexual guilt. Porn mags usually offered their images as serious studies of body-building prowess or as objects of 'high' artistic contemplation: *Body Beautiful* (vol. 2: 2, 'Studies in masculine art') has candelabra and a Shakespeare sonnet accompanying shots of a naked youth to rub home the 'artistic' message. By calling itself 'art' the porn pretends to play down its sex appeal. In doing so, it tacitly admits the guilt of real homosexual desires (hence the need to offer itself as serious culture). In queer novels the guilt is dealt with by making the sex objects clean and wholesome, the college athlete or the manly serviceman; which tells us that queers are not nasty effeminates (they can win races and fire guns), nor are they from the dregs of society (so they don't threaten blackmail). Orton's semi-pornographic images are not tinged with guilt. His young men are not identified as homosexuals and their appearance in sexy situations happens as a 'natural' result of the narrative. They are casual about how they themselves appear, but their sexiness is not underplayed. Orton thus resists the cop-out of some porn mags: the pretence to art and high culture. His young men are explicitly 'ordinary' lads. Happily there were in circulation visual equivalents of this, in the photos done by Robert Mizer for the Athletic Model Guild, which offer the male body, appropriately fetishised, for non-guilty enjoyment and sexual promise.

Orton also resists the propriety of queer novels, the confinement of homosex within safe middle-class behaviour. His lads are criminal and hooligan. Furthermore they – like Orton himself – are prepared to allow themselves to be photographed ('I've an appointment at the nude calendar shop. I've been commissioned to do February'; *Games*, p.22). By contrast, photos in queer novels were usually threatening objects: associated with improper lust, accidents of passion, and hence specifically with blackmail (and were in real life used that way).

Orton puts some of the problems about homo porn into *Entertaining Mr Sloane*. Sloane tells us he killed a man who took 'improper' photos of him:

> 'He wanted to photo me. For certain interesting features I
> had that he wanted the exclusive right of preserving. You
> know how it is. I didn't like to refuse. No harm in it I
> suppose. But then I got to thinking...I knew a kid once
> called MacBride that happened to. Oh, yes...so when I
> gets to think of this I decide I got to do something about
> it' (p.215).

The structure of the speech mimics the awakening of moral concern, the growth of a righteous worry about the impropriety of photography. When after this Sloane is threatened by Kemp's knowledge of his past crime, he kills Kemp. The old man's moral blackmail produces the photographic model's aggression. Pornography is placed within a context of immorality and violence. Yet, of course, in the play Sloane is a sex object, desired by Ed and Kath, and offered to the audience's desire also. His moral outrage at porn, and the associated violence, both *contribute* to his overall sexiness. Far from dignifying his 'porn' as art or propriety, Orton takes the opposed elements of moral outrage and pornographic violence and shows them to be two parts of one whole. The moral shock of Ed and Kath is closely related to their desire for what shocks them.

Orton's divergences from queer writing concern not just the sex object but also, importantly, homosexual emotions. He himself hoped that the portrayal of queers would change after the 1967 law reform, and his own work can be seen to implement some changes. Thus he refuses to perpetuate the myths of youthful innocence and lost Edens. The young men are characterised with a knowingness which, combined with a casualness about sexual pleasure, constitute a deliberate rejection by Orton of the traditional portrayal of homosexual desire. This is an example of such a portrayal: 'I knew I could do nothing whatever to stop the ferocious excitement which had burst in me like a storm' (Baldwin, 1957: 36). Desire is seen as a natural force, something bigger than the individual, but the poetic language is really an arty version of the stereotyped idea that queers can't control themselves, unlike proper men. Thus the sociologist says: 'His urges are powerful...He lives in perpetual fear of these longings getting the better of him' (Hauser, 1962: 91). And the queer novelist says: 'Deep within him, within the secret places of him, he felt a terrifyingly familiar phenomenon take place. It was as if a monster had stirred and sent upward a lazy, powerful tentacle to break the surface of his mind' (Barr, 1950/1965: 10). The homosexual desire, in whatever distorted form, may be like a force of nature in that it is bigger than the individual who houses it, but it is also monstrous, a weirdness in nature, something strange – something that needs to be *controlled* by the normal, something which is itself illegitimate.

So within the emotions felt by homo heroes we find a basic acceptance of what straight society says about homosexuals: 'the sight of him filling Harry with a tremulous, painful response, as debilitating as socially-acceptable love but even less dignified' (Lauder, 1962: 138). Even in happiness the joy is measured against guilt: 'He had plucked a forbidden seed and had achieved a forbidden life. Bright days of intoxication flowed with this knowledge over a forbidden threshold' (Little, 1956/1965: 224).

The sense of the forbidden, or the monstrous, comes from a knowledge that physical homosex is supposedly unnatural and definitely illegal. To counteract this sense, the queer novel claims to depict 'love' rather than 'sex'. Love is said to be of a higher status than sex, and it is a mark of the strength of love that it knows no barriers; it overcomes the forbidden. Love can be seen to go where sex may not tread. (Yet all the time, it's possible to enjoy the books on the basis that what is depicted *is* sex, despite the cover-up.) The choice of poetic language in many novels is an attempt to indicate how 'special' and 'unique' these feelings are. By presenting the experience of homosexual desire as something 'special', the queer novelist resists the implication that homosex is 'merely physical' and degraded. He thus resists the dreaded charge of promiscuity.

Promiscuity is meant to be a bad thing because it exploits sexual partners. Opposed to it are love and desire which 'express' the whole inner being. The opposition is, of course, nonsensical and queer novels unwittingly show this. The 'love' so often expressed reinforces masculine role-play. 'Love' is, firstly, conceived as possession: 'The secret of human love and desire was not mere longing of the flesh; it was a total longing to possess someone' (Little, 1956/1965: 52). Secondly, love or desire operate as a form of high-risk adventuring. In order to satisfy their desires the homo heroes have to reach for what is forbidden, to trespass and break the rules. To accept the rules would be to accept a repressive society. But, instead, something else is accepted – namely the sense of the forbidden. This usefully then provides an obstacle for the male hero to overcome, as a test of his adventuring courage on the lines of what is an old-fashioned masculine model. By contrast Orton's youths make themselves available to other people's desires. They have not internalised any notion of the forbidden or the special. They show no acceptance of homosexual weirdness or otherness. There is no break between desire and everyday life.

When homosexual desire is seen as something that is deep inside the man, a monster threatening to get out, there is an implication that this is the inner reality beside which the external surface is merely a facade. This way of looking at queers is aided by a feature that crops up in so much writing about them – the *confession*. Scenes in which a character 'breaks down' and speaks of his real inner feelings, or his real past history, are common both in novels and plays. Two plays of 1966, Christopher Hampton's *When Did You Last See My Mother?* and Charles Dyer's *Staircase*, engage audience sympathy for the moments when the cynicism or bravado of the surface give way to the 'real' inner turmoil: in the latter, Charlie's aggressive and camp patter is broken by the delivery of a police warrant for importuning and the act collapses, he 'looks old, tired, frightened' (p.29). The end of Mart Crowley's *Boys in the Band* (1968) has the bitchy Michael dissolving in tears of homosexual self-hate, realising and facing what he 'is'. The confession format implies that always below the mask are the real homosexual anxiety, guilt and self-hatred. It is significant that the confession is also used by books about queers, a good example being the BMA report (1955) which ends with a series of 'case studies' and statements by homosexuals converted to Christianity: 'I enclose an intimate and factual account of sexual experiences which I need hardly say I am very ashamed of, but which I could have been saved from, I believe, if I had only been able to meet up with a great driving force of "conversion"...earlier' (p.85). For the sociologist Schofield the 'sudden change of heart' after arrest is an opportunity not to be missed by the psychiatrist.

The confession in queer plays tells its audience that queers are all 'really' distressed. In fact, as we see from *real* cases, the confession is induced and then used by the authorities to get the frightened queer actually to *acquiesce in* rather than merely 'recognise' his guilt (since it's put there by those authorities in the first place). It is, hence, important to note that Orton rejects any sort of realism that implies we can discover the essential inner person, for that is a strategy used against queers. He specifically sends up the confession, at the end of *Butler*, for example: 'After a short conversation during which we discussed sex matters in an uninhibited and free-wheeling way, he asked me if I'd mind dressing up as a woman. I agreed to his suggestion having heard that transvestism is no longer held to be a dangerous debilitating vice' (p.77: note the joke about law reform and its limits; transvestism was very much a problem for law reformers).

2: *Trying Not to See Homosexuals*

Because Orton was breaking the 'rules' for representing homosexuals, many audiences could not recognise what he was doing. They tended to see the youths simply as hooligans and, similarly, the only clear homosexual in Orton's writing, Ed in *Sloane*, tended to be performed and seen as a stereotyped queer. Orton had to fight battles with directors and actors over Ed in order to prevent his being pigeon-holed as a type. The character is an exploration of the masculine homo, a type exemplified in the sympathetic businessman hero of *The Youngest Director*, who dresses soberly in suits rather than flaunts, who educates his working-class boyfriend into his own tastes. Orton follows the model: 'I've a certain amount of influence. Friends with money.' 'I shall dress in a quiet suit. Drive up in the motor.' 'Are you clean living? You may as well know I set great store by morals' (*Sloane*, pp.182-84). The dominant feature of Ed on stage is the element *The Youngest Director* plays down, namely lust: despite his claims, there's nothing altruistic about Ed and he's more powerful than the working-class Sloane. This reverses the novel's picture of middle-class sobriety (and hypocrisy). At the same time it tests its audience with the figure of the masculine homosexual. Ed is a difficult deviation from type, because although he is not a flaunter neither is he the accepted opposite, the chastely disciplined good queer; he has both social control *and* lust. Orton was pleased with the US production because it played Ed masculine and attractive, so the audience could not categorise him. Thus the portrait of a queer, rather than being a focus of pity, was actually a threat.

Orton observed that US audiences sympathised with Kath, and he delighted in how his play twisted expectations. It is precisely the rule-breaking which is the essence of his dramatic work and that, I think, constitutes the 'seriousness' of his plays, of which Orton was so proud. He said *Sloane* was as serious as Osborne's law-reform play, *A Patriot for Me*, and much more so than *The Killing of Sister George*. The latter play he attacked because it played straight to the expectations of middle-brow and middle-class audiences. It gave them what they wanted to hear about lesbians (and as Orton rightly observed, had little to do with lesbians: it was written by a *man* for godsake!). Although Osborne's *Patriot* is a serious play, its sense of itself as tragedy limits it (it's a case of 'typical' homosexual emotionalism again). Orton saw that realistic plays usually portrayed homosexual neurosis and panic, and that their production was mainly confined to theatres known for their 'commitment' (the most famous of these being the Royal Court, as a character in the novel *Winger's Landfall* remarks). And, as was notoriously apparent with *Patriot*, there was a third problem with the portrayal of queers: censorship. Osborne's attempt to show a sexual relationship between two men was banned from representation.

Now, Orton wanted to get his plays on, and to get them on in front of an audience that would be unsettled by them because it was not expecting 'problem' topics or rule-breaking. So he selected comedy as his form. *But* producers and audiences of comedy look for comic 'types'; they think they know where to laugh. Orton thus had a problem: he had chosen a dramatic form which he could use to avoid the homosexual stereotyping of 'serious' plays, but it was a form which is itself heavily dependent on stereotypes. So audiences and producers imposed their own (often comfortable) interpretations. They could not and would not see what Orton was doing. He noted that they laughed to assert their heterosexuality.

Thus, despite what Orton *wrote*, in production the presence of homosexual desire and imagery could be concealed (and often is). Against this, we need to stress that the product over which Orton had control, namely the written texts, does insist on its homosexuality. It does so in two major ways.

Firstly, the homosexual look. Not only do a couple of young men say they have been photographic models, but the staging presents them as objects to be looked at. After Ed's schemes for what Sloane should wear, Act 2 opens with Sloane lying on a settee in his leather jeans and boots; a newspaper covers his face, so that it is only the fetishistically clothed body which is seen. He is momentarily alone on stage and the audience has only his body to gaze at: a body wearing the clothes provided for it by another man, the body desired by that man, displayed on a couch – like a leather Madame Récamier.

Similarly, Nick is framed by a doorway in several stages of undress. That business gets its force from the fact that Nick has already been seen as the object of desire. He is offered to Prentice as a new secretary, so that in the classic comedy scene where the sexist boss (and the audience) appraise the newly arrived young woman, this time the focus is on a male youth. When Nick later undresses, his jacket slickly undoes 'from shoulder to hip' in a moment. Had he *fumbled* with buttons, it would be comic because it would show the male to be embarrassed over the loss of his clothes (particularly in front of another man). The jacket unzips instead like a garment in a striptease. He is not the clumsy victim of a farce routine, but the star performer in a different sort of show. The undoing of the jacket is a moment when the sexually secure gaze of a heterosexist farce audience is replaced by the erotic gaze of an audience at a male strip show. (Needless to say, it can be hurried out of the way in production.)

More complex is the use of a second character to control the way an audience sees the youth. The reaction of an onstage character often gives guidelines to an audience's interpretation. For example, *Boys in the Band* puts the straight Alan on stage in the queer party: the audience knows that Michael does not want to betray what he 'is' to his old friend Alan, so it watches always alert to spot any signs of give-away queer flaunting. We are encouraged to look through the onstage straight's eyes, learning to feel nervous about queer behaviour. By contrast, Orton engineers homosexual looks. In the first scene of *Funeral Games* Caulfield is being interviewed by Pringle. Pringle stares at him, Caulfield asks for an ashtray, Pringle 'puts it carefully' beside Caulfield, Caulfield flicks ash into it, Pringle asks him if he is for hire and Caulfield, after a pause, says: 'I won't be choirboy. I'm too old' (p.13). The reply develops out of Pringle's stare and carefully placed ashtray, the older man ministering to the younger. Caulfield's casual smoking, with his pause to consider, momentarily hints at a hustling scene. The interview becomes, briefly, eroticised through the way the younger man is looked at; his casualness changes its meaning.

As with the case of Nick and Sloane referred to above, a straight theatre production will remove or hurry over the eroticism. In heterosexist theatre the homophobic censorship does not necessarily need to come from on high, since it usually takes place as the performance is rehearsed. Directors and actors underplay or cancel out what is specifically homoerotic in Orton's work. Thus, as a small example, a production of *Sloane* at Manchester's Royal Exchange had Adam Ant as Sloane merely snoozing on the settee, not erotically *posed*. And where the sexiness did appear, it was labelled straight. The star name used to draw in audiences has a star sexuality which is carefully guarded and cultivated, precisely for this purpose.

To take another complex example of the look, this time from *Loot*: onstage, Dennis (holding a screwdriver), Fay, Hal and his father McLeavy. McLeavy speaks at length about the impropriety of criminals burrowing from the undertakers into a bank. He concludes that criminals must suffer because they are poor sleepers. Fay immediately asks Hal how he sleeps, to which he replies: 'Alone' (p.17). During McLeavy's speech, Fay has been looking at Hal and Dennis, suspicious of their criminality: the boys presumably avoid each other's eyes; Dennis (an undertaker) is holding the screwdriver, which could serve as much as a criminal tool as an undertaker's instrument. Fay, in looking at them, links them together; but her question moves from seeing them as criminals to seeing them as boys sleeping together – Dennis' screwdriver also has a phallic symbolism. McLeavy's speech ends in the unlikely place of having us think how criminals sleep; he has no idea that one of the criminals is his son and that he sleeps with another boy. The innuendo constructed implies there are two crimes hidden from McLeavy, one of them sexual. The business of the look, in silence, undercuts his own moral horror and positions the audience so that it *knows* about Hal and Dennis.

Secondly, let us look at the homosexual joke. Often these jokes are destroyed by performance; sometimes they are destroyed by the sort of biographical interpretation that Lahr indulges in. An example is this from *Ruffian*: 'We were happy, though. We were young. I was seventeen. He was twenty-three' (p.31). In Lahr's biography this is explained as a reference to Halliwell and Orton's relationship (he makes much of the difference in their ages) (1978: 115). But at one level it's a joke about the queer nostalgia for a time of innocent sex. Orton added it to *Ruffian*; it wasn't in the earlier radio version. Why? It makes the implicitly homosexual relationship of Wilson and his 'brother' (the man referred to in the quote) more shocking, in two ways. Firstly, at a time of scandal about 'dirty' plays and when homosexual law reformers were arguing for an age of consent of 18 or 21, one of the 'brothers' is distinctly under-age. Homosexuals were supposed to corrupt the young; here the young one enjoys it. Secondly, the play makes a sexual innuendo out of the relationship of 'brothers'. So often in fiction a brotherly relationship is used as a cover-up or euphemism for a male sexual partnership. Orton subverts this by playing with the notion of brothers as lovers. And here again is the Freudian Orton at work, insisting on the presence of desire in kinship relations which the dominant order depicts as a scene of innocence.

The status of the homosexual jokes is very much like this one from *Ruffian*: they creep in at the edges of the conversation. 'The doctor said he wanted to put the boy in some kind of club.' 'It's no good trying to do that. Boys cannot be put in the club. That's half their charm' (*Butler*, p.54). Rance's last throwaway sentence here undercuts our assumption that he is heterosexual, shakes his assumed sexual identity. A more pronounced example is when Dr Prentice tells Nick to take his clothes off; Nick (a hotel page and thus a classic homo sex object) asks if Prentice is going to mess him about, and tells him that other men usually give him five shillings. That could be the climax of the joke, which would allow the audience to laugh safely at all those other dirty old men who are not represented on stage. It's a laugh occasioned by Nick's misunderstanding and the audience's prejudice against queers (except that Nick's misunderstanding really comes from being too knowing rather than innocent). But the joke goes on, and Prentice replies: 'Five shillings! Good gracious the rate hasn't changed in thirty years. What can the unions be thinking of?' (p.41). The development suggests that Prentice too sold his body when young, and his horror is not at boy prostitution but at the inefficiency of the unions (working on the assumption that prostitution should be unionised). Orton uses a hoary old anti-union joke to taunt the audience to laughter at what most of them might find unfunny, the whorey young man.

The homosexual jokes undercut assumptions that people are heterosexual and innocent of homosexual practices. They take the audience one step further than predictable farce jokes. A last example, and one I don't much like: 'My wife is a woman. Intelligence doesn't really enter into the matter.' 'If, as you claim, your wife is a woman, you certainly need a larger income' (*Loot*, p.82). The first line is the climax of a series of sexist jokes about Truscott's wife, with Truscott pronouncing on the nature of women. It's a typical laugh line. What's odd about Hal's reply is the attention to Truscott's claim that his wife is a woman, as if that is an unusual thing to claim; it then proceeds into another sexist joke. But temporarily there's a problem: we had assumed all the jokes about Truscott's wife were jokes about women, whereas in Hal's mind they need not have been. His reply almost makes Truscott look silly for having married a woman – as opposed to a man? (Homosexuals, they always said, were wealthier because they did not have to support a wife and family.) The straightforward sexist joke is constructed in such a way that it wobbles straightforward sex role assumptions.

Clearly with the jokes, even more so with the looks, the effect depends on how they are performed. Although the witty style makes the plays seem so firmly written, the construction of the jokes and the way characters are looked at make the plays very slippery. They present themselves as if they were 'well-made plays', but they don't fulfil those expectations. That shift between what they promise, and what they do, is arguably part of the pleasure for a homosexual audience, in that the plays keep sliding away from jokes that confirm the usual oppressive sex roles and keep slipping into innuendo always most readily recognisable by those with homosexual knowledge. The plays offer positive homosexual pleasure, not by dealing in sentiment about the beauty and specialness of homosexual love, but by disrupting heterosexual expectations and by encouraging the complicity of homosexuals in the audience through shared innuendo and shared desire for the male sex objects. That desire is encouraged by the endings of the plays. At the end of *Sloane* Kath and Ed negotiate over Sloane. At the end of *Loot* Dennis, Hal and Fay are in a triangular tableau round the coffin, and in *Butler*, before the very end, Nick is in an incestuous tableau of the family. There is no sense that the boys have reached a satisfying or conclusive end to their stories, they are obviously dragged into dissatisfactory endings. They still await a proper relationship which will, feels the homosexual spectator, be fulfilled by his own desire.

The reason Orton's plays always remain susceptible to bowdlerisation by non-homosexual theatre production is that the homosexuality is unlabelled, confined to innuendo and throwaway lines. This is mainly the result of Orton's own strategy. The authority figures in the plays are undesirable straights; no open queer types can be opposed to them, since these types are the distorted products of that repressive society – neither the flaunting queen nor the masculine homo is an object of desire. The desired figures are the hooligans, and they remain desired only insofar as they are difficult to categorise.

For example, the deliberately Pinteresque opening of *Sloane* presents the youth as a 'typical' menacing hooligan in order to produce a specific set of fearful apprehensions in a non-homosexual audience. Yet Sloane is also recognisable – to a homosexual – as a bit of (suspiciously 'innocent') rough trade. That's his appeal for Ed. For a '60s audience Sloane doesn't fit into the available categories for a homo – he is promiscuous but not effeminate, manly but criminal. These categories have to be refused by the homosexual writer because they are invented by straight society. When Orton puts together Pinteresque menacer and rough trade, he produces a homosexual type which an audience can respond to not as a vulnerable casualty but as a sexy object of fear.

It was not possible, given Orton's attitudes and politics, to create a homosexual who is both secure and desirable, and clearly homosexual.

The plays are constructions of Orton's erotic fantasy, but he attempted to avoid making the obvious homosexual text. (Indeed he laughed at chunks of Genet's homoerotic *Querelle of Brest*.) So Orton could never fully declare the fantasy as his own (unlike Genet). It has always to be undercut, to appear on the edges, to disappear back into cynicism. Orton rightly refused the types offered by queer fiction and he was wary about having himself categorised either as a trivial comic writer or as a 'serious' homosexual writer, for that would have made him vulnerable to those he despised. He therefore produced texts that are both homoerotic and uncategorisable as homosexual. This means that performances can and do turn the written texts into banal heterosexual comedies, at which audiences laugh confidently to assert their heterosexuality...which always seems to *need* asserting, for some reason.

Chapter 7:
Misogyny and Mary Whitehouse

As attacks on the family and masculinity, Orton's plays may be seen as radically subversive. Their subversion is crucially limited, however, in one area: the representation of women. The plays invite their audiences to laugh at women who are trivial and silly and at women who are bossy and menacing. The laughter is a way of coping with an ancient masculine fear of women's sexual desire and women's social power.

This fear is masculine in general: some people would explain that it is developed in all boy children when at an early stage they realise they are biologically different from their mothers; others would see it as a nervousness produced by a combination of real dependence on women's labour alongside an unfounded claim to superiority over them. For male homosexuals, the relationship with women becomes especially complex, and it is this complexity which underlies all the twists and turns of this chapter. The male homosexual is a man in a world which gives power to men; through his biology he is offered a place in the dominant group. But through his sexuality he is oppressed and rejected by the dominant male group, he is not a 'proper man'. At certain periods some male homosexuals have seen how their oppression connects with (though it's not the same as) the oppression of women within a gender system which allocates power only to a certain definition of maleness. For some male homosexuals the link is sentimental rather than political, in that women are seen as more 'sympathetic' (less likely to beat you up). But these generalised links can become unstuck in the face of lesbianism. Far from there being a natural common cause in the face of anti-homosexual oppression, lesbians and gay men are groups separated by their different positions within a society divided on gender lines, and hence have differing experiences and differing objectives; insofar as they do make common cause, it is something they *work for* together. Male homosexual culture has tended to share with non-homosexual masculinity its contempt for lesbians. This contempt is often expressed in the stereotyping of women within our culture. Thus whereas gay culture may admire or fetishise the movie star whose glamour has been approved according to heterosexual norms, it perpetuates, without inspecting them, images of butch or powerful women as being ugly or malevolent. Lesbianism is separate in its sexuality, in which there is no place for men, no address to men; and often in its social organisation (its own clubs and meeting-places). It's necessary to make these points here, since this chapter is about men's images of women, and many of these images are based on (without saying so) a hatred of lesbianism. Lesbianism is in fact never explicitly discussed in the culture I am looking at here. Yet it is there all the time in the images we are looking at. We have to realise, and note, that we are dealing with an anti-lesbian homosexual culture, and that this is so even when links with women in general are apparently made.

In our period, the 1950s and '60s, male homosexuals faced specific problems connected with women. Before the Women's Liberation movement of the early '70s, much of women's political activity and organisation had been concentrated around moral issues, specifically seeking to uphold 'traditional' family values and sexual purity, and to oppose obscenity and 'deviance'. Of course this sort of activity still goes on, as a right-wing alternative to feminism (and in some cases has penetrated feminism too). Sexual purity campaigns threatened (and still do) the lifestyle and very existence of homosexuals. Women organised around these issues may hence be seen to be repressive. A domesticated version of this repressive role (though the book doesn't say it's repressive) may be seen in Jay Gilbert's *The Goose Girl* where a hetero couple put right a bitchy queer, and a woman is seen to become *properly* tough when confronted by 'unmanly' men. Thus, alongside any generalised misogyny, a specific hostility to repressive women characterised male homosexual attitudes at this period.

These events of the early '60s may be likened to the 1880s, when an embryonic radical feminism was sidetracked into the more conservative social purity campaigns; these led to the explicit criminalisation of male homosexuals. Indeed, the technical illegality of male homosex produced yet another reason for viewing male homosexuality and lesbianism as separate. By contrast, in the early '70s there were successful attempts to create alliances between male homosexuals and lesbians, and between homosexuals and the Women's Liberation movement in their collective opposition to the tyranny of traditional gender roles and the power of the family. It is a mark of how deep is the structure of gender in our society that many lesbians were in a short time alienated from these alliances by a combination of the acquired sexism and residual misogyny of many gay men. Nevertheless the effect of the early '70s was to teach us to criticise the gender system as a whole, rather than fetishise particular expressions of it. Thus, although women led one of the most recent campaigns against homosexuals – for example, Jill Knight and her Clause 28, Teresa Gorman and her homophobic diatribes, Elaine Kellett-Bowman and her support for anti-gay arson (affirming 'there should be an intolerance of evil'), Rachel Tingle and her pamphlet on education, *Gay Lessons* – and although a number of feminists are homophobic, this should properly be seen as a product of the gender system, a system principally serving and founded on male power. Indeed the very separation of gay men from lesbians may be seen as a product of the repression that this system produces in order to keep itself in being.

This chapter will attempt to explain Orton's mockery of women in terms of his situation as a male homosexual in the '60s and in terms of a masculine fear of female sexual desire. Although the problem affects many male writers, it is perhaps at its most difficult in Orton's work. On the one hand we can see his attack on masculinity, which would potentially link with the arguments of feminists, but on the other hand, the hatred of powerful women, which would serve to reinforce traditional misogyny. This hatred of powerful women had more in it than the hatred of purity campaigners, I suspect. There is probably a deep and uninspected hatred of lesbianism. (The image of a strong or independent woman frequently implies, without stating, lesbian sexuality: the independent woman doesn't need men.) The culture of the '60s offered few links between male and female homosexuals, either in terms of political discussion or shared social venues. For Orton, as for many male homosexuals, lesbians were a people apart. But it is perhaps deeper than that. Male homosexuals were taught that they could earn respect and tolerance by condemning those who flaunted their sexuality. A fear of being 'deviant' is used to police the behaviour and thinking of the social group. Using precisely the same learnt logic, male homosexuals could assert their own 'normality' by transferring onto lesbians the label of real deviance. By distancing themselves from homosexual women, homosexual men apparently draw themselves closer to the secure group, heterosexual men. The image (not the reality) is of men joining together in their condemnation of the one group that gestures its refusal of the gender system, those women who refuse to desire and serve men. The lesbian engages in sex that is unseen by men and that deliberately excludes men. Thus it becomes more mysterious and strange (to men) and hence an obvious target for misogynistic feelings. In the male homosexual's condemnation of lesbians, the enthusiasm for 'security' for queers within gender alliances is fuelled by a misogyny that is general to most men.

To bring all this to bear on Orton, it may be best to begin with a clear example of the tension between anti-masculinity and misogyny – in the novel published as *Head to Toe*. The book consists of a series of rambling adventures which work as various sorts of literary parody (which makes it pretty unreadable). The main parodic attack is on the spy thriller, with its usual celebration of tough masculinity. In an early section of *Head to Toe* the hero finds himself in a world run by women, being interrogated: 'He stared at Hogg's lips with intense concentration. But it was not in her lips. The signal came from her eyes. The man felt the steel bite into his neck; he winced, jerking forward' (p.42). Compare this with: 'The woman's eyes were still locked in Bond's. Out of Bond's sight, and not noticed by Mathis, who was still examining her face, the toe of one shiny buttoned boot pressed under the instep of the other' (Fleming, 1957: 207).

Orton makes a joke out of the thriller by having women in the tough roles supposedly reserved for men. But of course they are not always reserved for men, as my quotation from Fleming shows. For these sorts of thrillers also play with hetero masochistic fantasies, which Orton locates and mocks. The mockery is achieved not just through style, but also through deliberately confusing the female stereotypes that thrillers usually work to keep separate. While the tough woman is villainous, the pretty and submissive woman is desirable. Orton, however, makes his tough ruling women also conventionally 'feminine': 'A number of women rose and crowded round the Prime Minister as she entered wearing a wool two-piece, simplicity itself, yet with a sort of dash and elegance' (p.36). If the previous quotation mocked masculine thrillers, then this one mocks the genre of women's magazines.

The blurring together of the two sorts of women is more than a satiric device. It shows an anger at a gender system which requires women to demonstrate their submissiveness by dressing 'feminine' and dealing only with 'women's issues'; but it also scorns the woman who deviates from this gender system, who is tough and independent (and lesbian). This blurring together of apparently distinct targets will reappear consistently in the texts quoted in this chapter. This is why it is important to note here the extent to which they are not separate targets, but both together an expression of the male homosexual's discontent with the gender system. That the discontent is expressed in misogynist terms is partly a symptom of his oppressed condition: one of the effects of oppression is to reinforce ignorance and inherited prejudices. *Head to Toe* is preeminently a homosexual text. Its writing predates the plays, so that it comes from a period when Orton and Halliwell collaborated on literary projects. Much of their writing was done for mutual amusement. The original readership for *Head to Toe* was therefore a homosexual one, Orton and Halliwell as audience as well as authors. The piss-take of hetero thrillers and the jokes about women begin life as private homosexual jokes. The violent sexual desires of the women are at one level nothing to do with women (and at another level they are images that put down female sexual desire): 'she had struck with the fingers balled into a great fist. As in a dream...he felt her tearing at him, removing the forbidden garments' (p.25). The image enjoys the unclothing of the male; furthermore, as Elaine Hobby has pointed out to me, it reads very like an image of fist-fucking. So it has the thrill not only of envisaging things done to a man, but also because it teeters between Orton's (and maybe Halliwell's) desire and fear – Orton liked to be machismo but hated to be fucked (unless he was in control), and both, I think, feared/disliked SM as such.

I have extrapolated at this length because I want to clarify the tangle of issues: the differing female targets, the blurring together of these women, the anti-masculinity, the homosexual desire, the homosexual discontent. These are the areas we are handling, and they insist on mingling themselves together. They will, I hope, become clearer as the chapter progresses.

1: Fierce and Feminine Women

Orton liked the powerful women section of *Head to Toe* sufficiently to reuse it as a basis for his screenplay for the projected Beatles film. The screenplay, called *Up Against It*, can be seen as a development of the attack on a male world. It includes a parody of the Kennedy assassination, but in particular it sends up the image of the Beatles. Their manager wanted to present the 'boys' as clean-living lads in suits (they had abandoned the black leather of their early Liverpool days); although they were idolised by teenage girls, they were also loved (and bought) as nice boys by mums and dads. Orton's script subjects them to all manner of indignities at the hands of threatening women. He preserves at all costs the innocence so fetishised by their management, but reduces their sex appeal to nonsense: his script won't play the manager's game by allowing them both.

The original novel's sexist portrayals of women are also developed. In this respect the screenplay, far from poking fun at or undercutting contemporary culture, simply shares and reinforces its values. Orton's misogynist portrayals of strong women are of a piece with much popular heterosexual fiction of the period. For example, the hero of *The Spy Who Came in From the Cold* is on trial in East Germany: 'a shiver passed over him as he realised that the president of the court was a woman' (Le Carré, 1963: 179). Or, more explicitly, the arch-enemy faced by Bond in *From Russia With Love* is Rosa Klebb, a strong-willed Russian colonel with her 'sheen of nicotine-stained fur over the

mouth' (Fleming, 1957: 53). Both strong women are office-holders in
Eastern bloc countries, as it were products of the hideous equality
threatened by communism. They are a political nightmare dressed up
as, and fused with, a sexual nightmare. They are presented as the
antithesis of the fluffy desirable female sex objects of '60s Britain, so
that being strong-willed goes hand-in-hand with everything else that
is deviant for a woman in hetero culture, namely ugliness and
lesbianism. Insofar as we find Rosa Klebb's facial hair ugly we assent
to the heterosexist values implicit in the description. A different
example of frightening female ugliness may be seen in a 'youth culture'
novel already discussed, Leonard James Harper's *Teddy Boy Ahoy*
(1963). Part of Terry's initiation into the gang involves having sex:
afterwards, 'Terry saw for the first time the woman who had guided
him so expertly into his awakening manhood. She was old and ugly,
her hair hanging about her face in dirty matted strands. Her teeth
looked yellowed and ghastly against her curled, sneering lips. Utter
revolt gripped and tugged at his stomach, making him stagger
outside, where he vomited, much to the other boys' delight' (p.12).
This woman is also black. In making her black, the text demonstrates
how it sees all categories of the oppressed as more or less interchangeable – women, Blacks, (queers) – since they are all united in their
difference from dominant white male order. The sexually experienced
woman, like the tough official woman, deviates from the properly
submissive feminine role. Her deviation is automatically marked by
placing her in a category of 'strangeness' (that is, to straight white male
culture): this woman is black, Rosa Klebb was lesbian. Both are
negative categories. After sex with her Terry is nauseated by the *flesh* of
any woman who is not a sanitised sex object.

In another, more arty, genre of novel, the 'angry young man'
fiction, the woman is a representative of the 'system' which oppresses
the young hero. She is seen to interfere with or obstruct the male's
sexual or social independence, to impose moral obligations on him.
Here we have a stereotype that is perhaps less overtly expressive of the
sort of physical hatred than my previous examples showed. The
attack on woman as representative of an oppressive system seems to be
more 'political' in that it focusses attention on her attitudes (rather
than her body). But of course there were many more *men* who could be
attacked for being repressive; it's not a peculiarly female activity. So
this sort of stereotyping is not as far removed from an underlying
misogyny as it might like to pretend. Orton produces his own version
of this stereotype in his play *The Good and Faithful Servant*, which picks
up on various situations common to 'angry young man' fiction. Mrs
Vealfoy is the 'personnel lady' with a large firm, and through a
sequence of events she has the power to bully young Ray into

marriage.

The figure of Mrs Vealfoy is a product of the two strands of anti-female feeling: the attack on the powerful woman and the attack on the moralistic woman. This mockery of women is explained by Orton's biographer as motivated by Orton's personal reaction to his snobbish mother, but this is to blame Orton alone for what is in fact a cultural and social phenomenon. As a literary stereotype, the moralising housewife appears in an historical period when women's political activity is primarily engaged in social purity movements. Such a confinement of women to the 'private' sphere of life is a product of a male-dominated society; matters concerning the society's public existence, such as the economy, foreign policy and armaments, usually have men doing the talking. Woman is pushed into concerns such as the upbringing of children, personal conduct, moral education – supposedly 'private', 'domestic' issues. The division of gender roles was reinforced with particular intensity in the postwar years of reconstruction, when women were encouraged to seek fulfilment only as wives and mothers and when women's politics were centred on 'domestic' subjects. We can note such examples as the Housewives League of the late '40s, run by the extreme right-wing Dorothy Crisp (see Wilson, 1980: 167); in the late '50s, Lady Albermarle heading an enquiry into youth clubs; in the early '60s, the cartoons of Tory women leading a right-wing moral backlash; in 1963, Mary Whitehouse launching her Women of Britain Clean-Up TV campaign (and in the '80s, the women who have been encouraged to be vocal through so-called parents' rights groups and the associations for promoting 'family' values which are explicitly engineered by the Tory party).

Many male homosexuals were specific about the sort of woman who was felt to be oppressive. For example, Peter Wildeblood noted that when he was convicted as a homosexual, in contrast with the support he received from working-class women, 'a woman spat at me. She was a respectable-looking, middle-aged, tweedy person wearing a sensible felt hat. ...she looked very much like the country gentlewomen with whom my mother used to take coffee' (1955: 87). The focus on the middle-class woman arose, for male homosexuals, out of a political analysis (however inadequate) of the power which oppressed them as well as out of a simple woman-hatred. This can be illustrated from Orton's work.

Sloane appeared in the midst of a general moral panic about sex and violence in the arts. The play was denounced, along with other 'violent' or 'immoral' plays, by Peter Cadbury and Emile Littler. These two both had major financial interests in West End theatre; Orton was, by contrast, the struggling author. Cadbury and Littler were, in effect, trying to silence plays which questioned contemporary assumptions about the family and gender. What they saw as 'immoral' was that which questioned the structure of the world out of which they gained their wealth. The social purity panic was a backlash against social changes and its effects were to reinforce traditional conservative beliefs. Thus the moral panic which concentrates on the *personal* is useful to the power of the upper and middle class and capitalism in the *public* sphere. The person who busies her/himself with a social purity campaign is effectively preserving in power a world of male-dominated business, although that person may be only conscious in her/himself of dealing with moral issues.

Orton's analysis may be put in perspective when we see his response to the social purity campaign. At first he used his letter-writing alter ego Edna Welthorpe to fan the flames of outrage about *Sloane*, hoping to reveal the moralisings as idiocy. But in 1965 Pamela Hansford Johnson parodied the plot of *Sloane* as part of her attack on violent theatre (see Chapter 4). It is an interesting indication of contemporary sexism that, in order to be more extreme than – and hence parody – a plot suggesting male homosexuality, Johnson uses lesbianism. Once again the lesbian is presented as the ultimate oddity, suggesting that (gay) men were not alone in their prejudices about sexuality. A couple of years after this little episode Orton produced Mrs Vealfoy. Significantly he made her not a gossip nor a moral campaigner but a manager. The link between the middle-class female moralist and the structure of (masculine) big business is made evident in the figure of Mrs Vealfoy. Pamela Hansford Johnson seemed to think she was dealing with issues of morality alone. Orton shows that these issues are directly related to the capitalist management of labour. Mrs Vealfoy might be the 'personnel' lady, an appropriate 'private' sphere task, but she hires and disciplines the workforce. Orton's answer to the social purity campaigners was not, therefore, simply to use Edna in provocative parodies but to place the campaign within the economics of capitalist society. He had put his finger on one of the major elements that was to lead to the revival of Toryism and formation of the so-called new right as we know it – the force of conservatism gathered around a programme of moral clean-up and a return to supposedly traditional family values. Audiences now recognise in Mrs Vealfoy a horrific prophecy of Margaret Thatcher. Orton had spotted the birth of the monster with a clarity not shared by all homosexuals, then or now...

There is a second target attacked in Mrs Vealfoy. She is given stage business involving putting on a hat before she sees interviewees. Orton intends that this 'femininity' should be as much an object of mockery as her managerial role. Similarly the official women in *Head to*

Toe are trivially 'feminine': 'Put your strength into winning this election. Victory, I know, will crown our efforts. It is vital in the interests of the free world to stabilise the hemline' (p.38). Electioneering rhetoric combined with hemlines; Mrs Vealfoy's managerial system combined with her hat. Acting out a feminine role is as much to be disapproved as is moralising. The logic behind this argues that 'feminine' behaviour is, as much as morality, something constructed by a capitalism which depends on a division between genders, confining women to the private, moral, ornamental. Deliberately to act a feminine role is thus to play along with, indeed to reinforce, a gender system which is oppressive, particularly to gays (and lesbians).

It may be a sense of this oppression which leads to the specific antipathy to the feminine, the private, the housewifely, among gay writers. For, by contrast, in the spy novels the official women are seen as deviant because they are mannish or sexless: 'Her hair was cut short like a man's,' notices Leamas of the court president (Le Carré, 1963: 180). As against this there is the female schemer Mrs Curry in Angus Wilson's *Hemlock and After* (1952). Her house is full of chintzy frills and coy pictures of little children: 'her *pièce de résistance* was a little china girl in a bathing costume lying on her stomach. This object had a removable lid revealing the buttocks."So you've found my naughty little imp," Mrs Curry would say, and then taking the lid from the embarrassed visitor she would remark,"Let's make her comfy again, dear. Now she's all tucked up for the night"(p.42). The excessively 'feminine', the cosy and chintzy, is here felt to be claustrophobic and threatening.

But it's more than an attack on the feminine. As part of the horrors of Mrs Curry there is implied a lesbian and paederastic desire. The attack here on a manifestation of the gender system does not work to demolish that system, but instead keeps it in place by adopting its own definitions of deviance. Lesbianism is again seen as an absolute bad, and for as long as it is seen that way it sets severe limits to any idea of a genuine questioning of the gender system. This sort of attack is very different from that made by feminists against the 'feminine' as a product of the masculine, and both as products of an oppressive gender system.

The problem around responses to the moralistic feminine is seen very clearly in Orton's diary. He describes in Morocco 'a quartet of English tourists and one woman was saying "Well, the best holiday we ever had was in Plymouth, but we didn't have the weather unfortunately".' Here Lahr's note quotes a letter from Orton to Ramsay: 'Occasionally a cruise ship docks for a night and then we have clumps of the most terrible English middle-classery in flowered frocks sitting at the cafés looking as though rape was imminent. On one of these occasions I overheard a woman, with the sunlight dappling her C and A Modes hat, the exotic palms and the Arabs in their fezzes around her, saying in a loud voice, "The best holiday we ever had was in Plymouth." I felt like pouring my mint tea down her neck' (p.186). The diary merely mocks the English insularity of the female tourist, but the letter to Ramsay focusses its hatred on descriptions of the clothes; the hatred here is more obviously directed at class and sex rather than Englishness. Orton's response is violent: the desire to pour the tea, but also the scoffing at ideas of rape. He creates a picture of Morocco which is everything that England is not; not only are its morals freer (for men) but it is a male space, indeed sometimes seen as a male homosexual space. The larger anxieties about his treatment by reactionary sections of English society are expressed in an animosity specifically concentrated on a female middle-class tourist. But there is more to it than this. The diary, a text perhaps intended for publication, limits its expression of misogyny. The letter, addressed to a middle-class woman reader, expands on the topic; as such it constitutes an act of violence against that woman reader, but it is not a text for public consumption. We cannot dissociate what Orton says, however nasty, from the context in which he says it. The Morocco diary was asked for by his female agent; it is a record of his homosex in a place away from her; it speaks of his male 'otherness' but it is all the time a work set up by her. The diary thus acts out frustration with his own circumstances as he perceived them.

This frustration is more confused the closer he is to the society that oppressed him. Thus a diary entry describes him watching a discussion programme on tv with 'just three middle-class people': 'They discussed the proposed amendments to the abortion laws. Kept saying what is best for the "mother" and "of course, for the unborn child". As though anyone in their right minds would consider the unborn child. Any more than one would consider the feeling of a tumour or cancer. How I hate the liberal-minded, smooth, middle-class, "broadminded", "with-it" woman'(p.87). Again,what begins as a rather generalised class rage becomes focussed onto the figure of a woman. Furthermore, the rage at 'broadminded' women pops out of nowhere: for Orton would seem to take a somewhat brutal pro-abortion position against the more reactionary anti-abortionist. It is as if, again, Orton is concentrating his rage against certain aspects of British society – its class divisions masked by hypocritical liberalism – all onto the woman as the main offender. The presence of a deep hatred of women, which skews his argument, is evidenced in his deliberately violent comparison of a foetus to a tumour. This sees the product (albeit unwanted) of a woman's body as disease.

The 'broadminded' woman is like the moralising woman insofar as she claims a right to speak about personal behaviour, and thus may be seen to oppress homosexual men. But this analysis does not see who the woman speaks for. It sees the female purity campaigner as the originator of oppressive moralism, not as someone placed and used by a social system which depends on gender divisions. Orton must have known of male purity campaigners, such as Peter Cadbury, but he perpetuates contemporary stereotypes by making Mrs Vealfoy a woman. In the play, her activity constrains and disciplines a heterosexual youth. Orton's point, then, is not about what female moralists do to homosexuals, but about what they do to the sexual activities of men in general.

The blurring together of male homosexual and heterosexual sexuality crucially limits the expression of homosexual rage at homophobia. A Gay Liberation argument would say that male homosexuals are in positions similar to that of women in patriarchal capitalism, because both suffer (in different ways) from the denial of rights and equality to those who are not heterosexual males. We must remember that homosexual law reformers advised male homosexuals to behave as much like heterosexual men as possible. By being like hetero men, queers could earn themselves some legitimacy. Thus a number of them learnt to view themselves as essentially different from, and indeed better than, women. So we find, even in the supposedly 'outlaw' homosexuality of William Burroughs, that the line between women and men is drawn as firmly as that between straights and gays: 'God damned matriarchy. All matriarchies anti-homosexual, conformist and prosaic' (1959: 47). This sentiment defines homosexuality as male only; it cannot conceive of matriarchy as a lesbian utopia. It blames women rather than straight men for all that is oppressive to gays. In a shared contempt for women, men may apparently unite despite their sexualities. Thus in the following sentence there is little that specifies the homosexuality of the narrator in Simon Raven's *Feathers of Death* (1959: 92): 'I wasn't an ageing schoolmaster or a suburban housewife; I was an adult and educated man, who prided himself on his tolerance and knowledge of the world.' The man is defined in terms of his power and his sexual potency: the schoolmaster may be male, but he is old, and in his impotence like a woman. Both perform roles that service the men of affairs, and are thus less important economically. The reader is asked to identify with a man who is sympathetically associated with economic and sexual power, irrespective of his sexuality. Thus the male homosexual's insecurity about his place in an oppressive world is partly 'solved' by joining with the secure group in transferring the idea of real 'strangeness' onto the 'common' enemy, woman.

2: *Female Desire*

The 'strangeness' of the woman is much more than her place in the domestic sphere of life. It has to do, apparently, with a woman's nature rather than her social position. In the passage I quoted above from *Hemlock and After*, Mrs Curry's interest in children worked as an image of her general exploitative attitude to society. But alongside the attack on this interest comes an attack, by implication, on her lesbian sexual desire. Underlying so many of the hating descriptions of women, in writers who are hetero as well as homosexual, there is a hatred of woman's sexuality. This hatred is born out of a sense of an inability to cope with it. And for this reason, I think, the lesbian is always the most hated figure, for in lesbians female sexual desire is seen never to focus itself on a man, and therefore never to have the possibility of being 'tamed' and controlled by the male. In much of Orton's work, female sexual desire is presented as a threat to male sexuality.

Kath and Nurse Fay have predatory designs on the sex objects, the young men. This is seen as comedy, but it's also a picture of unnerving power relations. Fay's designs on Dennis split him up from Hal; the policewoman Connie won't let her man wear 'Daddy's clothes'; Kath gets Sloane's trousers off him in a classic scene of male humiliation. In Ed's service Sloane is dressed again, in leather; he becomes more fully fetishised as a sex object, and more powerful. Kath deploys both her moral clichés and her 'typical' femininity in order to get her clutches on Sloane's cock. In these portrayals Orton simply reproduces the negative, misogynist, attitude to female desire. But it has to be said here, on Orton's behalf, that his response to female desire was not only negative. To the extent that it fitted with his attacks on his other targets, he valued it positively.

I shall give an example of what I mean by this positive attitude by first setting out, in more detail, a negative description of female desire. In Eliot George (Gillian Freeman)'s *The Leather Boys* a fear of female sexuality is attributed to the sexuality of one of the boys: 'Horrified, his mouth touched hers, and her lips seemed to grow like the fleshy tentacles of a sea anemone and draw him into the wet, dark, devouring cavity within' (1961: 28). This description is homophobic in that it makes the fear of women a symptom of male homosexuality. And one wonders what anxiety the author herself is transferring onto her fictional character. By contrast with homosexuals, in fiction hetero men are always supposedly in control of sex. But enough evidence shows the fiction is not reality:

> Most therapists, as well as most women...have frequently heard complaints from men about fears of being dominated, controlled, swallowed up or suffocated. Underlying these fears, which on the surface appear to be concerned with autonomy and freedom, is a more basic fear about the disintegration or loss of their sense of maleness.
>
> (Tom Ryan in Metcalfe and Humphries, 1985: 22)

In *Head to Toe* Orton gives this nightmare of sexual vulnerability to his supposedly straight hero: 'A faint moan escaped his lips as she enveloped him; he completely disappeared under her; he was suffocating; he gave himself up for dead' (p.18). He deliberately has us laugh at a heterosexual hero who is threatened by female desire – and, through the stylistic parody, to appreciate that this sort of description is a sexist literary convention.

Orton's work can enjoy the idea of female sexual desire when it is of use in his larger project of attacking propriety. The fact that the project tended to be moral rather than political, and always to be based on a male-centred view of the world, led even here to confusion. An example may clarify what I mean. Orton presented a 'pornographic' sketch called *Until She Screams* for the revue *Oh, Calcutta!* (1967). He was clear about what he was attacking: 'It's supposed to be a parody of the school of playwriting beloved of Emile Littler and Peter Cadbury' (from a document in the National Theatre exhibition). In it, upper-class women talk about sex and frustration in the setting of a country-house:

> 'Never mind. Charles has promised to bring a friend of his over to poke you one of these days. You know that's all I can do for you.'
> *Lady Shane rises and walks to the magnificent eighteenth-century fireplace above which hangs a priceless Renaissance portrait.*
> 'I know, dear, but Charles has promised to bring this hypothetical man for so long. Every time he enters the room I wonder – is it this time? Shall I get my bit of cock this time?' (p.51).

The comedy lies in the contrast of the expensive detailed setting and the coarsely explicit language. The words are shocking in upper-class voices because that is not how the upper class usually has itself represented. There is also specific parody of the type of romantic Englishness represented in dramatic dialogue such as that of *Brief*

Encounter. Orton thought his sketch would challenge the tone of hippy, liberal porn that characterised the rest of *Oh, Calcutta!*, a show specifically designed to test the theatre censorship. For Orton the revue was too arty, and too modest sexually: 'Kenneth Tynan apparently said the revue was to be straightforward, and no phoney "artistic" shit. Since the revue is called *Oh, Calcutta!*, it begins with an artistic title. Anyway, they can have the sketch. If they dare do it' (*Diaries*, p. 91).

But Orton had a rather inflated idea of his own shockingness: they did dare to do his sketch. Orton's underestimate of the sexual 'liberation' of others is a mark not just of his vanity but of his isolation, I think. *Until She Screams* was written much earlier, in 1960, as a private joke for Halliwell. For Orton the piece came out of the couple's carefully private outrageousness, their cultivated difference from the world around them. It is almost innocent that Orton could not imagine either how conventional their own humour was or the way sexual liberation was spreading in society. The sketch is so obviously, conventionally, a joke between two men. Furthermore it is a joke between two men who do not understand, are separate from and fearful of, female sexuality. The end point of this 'shocking' sketch is in fact highly conventional and reactionary: the daughter Lesbia says: 'great aunt Eliza came in. She tried to interfere with me. I've spent the best part of half an hour fighting her off. She seems to have gone mad' (p.53). Lesbianism as the crowning silliness, the ultimate strangeness: this is not so much challenging as a piece of highly normal masculinity. Yet it was the same Orton who, in the course of attacking the sort of theatre and audiences he hated, could say of *The Killing of Sister George*: 'we're given to understand that it's about "lesbians"...lightweight piece of crap... That is why it's having a success with the middle brow, middle class audiences.' Female sexuality changes its status for Orton in different ways in relation to class on one hand, masculinity on the other.

We can in more general terms trace this doubleness about female desire, this celebration of breached propriety accompanied by misogynist horrors, in the other plays. While welfare state propaganda portrayed women as wives and mothers and insisted on their innocence and placidity, Orton created randy women characters with disruptive desires. The reason he disliked Kath being played as a 'nympho' was because that enabled the audience to place her as a stereotype: her desire had (notionally) to be surprising and uncategorisable. In *The Erpingham Camp* Eileen the young pregnant wife quickly becomes excited by the riot: she jumps up and down and screams 'I'm in the family way!', and when Lou tries to quieten everybody, 'Eileen runs across and smacks her across the face and pulls her hair. They fall screaming to the floor' (pp.78-79). The Greek original for the play is the story of the female followers of the god Dionysos who in frenzy tear the poet Orpheus limb from limb, in revenge for his lack of response to them. In Orton's version, the stable innocent family woman is the sudden source of violence. In *Butler* Mrs Prentice speaks openly of her sexual frustration: 'My trouble stems from your inadequacy as a lover! It's embarrassing. You must've learned your technique from a Christmas cracker.' Many of the laughs are with her against her husband. My guess is that Orton exploited Masters and Johnson's new work on the female orgasm in *Human Sexual Response* (1966), or at least the stir it caused, when he gave Mrs Prentice her 'shocking' openness: 'My uterine contractions have been bogus for some time!' (pp.15-16). The excitement of the line is constructed by replacing the more usual vaginal contractions with uterine ones. (Whether this replacement was deliberate or merely anatomically ignorant remains moot.) In Mrs Prentice's pronouncements there is something very much more forceful than the coy boss and secretary routine with which the play opens. That opening had carefully set up audience responses in line with conventional sexist, adult-comedy, expectations, in order of course to shatter these later on.

Now on the negative side: when the audience and Orton laugh at the pregnant Eileen they are not just mocking sentiment about the family, they are also laughing at maternity. Many feminists point out how the operation of patriarchy is seen most clearly in its exploitation and alienation of maternity. Orton encourages this alienation when he has us laugh at Eileen. Again, the laughter with Mrs Prentice is balanced by laughter at her. Her scream when she discovers Sergeant Match with his trousers down places her in a typical farce role, that of the woman frightened by the (almost) revealed penis. Just as her strength is not consistently shown, so too her sexuality is joked with. There are references to her lesbian friends and her own lesbianism, but lesbians are never shown on stage. The references are merely verbal, the topic for jokes. So on the one hand there is the confirmation of male potency offered by Mrs Prentice's shocked scream, and on the other the old idea that lesbians are both the ultimate horror and the never-to-be-represented. The framework around the 'explicit' Mrs Prentice is reassuring in masculine terms.

3: Compulsory Misogyny

Any explanation of the doubleness of Orton's thinking about women must take seriously his situation as a homosexual in the '60s. His rage at sexual hypocrisies and 'norms' was, as an analysis, somewhat inarticulate. But it happened in the context of, and was continually influenced by, the extent of misogyny within sections of male homosexual culture.

I want to illustrate the shape of this misogyny in more detail, but before I do so it is important to recall three points. First, that the woman who was engaged in a social purity campaign was a potential threat to male homosexual existence; and a slippage occurs from this sort of woman to women in general. Second, that misogyny is most definitely not confined to male *homosexuals*: much hetero male writing sorts out women into ugly threats versus vulnerable sex objects, as a way of coping with hetero male fears. Third, that a hatred of lesbians is not the same thing as a hatred of women in general: male homosexuals showed a preference for women who acted their 'proper' role in the social structure, which is to say women who did not trespass on sexual mores or display a different sexuality. By expressing anti-lesbianism, as by expressing racism, the white male homosexual could try to participate in the cosiness of dominant heterosexuality.

Another point needs making. In part it anticipates the argument of this whole section, but it also needs saying at the start. This chapter does a lot of blaming of male homosexuals. While I have no regret about blaming reactionary queers, we must not lose sight of the fact that *male homosexual attitudes are the product of a society that is run by (officially) heterosexual men*. It is one result of his insecure position in society that the homosexual man learns to speak the language and reproduce the attitudes of the secure and dominant heterosexual male. This can mean learning a hatred of lesbians, and a complexity of response to women in general. Such attitudes emerge from the ambiguity of homosexuals' position. In the public sphere of society, the structure of social relations that produces wealth for example, the male homosexual has, particularly if he's closeted, all the power of men. In the private sphere of society, the structure of sexual relations that produces families and children, the male homosexual is 'weird' and weak. The cowardly, self-oppressed homosexual flexes his strength in the social relations of production, insisting on the division that preserves the public as the (comforting) male sphere and consigning the women to a private sphere. The women may then be tolerated, indeed welcomed, as 'personal' friends or mocked as aliens. Either response only happens once the primary division is insisted upon, the division which confirms the male homosexual's power as a man over and above the woman's lesser status. This attitude works to keep in its place the private sphere within which there is such potential anxiety. Thus the male homosexual is first made insecure, then taught to agree to the unequal division of men and women, because he can benefit from it.

Law reformers insisted that tolerance would only come from obeying the rules, copying the image, drawn up by those doing the tolerating. Women had no power and thus did not need appeasing. The woman who apparently sought power had to be resisted because she complicated the delicate truce. The document that recommended homosexual law reform, the Wolfenden report, was drawn up by nominal heterosexuals. Its liberalism towards male homosexuals was in the same report accompanied by recommendations to strengthen laws against female prostitutes. The text of the report not only offered tolerance of a 'disciplined' as against a 'flaunted' sexuality; it accompanied that distinction with a contrast between male and female. That report expressed heterosexual male thinking; it clearly, inevitably, shaped homosexual thinking.

With these points made, I can move on to look at modes of describing women, and then to argue that such modes perform a defensive function for male homosexuals. Descriptions in queer novels often focus on a woman's sexual anatomy: 'Her breasts were large and the dress stretched over her protruding stomach. Her hair was a dirty blond' (Little, 1956/1965: 44); 'a million dollars woman pressing her udders against the counter' (Garland, 1966: 70). What the hetero world claims is desirable is here made ugly for an assumed male reader. What is conventionally (hetero)sexy about a woman is thought of specifically as a threat to men. The image of woman can become a threat to the young male homosexual when he discovers that he is expected to desire or fall in love with a woman and make a family of his own. In a heterosexist society he experiences pressure to find attractive someone of the opposite sex and to keep silent about his own sexual desires. Where feelings of desire would be focussed on the male sex object, the forcible replacement of that male sex object by a female produces a reversal of these feelings into disgust. The one gets the stronger the more the other is frustrated.

Not all women are viewed with disgust, however. Traditionally within homo ghetto culture, certain women – mainly film stars or cabaret performers – are approved and, in a sense, desired (see the work on this done by Richard Dyer or Michael Bronski). This approval has been explained by Dennis Altman: 'Such women represent both the qualities that men are denied in this society and the defiance of traditional values...that have kept down both women and homosexuals' (Altman, 1982: 154). To this argument I would add that the stars have an image either of a basic innocence or of overdone theatricality which guarantees that the act is an act, and ultimately harmless. A homosexual male audience can watch a female performer playing at being sexually hungry for a man. Being an act only, her desires work as flattery rather than threat to the audience; they enjoy her looking at the male sex objects that they themselves look at, and identify with. The *safely* voracious woman makes it legitimate – as part of the act – to flirt with and express desire for men.

Here is another function of the woman in queer writing. The portrayals of sexually voracious women permit the writer to present young men not simply as sexy but as those for whom desire is expressed (what is illegitimate in non-homosexual society is not male sexiness but the desire for a male sex object). So in the work of Ronald Firbank, a stylist admired (unfortunately) by Halliwell and Orton, the frequently silly women have conversations which centre on men: the black woman in *Valmouth* says: 'He was a little blonde Londoner – all buttoned-and-braided, one ob de *chasseurs* at your hotel' (Firbank, 1919/1982: 44). (The sex object is traditional, the hotel page, with the horrible addition of racist prose which reminds us of the division between the black female desire and its blond male object.) Kath's lecherous gaze at Sloane is an echo of Orton's own (he insisted that the actor of Sloane be sexy); and indeed of the audience's.

In gay bars you can sometimes come across conversation about women that, on one hand, seems to hate female sexuality where it threatens the male – so such women are insulted; on the other hand it approves of stars, because they offer little threat. This double attitude reappears in Orton's diary, where his appreciation of his actresses coexists with his contempt for women in general. The gay bar conversation works as a filtering device, admitting and disallowing selected aspects of 'woman'. This filtering, even more clearly than novels' descriptions, works as a defensive device in and against a world which pressurises men to find women sexually desirable. The hatred for the 'slag' expresses all the frustration of a desire which cannot publicly focus on its real (male) sex object. (Remember that one of the objectives of Gay Liberation was to redirect the anger and frustration out towards a gender system that reproduced roles in which people felt trapped, and towards the masculinity which connived at such a system.) For the male homosexual who feels guilt about his sexuality or who sees himself threatened by ideas of social purity (as, say, is happening now), the anger is misdirected – away from masculinity – to focus instead on the woman, who is herself also oppressed in specific ways. The '60s saw little of the analysis of the sort made by the Gay Liberation Front and the Women's Liberation movement, which linked gay men and women as groups of the oppressed. By contrast in much queer culture there was an ignorance about women's activity and organisation. So even where homosexuals came out and assumed a homosexual identity, that itself took particular forms with particular (uninspected) prejudices.

Thus although Orton was fairly open about his sexuality, that openness was not shaped by gay consciousness. His sexual questioning was moral rather than structural, in that he attacked hypocrisy rather than a gender system. His sense of himself centred specifically on his homosexual masculinity, so that he celebrated his difference not only from non-homosexual men but from all women. When he says that he is not in favour of 'Arab girls becoming freer sexually', it is because 'the more girl-conscious they become out there the less boy-conscious' (*Diaries*, p.237); the subjugation of women benefits his 'open' sexuality.

Orton's homosexual masculinity, as we know, defended itself as tough against other queers. This led to deliberate abuse of the camp enjoyment of female stars. When *Sloane* was on in New York, Orton observed that 'Sheila is the pride of the faggots. They treat her like Judy Garland or Dietrich. Irritates me' (Lahr, 1978: 216). Orton, being the proper professional, admires Hancock but not as an object of queers' camp. As an opposition to a form of homosexual sexism, this is positive. But alongside his opinion of Fenella Fielding ('I don't like her – she's a camp lady'; *Diaries*, p.53), it would seem that what is controlling his opinion of women is a reaction to camp rather than to the women as women. In this connection, recall that Orton has the macho queer's response to 'effeminate' queens: he complains of the 'influx of limp queens' in Tangier, 'wetly complaining of the "trade"... Unpleasant to hear them talking so loudly' (*Diaries*, p.219).

I suspect that the antipathy to Garland, Dietrich and Fielding is not only the camp, but their power as professional women. Orton could enjoy Hancock because she was 'his' actress, in his play. And in this context I wonder whether the meticulously recorded misogyny in the diary isn't partly calculated as a piece of verbal violence against another powerful woman, the one who suggested the diary, his agent Ramsay. 'We discussed women for a bit and I wrote them off as a mistake' (*Diaries*, p.187). The voyeuristic peer into queer sex lives that the book-buying public might obtain from the diary finds itself looking at misogyny: 'I heard one of the tourist ladies asking for tea. "We asked over half an hour ago," she said so desperately that I had a twinge of conscience. "I come," Abdul-Aziz said. "He'll fucking come," George said, "right up your smelly cunt, if you ask him." ' (p.178).

The jealousy of female power reveals the other aspect of Orton's attitude: his masculinity, his assertion of his power, even as a queer, over women. He spells this out in a story from Tangier about a woman called Vipsil:

> She talked all the way of how in Islam women were
> 'treated so bad you know'. How she couldn't walk down
> the street without 'the bad things being said to me, you

know'. And I thought, what a beautiful cow, and how
right the Arabs were about women. I enjoyed the looks of
envy as I walked along with her. In a shop a shopkeeper
lifted a silver chain and offered it to her... I took it from
him and put it round her waist. He completely accepted
the reason for my taking the waistband from him,
accepting also that she, whilst in my company, was my
possession. And so, in fact, for a morning's walk around
the town, I possessed the most beautiful and desirable girl
in Tangier. I was curiously excited by this fact (p.173).

Orton's excitement comes from possessing, temporarily, the
woman whose value is acknowledged by others. She is a rich
commodity, but her value doesn't alter his contempt (expressed in the
word 'cow'). He is excited by the display of his own masculine
potency. In Tangier he was openly homosexual, so this display seems
to have little to do with passing for straight (unlike, say, in the novel
No End to the Way where the hero enjoys playing the straight manager
with his female secretary). For Orton his own homosexual potency is
confirmed in that he is walking with a white woman tourist who
would be desired by the native boys that he himself desires. His sexual
ownership is compounded by a racial superiority. By possessing the
beautiful woman Orton could prove his right to a place in a social and
racial elite.

Orton's turn-on from the potency bequeathed by public ownership
of a woman was not something peculiar to him. In *City of Night* John
Rechy describes the sexual thrill for the male hustler with his 'cover',
and the excitement is similar to Orton's: 'It felt good to be sitting here
with this girl, to be seen with her by some of the men I had scored
from'(1964: 145). Rechy describes the hustlers speaking frequently of
their relations with women, and appearing with them, to sustain the
image of being straight, which in turn increased their appeal to their
customers. The capacity to possess the company of a beautiful woman
is a turn-on because it confirms the masculine potency of the male in
the eyes of other males, who are thought to value what he possesses. It
is also exciting for the male homosexual because it is a demonstration
he can pass as straight. The pleasure in this derives – in the long
run – from the pressure on him to conform sexually. In the case of
Orton in Tangier the particular pleasure was, as I've said, to do with
another form of security, his capacity to belong to a social elite (like
having the Evening Standard Drama Award). All of this eventually
links back to an insecurity composed of mutually reinforcing social
and sexual alienations.

The idea that a woman is the only acceptable sex object potentially oppresses the male homosexual. The resulting hostility tends to be directed at the women-figures who play the greatest part in shaping and inhibiting homo sex life. We have seen some attitudes towards the threateningly available sex object; but another target is the mother. She can be responsible, if she is heterosexist, for oppressing the desires of the young homosexual. But the specific '60s focus on the mother rather than the father derives from contemporary theories about homosexuality. Families with domineering mothers, we recall, were said to produce queers. Thus the guilty queer was taught to blame the mother, not simply as an inhibitor of his desires but as the *creator* of such inadmissable desires. Let us take two examples to clarify this. In Montague Haltrecht's *Jonah and his Mother* (1964), Jonah is spoilt by his mother Frederika and is picked up by Gray, an antique dealer (!) at the opera (!); they both move into Gray's flat, Frederika accepts the relationship, because she considers that neither Gray nor Jonah is a real man: 'She still had her power, and was clever enough to enjoy it' (p.70). She concentrates on developing her role as a womanly woman (i.e. being a sex object). Then Jonah starts going out with Susan who looks set to put him back on the straight and narrow, which is a threat to Gray's sex life and Frederika's power. Susan, however, is nauseated when she finds out what Jonah 'is', and her influence soon wanes when, in his misery, Jonah goes not to her but to his mother. The novel ends with Frederika and Jonah leaving the flat for a hotel. They have discovered that not only do they belong together but that they have an easy way of satisfying Frederika's dominant desire for wealth: Jonah becomes a high-class hustler to support himself and his mother in luxury. The book attempts the 'shocking' cynicism of the '60s by showing how the queer is here to stay, how stories of conversion to heterosexuality do not work. It also places the mother as culprit: it is she who originally spoils Jonah, she who wants the wealth and power (another of her type is the mother of Tim in *Quatrefoil* who uses him to get the family wealth).

In my second example, *Child of the Sun*, the young Antoninus has a domineering mother and grandmother. They both mould him to serve their political ends, namely to gain the imperial throne of Rome. When he shows signs of independence developed under the influence of his sober lover Hierocles, the grandmother stages a coup. By this time the mother is too busy having sex to be in politics, but her influence remains, for when Antoninus decides to marry (for reasons of state) he can find no woman who matches up to the sensuous beauty he appreciates in his mother. It is suggested here, as with Frederika, that the mother has an unhealthy interest in her own sexual potency. Woman's desire appears again, deforming men.

Antoninus' female kin are responsible for making him effeminate in his youth: he 'was to have no mind of his own – only his body' (Onstott and Horner, 1966: 9). No other women are to be permitted a place in his affections, so that the mother can carry through her political ambitions unopposed. The ambitious mother creates the effeminate queer, as the story has it. The powerful woman is constructed as a precise inversion of the powerful man: when she becomes controlling, he becomes merely pretty and ornamental. Thus the story teaches the homosexual reader who hates his 'condition' (and fears his loss of rightful power) to blame his mother. Guilty homosexuals, therefore, added their voices to all the *non-homosexual* men who were resisting women's bids for autonomy. Opposition to the 'dominant' woman unites the queer, sadly, to the anti-queer.

I have related the 'homosexual view' of the mother back to the hetero view, because this is where it belongs. Far from being a natural part of the 'condition' of male homosexuality, misogyny is produced by heterosexual masculinity. The straight sexologist D. J. West argues: 'Maybe male homosexuals who have got away from binding, maternal attachments, and are freely practising their perversion in the community at large, are better able to express their resentment of maternal domination than a group of anxious, neurotic homosexuals' (1955: 187). Notice how this quotation tends to favour the 'free' expression of resentment of the mother rather than a 'neurotic' silence about it. While West defines homosex as perversion, he nevertheless also sees it as necessary masculine rebellion against women's tyranny. The ideas at the back of West's mind are precisely those we have already seen in the ideology of the rampant penis. This ideology defines sexual freedom as the operation of male sexuality in a world threatened by female power. It views women as spoilsport moralists and supporters of the oppressive 'family'. Clearly it has little notion of lesbianism as a distinct, and oppositional, sexuality. Insofar as it attributes any sexual desire to women, it characterises this as unpleasantly aggressive and demanding.

Male homosexuals, only too conscious of their oppressed sexuality, looked for some form of escape. A recipe for 'freedom' was apparently offered by a masculinist concept of sex as rebellion. Hence queers learnt these ideas, and William Burroughs could say that 'Homosexuality is a *political* crime in a matriarchy' (1959: 54). The irony is that it is a masculinist gender system that oppresses queers and women in the first place, and then divides the groups against each other in order to maintain its own power.

Earlier I suggested that Orton might have found attractive the idea of the penis rampant. But I don't think we can entirely explain his thought this way. The argument here has tried to show how Orton's fairly traditional misogyny is interlocked, inextricably, with his subversions of accepted views. Just how complex this is may be restated, if only to stress its positive side, in examples from the plays. In the figure of Ed in *Sloane*, masculine definitions of women are shown to serve the interests and power of men. Ed, the masculine homo, is identified as woman-hating: 'I generally spend my holidays in places where the bints have got rings through their noses' (p.183). Ed tries to teach Sloane his own misogyny, in order to keep Sloane for himself. The joke is that the very mark of Ed's 'discipline', what makes him a *good* (i.e. manly) queer, is his attack on female sloppiness. This attack, however, suits his own sexual interests, as a *queer*. The text is playing with sexual stereotypes, to 'reveal' a set of power relations. This happens despite, or indeed because of, the closeness of Halliwell and Orton to Ed. They too spent their holidays where they knew women to be humiliated, and they put *their* favourite (misogynist) joke-word for heterosexual desire – vaginalatrous – into Ed's mouth.

Many of the sexist lines in the plays are given to men. In *Butler* Orton shows Dr Prentice desperately trying to control and silence his wife. He and the other doctor, Rance, attempt to maintain order by threatening with their phallic guns in the interests of 'sanity'. This leads to a stage image near the end when both women in the play are placed in straitjackets. The picture of men being self-righteously rational contains within it forcibly restrained women. This is a very different set of images of masculine power from that of the rampant penis. It is masculinity measured by what it suppresses. And yet the play itself may be measured by its suppression of lesbianism (through its jokes and marginalising of it) and of female desire (again through its jokes and deliberate distortions). It remains a very male-centred text, although not a heterosexual one.

To speak of Orton being 'male-centred' requires, finally, that I repeat that his need to be 'masculine' partly grows out of worries associated with being queer, worries for which of course the dominant straight order is responsible. This may be exemplified in his feelings about Ed in *Sloane*. He enjoyed the US production of *Sloane*: 'as Eddie is being played right the audience are very worried that this attractive masculine man should be a power and a threat to them (they identify with Kath – Sheila gets rounds of applause on some of her lines – but it's only that they want to show their solidarity)'. He loves the homo character that for once a straight audience feels threatened by; and he consequently mocks their attempts to side with Kath. In interview, when he was being deliberately homosexually aggressive, he said: 'only a man who's had experience of women can dislike them. The adorers of women tend to be impotent: the priests of the mother-goddess were always eunuchs. But Ed's hatred isn't violent or vitriolic, he's had the sense simply to see the obvious alternative' (*Plays and Players*, August 1965). Again, Orton is enjoying his invention of what might be said to be a *positive* homosexual type, as a campaigning position. We might contrast this with a letter to Glen Loney about the US critic Taubman's attacks on *Sloane*: 'Nice and kind of quaint to hear people still referring to "epicenes". Gives a very Yellow Book flavour to "Sloane". And the idea of all those Wildean aesthetes (right spelling?) leering secretly at the humiliation of women is charming. Doesn't Taubman know that most "epicenes" (or all the ones that I've ever met) adore women. They'd tear you to pieces rather than allow you to humiliate a woman.' In mocking a clearly oppressive image of homosexuals, Orton is mocking the sorts of homosexuals who contribute to the image by being woman-adorers. *But* he's surely also wanting to mock Taubman's lack of knowledge of homosexuals in general, and to assert, in however ironic or embarrassed a way, that homosexuals in his experience are not women-haters. The embarrassment about this admission would come precisely from a fear of heterosexist categories: he doesn't want to be an effeminate 'epicene', because that is an oppressive role, so he clings to an image of the masculine homo who feels free and tough enough to mock women if he wants. We could say that society's oppression of homosexuals is playing its part in shaping Orton's misogyny.

There is no neat conclusion to this chapter, since we are dealing with something that is both contradictory and deeply embedded within male homosexuality at that period. The general problems with 'women' within a heterosexist gender system are given specific edge by Orton's particular circumstances. His relations with women were bound up with his relations with the social class which he was trying to enter professionally. Through walking with Vipsil he demonstrated he could belong to a male elite; through being partnered by Ramsay at the Drama Awards lunch he escaped embarrassment in his new success world. Owning the woman was apparently the key to easy entry to the class Orton desired (or needed) to enter. This is what gave the thrill. But needing to be partnered by a woman revealed the vulnerability of the sexual identity. This is what produced the rage. Woman thus became obsessively – misogynistically – fetishised as both social key and social obstruction.

The diary's misogyny is partly a vengeful fantasy directed against England, made more aggressive because Orton knew he depended on that England. The misogyny may not be separated from the anxieties produced by social inequalities and an oppressive (heterosexual) gender system. It was indeed shaped by these anxieties, but they themselves were huge, complex and difficult to grasp. The misogyny, sadly, offered itself as an easier option, a more graspable solution, to express those anxieties.

Chapter 8:
The Physique of a Nation

From sexual politics we move to the state and nation. The step is necessary because gender roles and ideas are shaped by the interests of a dominant class in a state. We shall see that the deviation of queers from proper family lives was not merely a matter of their *personal* failings but a very public symptom of their bad citizenship and lax patriotism.

In a sense this chapter is trying to make something out of an apparent nothing. Much homosexual writing concentrates only on personal issues – around sex and family – because it is here that anti-homosexual oppression is most clearly felt. By contrast there's very little explicit homosexual commentary on ideas of state and nation. The reason for this may be, in part, that homosexuality is most often thought of only as a private 'personal' topic, irrelevant to questions of state.

Nevertheless, questions of state and feelings of nationalism are forces which shape not only homosexual ideas but homosexual lives. In the '50s and '60s there were national panics about homosexuals. They were seen as 'security risks' because they were not proper family men, had no sexual discipline and might, through being vulnerable to blackmail, become spies. In response homosexuals attempted to demonstrate that they were loyal and patriotic, but in doing so they dissociated themselves from the homosexual community and explicit homosexual identification. The effect of the national panics was to make homosexuals more loyal to the state which oppressed them (or if not them, other homosexuals...one guesses that Godfrey Winn and Lord Mountbatten were comfortable enough).

Much of this chapter is concerned to describe, in general terms, the panics so that we can the better appreciate that rare thing, a public and critical homosexual response. The more general sweep of the chapter therefore eventually leads into a specific reevaluation of Orton as a homosexual writer consciously critical of state and nation.

1: Naffionalism

First some quotations:

> I am convinced that the majority of British people agree
> with me that few things lower the moral fibre and injure
> the physique of a nation more than tolerated and
> widespread homosexualism.
>
> >   (Lord Winterton, House of Lords, May
> >   1954)

> Just as we have today found our way back to the
> old-Germanic view on the question of miscegenation
> between different races, so we must similarly return in our
> judgement of the race-destroying and degenerate phe-
> nomenon of homosexuality to the moral idea of eliminat-
> ing the degenerate.
>
> >   (Heinrich Himmler, 1936)

> I am against any suggestion that we should weaken the
> law as it stands at present. My main reason is that a
> weakening of the law will strike a blow at all those
> devoted people who are working to improve the moral
> fibre of the youth of this country.
>
> >   (Field-Marshal Viscount Montgomery,
> >   House of Lords, May 1965)

> Jews, Quakers, Jehovah's Witnesses, homosexuals, and
> many others went to Dachau and other camps, and there
> they died. There are no concentration camps in Britain,
> but there are jails for homosexuals.
>
> >   (Douglas Plummer, *Queer People*, 1963)

In the opinion of the BMA Report on *Homosexuality and Prostitution*
(1955), 'the virility and soundness of the national life' depended not
only on physical and mental health, but on 'social responsibility and
stable family life' (p.8). This statement takes us some way towards
explaining why homosexuality was said to cause national degeneracy.

Firstly, the nation is thought of as a masculine entity, which is tough
physically and morally disciplined. This ideal of masculine nationalism
is undermined when the men stop being proper men and become
effeminate queers: as Godfrey Langdon (Conservative) said in the
House of Commons in June 1960: 'In my opinion, in the general run

the homosexual is a dirty-minded danger to the virile manhood of this country' (Hyde, 1970: 242). Thus after the law reform of 1967, homosexual acts remained illegal in the armed forces.

Properly virile young men are apparently only produced from a 'healthy social environment, springing from secure and happy homes which give a sound background of character training and where sex is kept in its rightful place' (BMA, 1955: 41). The second factor at work in the notion of homosexuality causing national degeneracy is that homosexuals contribute to the breakdown of the family. The 'rightful place' for sex, according to the BMA, is its use for making babies. Babies were necessary in order to enlarge the workforce of the nation in the postwar reconstruction period. Thus an individual's attitude to sex indicates his national loyalty (the Report only addresses 'him') 'the proper use of sex, the primary purpose of which is creative, is related to the individual's responsibility to himself and the nation' (p.9). (This sort of thing was still being heard, more than thirty years later, from Tory benches in the House of Commons, as if the endless repetition of an idea somehow made it true.) Homosexual sex is conspicuously non-creative; its only motivations are desire and pleasure; thus homosexuals have to be blamed:

> Personal discipline and unselfishness have little place in their thoughts. If this behaviour is multiplied on a national scale the problem to society is apparent, for widespread irresponsibility and selfishness can only demoralise and weaken the nation. What is needed is reponsible citizenship where concern for the nation's welfare and the needs of others takes priority over selfish interests and self-indulgence (p.10).

As much as with the family, the idea of national duty is enforced by associating any threat to it with the behaviour of despised and unnatural queers.

Although with the 'liberalisation' of the '60s homosexual 'love' came to be seen as something allowable (as long as it was serious), the threat of homosexual 'selfishness' remained. This constitutes the third reason why homosexuals contributed to national degeneracy: they are – supposedly – not merely selfish in refusing to discipline their personal desires, but they are economically selfish. They were seen as being wealthier than men with families: 'The economic conditions in society are heavily weighted in favour of the homosexual and against the young family head' (Hauser, 1962: 117). Not only does the homosexual not have to support wife and kids but, as Bryan Magee argued, he had no incentive to save for the future (1966/1968: 43). The extra wealth possessed by the homosexual was bad not simply because it was unfair but because it could be used to corrupt youths and to aid the process of proselytising. The main objection to fixing the age of consent at 18 (as recommended by Wolfenden) was that even older teenagers are 'susceptible to the influence of an older and possibly richer man'; until he has an 'independent career' the teenager is 'impressed by gifts and social status' (Chesser, 1958: 48-49). The prosecution in the trial of Lord Montagu and Peter Wildeblood (in 1954) alleged that two young airmen had been tempted into committing 'immoral acts' under the 'seductive influence of the lavish hospitality' of the older men (which in fact consisted of a bottle of cider shared between four, and the occasional scrambled egg) (Wildeblood, 1955: 63). Not only was the nation threatened when two young airmen were (perhaps not unwillingly) seduced, but class barriers were improperly crossed. Wildeblood suggests that Lord Montagu's real crime in the eyes of 'society' people was his acquaintance with a man 'infinitely his social inferior' (p.32). Homosexual wealth apparently exploits and infringes class structure.

The seduction of youth with money did not only constitute a sexual threat but it also encouraged the worst aspect of youth, their 'wasteful' expenditure on luxuries. Homosexuals and youth culture could be connected both in their attitude to money and in their 'freedom' about sexual morals. Benjamin Morse pointed ominously, as I noted elsewhere, to a 'close relationship between juvenile delinquency and male homosexuality' in the United States (1964: 128). Youth culture, like homosexuality, was seen as a threat to the nation, often because of its attitude to wealth: 'Blackguarded, blackmailed by the cult of youth, the cult that is, of early school-leavers in dead-end jobs with more purchasing power than any consonant generation in history, the English were beginning to lose their nerve' (Johnson, 1965: 122).

Open homosexual behaviour threatens to cause national degeneracy because it is seemingly anti-virile, because it stands outside and refuses to reproduce the family, and because it has a spending power that is not constrained to invest in the domestic economy of the family.

The threat of homosexuals to the nation was confirmed (that is, partly manufactured) in the publicity given to a sequence of spy scandals. In 1951 Burgess and Maclean were rumoured to be spies for the Soviet Union, and homosexuals; in September 1962 the homosexual Vassall was arrested for spying for the Soviet Union; in the United States in the summer of 1960, William Martin and Vernon Mitchell, both homosexuals, defected to the Soviet Union. Homosexuals were consistently seen as security risks in government posts, because their sexuality, being illegal, made them vulnerable to blackmail. This idea is really only a version of the stereotyped picture of the homosexual as a man who cannot control his desires, what D. J. West calls Vassall's 'seducibility'. The theory here is that the homosexual will always fall for blackmail because he is permanently in the grip of his desires. The connection between homosexuality and spies was kept in public consciousness by spy thrillers: Robin Maugham's *The Man With Two Shadows* (1958) has a scene of a boy being set up as queer blackmail bait (and the youth, being a corrupt 'youth of today', takes to it readily); the agent Ashe in *The Spy Who Came in From the Cold* (1963) is described as a pansy.

The panic about homosexual spies was reinforced by one aspect of the traditional image of homosexuality – that of the proselytising religion. This image implies a secret faith, perhaps operating in a network, always looking for converts. The BMA spoke of homosexual practices which 'insidiously invade certain groups of the community which would otherwise be predominantly heterosexual' and adds that homosexuals arouse public hostility because of 'their alleged tendency to place their loyalty to one another above their loyalty to the institution or government they serve' (p.16). Such thinking was sustained by the vocabulary of newspapers which spoke of 'unpleasant freemasonry', 'secret brotherhood' and 'social disease' (Plummer, 1963: 20). In 1964 Masters wrote of a ' "cell" of inverts in the {US} State Department' (p.126); in 1965 Kilmuir (Conservative) in the Commons spoke of 'sodomitic societies and buggery clubs' (Hyde, 1970: 262). After being forced into a ghetto by society, that ghetto existence was taken as evidence of the homosexuals' plot against society.

Emphasis on the 'proselytising' aspect of homosexuality converted the possibly pathetic picture of the queer as helpless victim of his sexual desires into a new, less sympathetic, picture of the queer as conspirator. In the years of the Cold War the homosexual plot to make the nation degenerate would be readily explained as something to do with communism: thus the Moral Rearmer Peter Howard explained in *Britain and the Beast* (1963) that 'The disturbing increase in homosexuality...is the result of a Moscow-directed propaganda, expressly designed to corrode the tissues of capitalistic society' (Schofield, 1965: 182). In the United States the witch-hunt of communists associated with Senator McCarthy had already tracked down homosexuals in the '40s, and it continued into the '50s with, for example, Senator Dirksen promising a campaign in 1954 against 'reds, pinks, psychopaths and homosexuals' (Masters, 1964: 150). Like all things lovely and North American, this was exported to Britain. In October 1953 the London correspondent of the *Sydney Morning Telegraph* explained that the new police drive against homosexuals 'originated under strong United States advice to Britain to weed out homosexuals – as hopeless security risks – from important Government jobs' (Wildeblood, 1955: 50). This explanation was not printed by the British press, who presumably, as ever, had the interests of the nation at heart.

Just after this police drive had started, and in the year of the Montagu-Wildeblood trial, Rodney Garland's *The Troubled Midnight* (1954) appeared. The novel works as an apology for McCarthyite witch-hunts, and in parts appears based on the Burgess-Maclean story. Its homosexual villain speaks of the United States: 'Innocent people being accused, kicked out of jobs. Half the population suspected. Just like the Gestapo. And they want to extend the same thing to England' (pp.160-61). This is the traitor speaking, so he must be wrong says the book. The hero of the novel is non-homosexual, but he is mistakenly accused of being queer early on; he spends the rest of the novel demonstrating his heterosexuality by helping, as a double agent, to catch the homosexual traitors. One of the traitors went to communist meetings when he was at Oxford university, motivated to attend, thinks the narrator, not by a political principle but because he was alienated from his father and 'A religion is always a parent-substitute' (p.61). In this statement pseudo-psychoanalysis is employed to link failure in family life with national treachery, another function of the 'Freudian' theory which oppressed homosexuals. This quotation suggests that queers will always be *naturally* susceptible to communism, because queers come from broken homes and are therefore looking for parent-substitutes.

The Troubled Midnight works as a vigilante novel, asking for greater efficiency in the hunting down of homosexual traitors. The British secret service is shown to be embarrassed by what the United States will think of them when the two diplomats defect: 'What price British security? You can just hear Senator McCarthy on that one' (p.152). The narrator feels that for all its panic the US is showing the way: 'The Americans may be hysterical, but in his case their fears were justified, I thought. It was strange that our own intelligence services suspected nothing about Alan until the Americans had sounded the alarm' (p.177). The anxieties generated in this revolting book connect directly with the appeal of the successful British agent, Bond. The Bond novels started to appear in the mid 1950s and, although at first they had a cult following, their heterosexist, masculinist, racist, imperialist (what a list) fantasies were soon taken up by a wider audience. Here the proper hero for the age had been found.

McCarthyism did not go unopposed. For instance John Osborne's first play, performed in 1951, generally attacked McCarthyism and had a scene in which a character was smeared (!) as a homosexual. But I am interested here in the *homosexual* response to the national panic. This response was governed by the insecurity of homosexual existence.

Thus it was not so much an open opposition to, but a damaging internalisation of, the panic. I shall try to show how the witch-hunts and the concept of national degeneracy shaped homosexual thinking.

The implied association of communism with homosexuality precisely strengthened anti-homosexual feeling in the years of campaigning for law reform and liberalisation: it converted the issue of sexuality from one of potential 'private' individual choice back into public 'responsibility'. At a time of apparent homosexual unity behind law reform campaigns, the witch-hunts produced disavowal and dividedness. The homosexual in Julian Mitchell's *Imaginary Toys* (1961) is said by one narrator to be close to the Communist party –, which I, as a good middle-of-the-road Socialist, regard as far more perverted than being homosexual' (p.13), but the homosexual himself later disavows his communism: 'Communities are a pooling of selfishnesses, so that everyone can do what he wants. When I say this sort of thing I am accused of being a Communist. But a Communist has some misty goal – ' (p.106). A much more acute form of disavowal is presented in Robin Maugham's *Man With Two Shadows* which is not on the surface a queer novel. In it the hero has a split psyche; when he blacks out, his other self acts in ways unknown to him. The hero is associated with the British army and foreign service, but his other self is committed to communism (his 'double' conduct is reminiscent of that of Guy Burgess in North Africa). At one remove this novel is about the 'queer problem', the uncontrollable sexual desire that leads to national betrayal, but it is presented here as a definitely *medical* condition.

Peter Wildeblood describes the panic that accompanied his trial: 'every pansy in London was telling "Montagu stories" in a feverish attempt to divert suspicion from himself' (1955: 49). This dividedness among homosexuals is contributed to in such fiction as Stuart Lauder's novel *Winger's Landfall* (1962). The story is set aboard a passenger ship. The passengers themselves are non-homosexuals, and they remain outside the plot which takes place amongst three groups of homosexuals. The first two are the usual ones: outrageous, but sometimes affectionately seen, flaunting queens, and the masculine homos (including the 'straight'-looking narrator-hero) who are more circumspect about their desires. The book's hatred is directed at a third group which comprises younger boys who are organised into a secret club by the character Bernard, who is religious, doesn't drink or smoke, a fixer on the ship. His attitude to the boys is 'fatherly', and he claims to protect them from the corruptions of the ship's society. The boys are supposedly trained in a form of religious service, which the hero (and reader) suspect is simply a cover. Bernard, for all (because of all?) his moralising, is easy to dislike: he is the implied paederast. He has a vision of his organisation, though he denies it's subversive, spreading through the merchant navy, spiritually regenerating it; proselytising. In making the reader suspicious of this so-called idealism, the novel takes up the language of the queer conspiracy in order to shift the blame away from homosexuals in general and onto paederasts in particular. The hero is a masculine homo, restrained, questing into the mystery of his cousin's death; his enemy is the figure that embarrassed all homosexual law reformers, the 'corrupter of boys'.

In its attack on homosexual conspiracy and homosexual 'idealism' Lauder's book shows itself to be shaped by the attitudes of moral panics. The publicity language of the witch-hunts had made any homosexual idealism suspect. Burgess and Maclean were associated with Cambridge university; *Troubled Midnight* has its traitors go to communist meetings at university. To be a homosexual and to be an intellectual meant more or less to be a traitor; being an intellectual meant embracing causes or ideals that departed from national policy. Nicholas in *Imaginary Toys* is said to embrace causes, and in his wondering if he is so different from heterosexuals he says: 'I would give the whole of NATO's stockpile to Mr Kruschev if I am' (p.133). The thinking homosexual is dangerous. James Bond has an argument with the Head of Admin. in the Secret Service who tells him: 'you suggest we should staff the organisation with long-haired perverts... I thought we were all agreed that homosexuals were about the worst security risk there is.' Bond tries to tell him that all intellectuals aren't homosexual, but the point isn't taken (Fleming, 1957: 83).

These sorts of descriptions and language had their effect. To defend themselves against witch-hunts many homosexuals sought neither to claim for themselves any 'idealist' political commitment nor to behave like intellectuals. Instead they demonstrated their ordinariness and their loyalty to English nationalism. Douglas Plummer argued that queers were not 'bad security risks' but 'intensely loyal' (1963: 24); Peter Wildeblood described a conversation with a queer ex-naval officer who was 'well-built, masculine, and neatly dressed' (1955: 29), and his book reminds us that he too had fought in the war.

Pro-homosexual novels take up the mission of demonstrating that their heroes are as loyal as naffs. Mary Renault's classically mawkish *The Charioteer* (1953) has a hero who is severely wounded at Dunkirk and coincidentally rescued by the man he loved at public school. This man has himself lost the use of a hand in action. Our maimed duo are both quiet heroes of war service with impeccable English pedigrees (though one of them left public school in a homosexual scandal, and joined the navy). The novel insists on the difference of these two from the frivolous and bitchy world of the homo ghetto; its jealousies nearly destroy their love. Division happens again: on the one side the horrid queens, on the other the noble love of two worthy soldiers. They may be queers but they are disciplined and brave. In Simon Raven's *The Feathers of Death* (1959) the central character, Alistair Lynch, is courtmartialed for murdering his troop's trumpeter. The prosecution accuses him of killing Drummer Harley because they were lovers and had a quarrel, threatening separation, the previous night. Alistair claims he killed Harley for disobeying instructions while the small troop was under attack from natives. A situation is constructed in which the hero has to admit both his love and its permanence in order to disprove the murder charge. The court decides he behaved heroically under fire as leader of his troop. The troop themselves all support their leader and regard the affair with Harley as a private matter which does not affect them, since Alistair in all other matters is a good soldier. This reflects the liberal tone of the book, which criticises the racism and narrow-mindedness of conservative elements in the army. Alistair, having been cleared by the army, is literally stabbed in the back (!) by Harley's obsessed 'friend' from the ranks. Again, undisciplined homosexual passion is seen as a threat, even where an individual homosexual can demonstrate himself to be a proper public-schoolboy and soldier.

This division of the good homosexual from the queers is characteristic of queer novels. But here we can note how the division is created by an atmosphere of national panic about treachery. The good queer is the one who serves his country; and by way of reward, as it were, discovers that nationalism is more than duty, it is desirable. Thus, in *The Youngest Director* the sex object is the more attractive because of his Englishness. The hero's boyfriend 'had one of those open, English faces that look so well on recruiting posters' (p.16). His English good looks not only make him a proper partner for a manly businessman hero but they make him more sexy (as well as more virtuous) than the rest of the queers. Nationalism becomes eroticised. It succeeds in dividing up homosexual society at the deepest level. *Duty* to nation may be argued against; *desire* aroused by nationalism is felt as natural gut-reaction, beyond argument.

Yet the witch-hunt should have taught these queer writers different. Peter Wildeblood comes close to articulating what his trial meant: 'I did not believe that such things could happen in England, until they happened to me' (1955: 54). England itself is brought into disrepute as a society. He remarks that Montagu 'had about as much chance of a fair trial as a Negro in the Southern States of America' (p.67). The witch-hunts potentially revealed that English law and society were not the model of civilisation that blind nationalism assumed they were. What all too often prevented homosexuals seeing the truth about their nation as a whole was a conviction that homophobia was confined only to one element of that nation, namely the middle class. Plummer, Wildeblood, Orton all speak of the middle class as the enemy; Wildeblood says that the upper class and the working class are tolerant of homosexuals; the narrative of *Feathers of Death* has an upper-class officer's desire tolerated by his lower-class troop, with trouble for him being created by a character who has clearly identified petty-bourgeois ideas about work and wealth. The failure of many thinking homosexuals to realise what was really happening to them is indicated by their sentimental idea that they could achieve a form of 'classlessness': there are stories of love that transcends class barriers, and of homo clubs in which everybody is dressed alike and hence is 'classless'. The society of this period (as now) remained rigorously divided by class and hideously bound by a form of nationalism. An aspiration to classlessness was going to combat neither middle-class power nor the links between the middle class, nationalism and homophobia. Homosexuals were right to see the middle class as their enemy; but wrong to see the antagonism as something only caused by moral prudery. A witch-hunt organised to demonstrate that Britain was a worthy member of the North Atlantic Treaty Organisation served specific class interests. Those with investments in the arms industry, in multinational companies, in international banking – in other words, those with investments full-stop – had an interest in Cold War nationalism in Britain, and in the struggle of the Anglo-American empire for world domination. The very same class constructed, upheld and depended economically on a particular model of gender roles and the family. This model oppressed and hated queers.

But there was resistance to nationalism, and after the negatives of this chapter we must move to the positives.

2: *Fairies Against Fascism*

I have spent some time outlining the scale of homophobia as a national panic. That description was necessary in order for us to give proper weight to the apparently incidental jokes made by homosexuals. In these jokes was contained the criticism of and resistance to the panic that was so dangerously internalised by many homosexuals. Lenny Bruce told jokes about homosexuals which played on their subversive connotations; as Marowitz said in 1962, Bruce used the queer to 'mock the brawny, heterosexual vision of the world which, in America and elsewhere, is itself a desperately-maintained fiction' (Marowitz, 1965: 257). The man-hating Myra Breckinridge doesn't care that she is thought to be a commie. And in Britain, among others, there was Orton and his anger. He may have been confused over class, but his diary is peppered with raging remarks about the hypocrisies and conservatism of English society. He gave to English society the name that Plummer and Wildeblood for all their remarks about concentration camps and the American South kept back: 'If you really wanted to spot the nasty equivalent of fascism in England you have to read the letters to the *Radio Times* and the *TV Times*' (Lahr, 1978: 138). Or again, in a letter to Ramsay: 'scratch a Liberal and you'll always find a Fascist bleeding'. With a degree of accuracy, he put his finger on the reactionary self-righteousness of middle England; but his hatred was not confined to the middle class. He noted down the immature repetition of imperialist thinking that he and Halliwell overheard from the mouth of a petty-bourgeois Black on the airport bus, and he especially noted the violent and stupid remarks about communism. British imperialism and anti-communism were topics to mock. So too was the figurehead of the nation herself; the Christmas messages from the queen and the pope are described as 'Pilate and Caiaphas celebrating the birth of Christ' (*Diaries*, pp.38, 104).

The anti-nationalist anger was put into the plays. In *Loot* Orton sharply juxtaposes propagandist ideas of the 'fair' British system with a grimmer view of that system's reality. It is the *Irishman*McLeavy who so foolishly says: 'I know we're living in a country whose respect for the law is proverbial' (p.60) – the racist joke about Irish stupidity slips into a joke about English hypocrisy and unfairness. It is Truscott the policeman who knows the real Britain: 'Under any other political system I'd have you on the floor in tears!' – to which his victim Hal replies: 'You've got me on the floor in tears' (p.47).

Orton asked that *The Erpingham Camp* be performed as the Royal Shakespeare Company performed Shakespeare's history plays. What he presumably had in mind were the productions done to celebrate the 400th anniversary of Shakespeare's birth in 1964. That occasion was, however arty, dominated by nationalism. Shakespeare was (is) seen as the national poet; the works of his chosen for performance were not the acknowledged 'greats' but those that depicted and celebrated the nation of England as an entity. The RSC's share of Arts Council money was (is) disproportionately large, and the audiences mainly upper- and middle-class. (In recent years the theatre has become a showcase to display *English* art to *foreign* tourists.) The values associated with, and reinforced by, the occasion of the Shakespeare anniversary were the target of Orton's attack.

The play depicts England as a holiday camp run by a man who combines rampant moral piety with a manic imperialism (for lots more camps). The holiday-makers are to be kept under control by offering them entertainments; but things go wrong and the holiday-makers revolt. In the anarchy that follows it is difficult to tell who is most crazy, the camp owner or the rioting families. There is no clear opposition to Erpingham's semi-fascist lunacy. He is supported in his rule by a chaplain and the ever-obedient – but mutually jealous – redcoats. The holiday-makers are divided between the worthy Conservative couple (Lou is involved with civil defence; Ted met her outside the Young Conservative club) and the nearly fascist Kenny and Eileen (who are overtly anti-Tory), who do violence in the name of the family and a sentimentalised (sexist) version of motherhood. The political positions have in common an infantile rebelliousness. Those seemingly respectable adult, *national* causes – civil defence, family unity – are shown to be founded on violence and symptomatic of basic immaturity. With opposition of this sort, the Erpinghams will always win. Significantly the victory is not obtained through the use of direct force, indeed Erpingham himself dies in battle, but through the appropriate decorums and reverence to which most people are habituated. At Erpingham's funeral, the holiday-makers are penitent: the ritual makes them submissive and restores the owner's order.

Orton's picture of an order which tries to maintain control by entertaining people, by apparently giving them satisfaction and pleasure, and his constant questioning, throughout all his plays, of the sanity of an authority that claims to be rational, are both very close to the radical political thought of his day. The seminal conference on the Dialectics of Liberation held in July 1967 was addressed by, among others, the Marxist Herbert Marcuse who pointed out how the 'subjective need' for social change was repressed 'firstly, by virtue of the actual satisfaction of needs, and secondly, by a massive scientific manipulation and administration of needs – that is, by a systematic social control not only of the consciousness, but also of the unconscious of man' (Cooper, 1968: 182).

The control of people's unconscious is shown by Orton in the characters who always use second-hand journalism and clichés without realising they do it; they have as it were absorbed what the manipulators want them to think. Marcuse had written more extensively on this topic in *One Dimensional Man* (1964: 22): 'in the most advanced areas of this civilisation, the social controls have been introjected to the point where even individual protest is affected at its roots. The intellectual and emotional refusal "to go along" appears neurotic and impotent' – as, for example, Geraldine's desire to get out of the mad logic of the psychiatrist's room and her insistence on truth make her seem as neurotic as anyone. Marcuse goes on to say that the products of 'civilisation', in which he includes the entertainments industry, bring with them habits, attitudes, expectations of a lifestyle which affect the consumer: 'The products indoctrinate and manpulate ... And as these beneficial products become available to more individuals in more social classes, the indoctrination they carry ceases to be publicity; it becomes a way of life' – a way of life that militates against change (p.24).

In *Erpingham Camp* Orton uses over-the-top effects, particularly absurd combinations of music and words, so the audience is not so much 'indoctrinated' by the entertainment effect but becomes very conscious of it; speeches done seriously on stage are in fact laughable. When Erpingham makes Riley the Entertainments Officer, his ceremony of investiture is carried out to the coronation anthem, 'Zadok the Priest' and then Erpingham delivers a speech accompanied by 'Land of Hope and Glory'. The moment we laugh at the overdone solemnity is simultaneously the moment we laugh at bits of English nationalistic ceremony. Orton is not only critical of English nationalism but attempts to get his audience to understand how they are indoctrinated by it, and to refuse that indoctrination through laughter. The play is crammed full of clichés about order, society and civil unrest: all of them made comical. When Erpingham dies, he is laid out on a bier; the 'Last Post' is played on a solo trumpet and four dozen red balloons fall. This combines the lying-in-state of Winston Churchill with the annual Remembrance Day ceremony in the Albert Hall, when poppies are dropped from the ceiling.

Continually the plays mock the ceremonies, and above all the *images*, which reinforce nationalism. In *Good and Faithful Servant* George, the pensioner-hero, speaks of the Memorial to the Fallen: 'Who are these people who have no respect for the dead of two world wars? I'm bitter about it, I am. We fought for that Memorial. Men died for it' (p.84). (The Memorial, of course, not being the thing supposedly fought for: real World War I veterans demonstrated against them.) When in *Loot* banknotes are hidden in Hal's mother's coffin, Orton's text reminds us of a detail of those banknotes: 'Every one of these fivers bears a portrait of the Queen... Twenty thousand tiaras and twenty thousand smiles buried alive! She's a constitutional monarch, you know. She can't answer back' (p.82). The attention to this detail completes the cluster of images at the centre of the play: a corpse interchangeable with money, a dead mother, the figurehead of the state. Orton was beginning a play about Edward VII when he died: it was to be called *Prick Up Your Ears*.

Orton's most extended anger was, however, reserved for a male figurehead who had explicit associations with nationalism. In *Butler* he turned his attention to Churchill. To appreciate Orton's daring we have to recall the extent of national mythology surrounding the man.

The state funeral, the biggest national bunfight since the Coronation, was watched on tv by an estimated 350 million people. It produced journalism such as this: 'The last frail petal of one of the great red roses of all England falls. And the sword sleeps in its scabbard' (whatever that might mean)(Booker, 1969: 251). In Orton's play the statue of Churchill is blown up in a Gas Board explosion, leading to the castration of the replica of the national hero. The play's attack is aimed precisely at the combination of ideas represented by Churchill: propriety, tradition, masculinity, nationalism; and at the making permanent of these ideas in statues to the hero. These too were the ideas taken up and absorbed by so many homosexual writers who, in a bid to make themselves respectable, contributed to their own self-oppression. Finally the attack is a *gay* attack on virile nationalism: the play involves anarchy of sex roles, ending with the rediscovered penis of the statue, held aloft by a policeman in a dress. The stage direction calls the penis the 'nation's heritage' and all draw in their breath at its revelation, as if in awe.

But it's not a symbol of authority – it's a comic penis. The tableau's outlook is specifically gay: the penis is viewed by a family whose unity is ridiculous, if not incestuous; in it the boy and girl have swapped gender roles; the penis is held by a man in a dress, a policeman whose law-and-order authority has been demolished by gender anarchy. And what the tableau does to the penis belongs more with gay culture than with straight. In dominant non-homosexual culture it is taboo to make sexual advances to a man and it is taboo, as we've seen, to represent the erect penis. Both taboos preserve the dignity of the penis, defining it as a symbol of power and order. Conventional masculinity is founded on the notion that biological possession of the penis gives a person cultural or social power. Radical gays attack gender roles and, in particular, masculine privilege. They insist on seeing the other man's penis as an object of fun and desire rather than authority. Orton's tableau has us look with a mocking gay look at the combination of elements – family, naff gender roles, nationalism, masculinity, propriety – which make up English fascism.

The first production, we know, censored the penis display. Instead an attempt was made to create innuendo around Churchill's cigar. The bowdlerising shows how taboo is the mockery of the penis; the innuendo keeps the penis sacrosanctly hidden. But, luckily, by this time Orton's play had already done its work: audiences yelled, waved union flags. Orton had produced the *open* display of what he so much hated, English fascism, and he had done it as a gay writer.

Unfortunately, because he was also a queer, he and his lover were by this time dead. Killed by a polite version of the fascism and heterosexism they hated.

This chapter has to end grimly, because the society is finally bigger than the author or artwork. But as readers of the artworks we may at least consciously celebrate those incidental references and one-off jokes in which Orton does battle with that most dangerous of topics, for homosexuals, nationalism. He remains all too rare as a writer opposed openly to the combination of English masculinity and fascism.

As in the previous two chapters, I have tried to highlight the subversive side of Orton (where I could: it's less easily done with the subject of women). But there remains the problem I noted before: the meaning of any particular play depends on what the director and actors make of it. Dramatists in professional theatre have all too little power. Being dead doesn't help. There's nothing to stop theatre companies from turning Orton's plays into reactionary sex comedies. There are, unfortunately, all too few radical and openly homosexual men with the institutional power to insist on presenting a gay Orton. So far it has been impossible to break the control established by the Orton industry. That control is maintained, with regard to many others beside Orton, because most people are unaware of how it operates. Therefore we have to finish with a look at the Orton industry and at what it manufactures, a safe and sanitised Orton.

Chapter 9:
Cottage Industries

A few years ago *Loot* reached the A-level syllabus. Orton was definitely dead.

The interest in the work and death of Orton has expanded considerably in recent years, so that, as *City Limits* put it, he was 'flavour of the month' in the 1980s. Very few obviously gay writers have occupied such a position in British culture, read about and enjoyed by straights.

This chapter surveys the development of the Orton industry. During the years of my work on Orton, the ways in which he has been sold to modern society have come to be one of the most important aspects about him. We therefore decided to hold back publication of this book until the diary and the film biography had appeared. For the products of the Orton industry can tell us not only about what non-homosexuals do to gays but about power structures in this society.

1: An Edited Life

The publication of the Orton diary in November 1986 apparently gave us the 'key' text for understanding Orton's life and work. In his preface, the editor John Lahr announces that he has reached the final climax of his work on Orton. Lahr had already drawn heavily on the diary for his biography of Orton, and in doing so had established certain significant features of the Orton legend, as we've seen. With the publication of the diary it became technically possible to unravel Orton for oneself, but such is the grip of the legend that many reviewers of the diary continued to reiterate the features of Lahr's Orton. Indeed it is quite difficult to make a different reading of the diary because Lahr's method of editing it confirms his own analysis.

The two main instruments available to an editor are the introduction to a text and the footnotes. Lahr's introduction does at last reappraise his view of Halliwell, in a limited way. But his picture of

Halliwell and Orton's lives remains highly selective. He speaks of their 'rare' happiness and emphasises a secretly weak and unhappy Orton: the 'enemy was within'. Halliwell is 'explained' by his 'traumatic' childhood; his 'possessiveness' is what destroys the relationship. These phrases repeat '60s prejudices about queers being lonely, weak, jealous and destructive, and never happy. Furthermore the diary is said to symbolise 'Orton's retreat' into himself. In presenting it as a tragic text Lahr gives it 'serious' cultural status; and of course invites people to read (and buy) it. Much is made of the diary being unfinished, with its possible missing pages, and Halliwell's ambiguous death-note. Thus the diary is presented as a never-solved mystery, shrouded in the same darkness which surrounds the doom-laden homosexual lovers, offering its reader a share in the macabre.

Apart from reflecting anti-homosexual ideas, the introduction gives a rather unbalanced interpretation of the diary. Lahr says Orton was 'compelled' to recognise Halliwell's talent in writing the diary – which in the context implies, I think, that Orton really knew, as does Lahr, that Halliwell had no talent. Meanwhile the diary itself celebrates Halliwell's witty remarks and observations, and his ideas for Orton's plays. (Lahr himself must have found at least one of these ideas attractive, since he stole from Halliwell the title of *Prick Up Your Ears*: that theft was only *explicitly* acknowledged years later in the *Diaries* introduction.) Arguably the diary played its part in both celebrating and provoking the Halliwell-Orton relationship. Orton's blame of himself in some situations and Halliwell in others could defuse or joke away causes of friction. If the diary is simply read as a 'personal retreat', none of this creativity can be seen for what it was. The ability of the couple to manage their relationship is played down, perhaps because they are more culturally attractive as passive and tragic victims.

The introduction quotes Penelope Gilliatt's description of Orton's rage at 'people's ribaldry about camp' (p.17). That rage is expressed both in the diary and the plays against those non-homosexuals, in particular, who moralise about and get a thrill out of queer activities. The diary is clear about Orton and Halliwell's hatred of many theatre people and those with privileged class positions. There is scorn, too, for homosexuals who are guilty, frustrated and possessive. While these opinions can be inferred from Orton's other writings, the diary puts them most blatantly. But instead of highlighting this attack on a hostile outside world, Lahr pictures Orton as a man with an enemy within both his relationship and himself. To read the diary as an attempt by a secretly weak man to laugh at the world is to deflect attention from its positive animosity towards a world that many people, rightly, view with contempt. For a number of other people, by contrast, the job of work done by Lahr in locating the blame and difficulty only within the 'tragic' relationship must be pretty attractive. The closet queens and theatre folk wanted to explain the tragedy by focussing on Halliwell's possessiveness or Orton's selfishness, rather than acknowledging their own violent desires and exploitation. The cultural establishment has not changed much, and it still refuses to admit to its socially privileged place and its competitive aggression. There is, therefore, little interest in remembering Orton for his attacks on class and privilege (and closet queenery).

Our reading of the text of the diary is potentially influenced by Lahr's notes. I'll list a few examples. Orton remarks, in the context of problems over their Libyan visas, that Halliwell's passport shows him 'with a shaven head' and since then 'he has bought his wig'. Lahr footnotes a letter from Ramsay: 'Kenneth improved when he began wearing a wig. He was quite bald, and was very ashamed of his baldness... The first money Joe earned was spent on a couple of wigs for Kenneth' (p.90). The diary says next to nothing about wigs (and calls Halliwell 'shaven'), but it's important for Lahr's analysis so he ensures the reader attaches importance to something which for the diary itself is a passing detail. In effect, he *invents* what Orton should have found important but didn't. Here, as elsewhere, much use is made of quotations from those who knew the pair. Apropos of a disagreement about who arranged a date for sex, Rattigan is quoted on Halliwell's jealousy, his 'obviously phoney' erotic triumphs, and how he 'lied about his age' (as in fact did Orton, in almost every interview he ever gave) (p.160). Orton's description of the effects of hashish speaks of gazing at himself in the mirror 'without self-consciousness'; this is footnoted from Kenneth Cranham: 'His real buzz was himself. When he'd leave a room, he would stand in front of a mirror...' (p.182). Orton's point is about the effects of dope, Lahr's note transforms it into the usual queer problem of narcissism. In these sorts of notes, Lahr's additional 'information' functions to promote in the reader's mind thoughts which Orton's text might not on its own have suggested. The notes might claim to give context to the diary, but they themselves need contextualising. Maybe we ought to recall Orton's contempt for Rattigan when we read Rattigan's note; maybe we should see all that Willes says in the light of his own apparent jealousy. Cranham's remark about the mirror is very interesting: the diary makes it clear that Orton was fascinated by Cranham, and we might wonder how much Orton performed for Cranham's benefit. In other words, we might ask how much Cranham's (or anyone else's) picture of Orton had been already influenced by Orton's attitude to him.

The role of editor is very powerful. If Lahr had been properly scholarly, he would say where he made cuts in the text, where he substituted names. (We still don't know what Orton *really* wrote.) It sounds pedantic, but it would be useful to know about the handwriting, the deletions, the general state of the text. These things can sometimes tell us how much pressure the writer is under: does the handwriting in the final weeks show signs of tension? Does the diary show a pattern of tension? An editor is paid to do this donkey work, which is at least potentially useful, unlike this sort of thing: 'Paul VI (Giovanni Battista Montini) (1897-1978). Became Pope in 1963. Travelled more widely than any previous Popes' (p.177). Ah, scholarship!

In his roles of editor, biographer, critic, and now playwright, Lahr insists on his own centrality: his biography is 'the' biography, his own introduction to the plays is (he says in the *Diaries* edition) 'useful' (whereas I'd suggest Maurice Charney's is much the best). As a reflection of this, in the film *Prick Up Your Ears* there are four major characters: Orton, Halliwell, Ramsay and Lahr. The two lovers cannot be dissociated from the agent and the biographer; they are always in our culture surrounded by the industry that popularises and makes money out of them. While the biography was being turned into a film, Lahr was turning the diary into a play: 'Joe Orton's Diaries – Dramatised by John Lahr' (note the always inevitable pairing of names: Orton's unpublished text comes to proper public fruition through Lahr's kind agency, twice.) By emphasising his own closeness to Halliwell and Orton – which was historically non-existent – Lahr constructs his own scholarly authority. This authority has been made real by the extent of his control over the unpublished papers. Those papers did not seem to be available in a public place; as a researcher I could never find out where they were, nor would the agent state their precise whereabouts (though they turned up in an exhibition at the National Theatre). Now the Orton papers have been deposited in Boston university, placed there as part of the '*John Lahr Collection*'!

People who try to work on Orton and Halliwell come up against this power over the papers. In my own case, I originally wrote to Orton's agent to ask if I could read the diary. She helpfully agreed, but pointed out that there were (at that stage) legal problems over its publication. A number of months later, not having had time to get to the diary, I wrote again. This time I learnt it could not now be read. I understood: there were rumours about it naming names, and closets – unlike other furniture – have power. But I asked about the other unpublished material: the novels, the Edna Welthorpe letters, Halliwell's collages, the *Sloane* scrapbook, the first drafts of the plays, the unpublished plays. I knew this vital stuff could not be legally problematic, because it had been photographed and quoted from. So I asked to see it, and received in reply this letter:

Dear Mr Shepherd

JOE ORTON

Please do not write to me any more about Joe Orton! You
can get the full list of the material he has written on the
back of the publications of any of his plays. Anything else,
has been fully researched by John Lahr in his book. I gave
John every piece of information and there is nothing more
to be said.

You can catalogue anything you like from the Orton
book and from the plays – there is no more. {This in
reponse to my saying the material should be properly
catalogued, since Lahr's biography only listed what was
published.} I do not hold the material of the spoof letters,
but it is in John Lahr's book.

Certainly John Lahr's publisher would not give you
anything and John Lahr has done all the work for you
already regarding the spoof letters and there are no more.

Please realise that we have a lot of living authors and
that we have done everything we could during his lifetime
and that we helped John Lahr's compilation, which is
definitive. Islington Library will certainly not give you his
defaced books, and the best thing would be for you to
write to Lahr himself. {I did, c/o his publisher, but the
letter was returned undelivered.}
Sincerely yours

Margaret Ramsay

Do remember that Joe died 13 years ago – and if he
not been murdered there would not be this
unseemly interest in him – HIS *PLAYS* remain *available*.

My response to this letter, beyond a reflection that Orton hadn't
learnt his control of syntax from his agent, was that it was misguided,
severely misinformed and downright impertinent. If the agency really
cared about their dead author, why did they discourage research? And
if they couldn't handle the unpublished papers, why not deposit them
in a *public* library? See how the barriers are constructed: Lahr's
biography is 'definitive' – but what values does it define? What we
should be really interested in are the plays – but aren't the plays now
seen merely as adult sex comedies? Research into Orton's life is said to
be 'unseemly', only interesting because he was murdered. The

particular obnoxiousness of this remark is that it excludes any notion that Orton might be interesting as a gay writer who has not been well served by the only people who had full access to the papers (and how did they get hold of them: were they officially bequeathed?). In *The Times* (10 March 1984) Ramsay allowed herself to be photographed in front of the collage Orton and Halliwell did for *Loot*. The photo indicates how Orton and Halliwell have been appropriated. (Indeed Osborne's review of *The Orton Diaries* in the *Spectator* suggests that Ramsay pinched the diary from the dead man's room!)

In pursuit of more information, I wrote to Maurice Charney, author of a recent critical book on Orton. He told me that a research student of his had encountered great difficulties in reading the unpublished papers, so much so that it discouraged Charney himself trying to read them. He went on to remark that attempts were made to prevent his own book being published. Similarly, when the biography was published it carried a prohibition on quoting from the diary chunks included in the text. Something was/is being protected, and that something was the control of a money-making little industry. The control is not just economic; it is also sexual. Most gay men I know find Lahr's biography unsympathetic, to say the least. The industry creates a heterosexist version of Orton's life and work. When Orton's papers were deposited in Boston under the name of John Lahr, the straight journalist literally eclipsed the gay writer.

2: *Queer Plays for Straights*

The management of the Orton industry is a blatant, but not a new phenomenon. For years theatre companies have been appropriating individual plays. This activity began in Orton's lifetime, when he had to argue with producers and actors over the correct way of doing his plays. Now he is dead he is easier to walk over, and productions regularly encourage audiences to do precisely what Orton tried to stop, laughing to assert their heterosexuality and political complacence. He had only been dead 18 months when a professional company foisted its bowdlerised ending on the first production of *What the Butler Saw*. The commercial control over his work was consolidated when his agent allowed Methuen to publish the play with its fabricated ending, without mentioning that Orton had written something different.

Instead of writing a detailed history of Orton productions, I'll make two general observations about what happens to them. *Erpingham Camp* becomes an opportunity for kitsch singalong and games, by expanding the camp entertainments so the audience can join in.

Students like doing this; also some versions of 'community' theatre. Brechtian pastiche, nationalist parody, analysis of British fascism all vanish, leaving an aimless but often snobbish giggle ('so that's what Butlins is like...how frightfully uncool!'). *Sloane*, *Loot* and *Butler* become adult sex comedies, the stock-in-trade of reps engaged in putting bums on seats by putting bums on stage; the emphasis is on being risqué and naughty ('Whoops, you nearly said fanny there. Oh ho ho!'). (The leaflet for a production in Chesterfield of Lahr's dramatisation of the diaries doesn't have a word about homosexuality, unless I suppose you read the code: 'Lively, scurrilous and perversely {!} enjoyable throughout'.) The plays start to be challenging for an audience only when their sharp changes in style are marked in performance, when the violence is played to cut through the laughter, when – as Orton said of *Loot* – the audience stop laughing. To even out the tone and to underplay the violence is to make the plays less surprising and more cosy. Professional companies adopt a style which thinks 'Ortonesque' means tasteless and kitsch. (The A-level text of *Loot* tries to ensure that sixth-formers do likewise; one of its oddly Ortonesque footnotes kindly informs that 'The "large wreath marked off into numbered squares" is a representation, in somewhat bad taste, of the kind of card used to play bingo'; p.90.) As they're usually done, the plays seem to show ignorant or silly people to an audience that prides itself on its taste and 'broad-mindedness'. If you underplay the aggression of the comedies, there are no problems for an audi-ence – no clear opposition to petty-bourgeois Britain, no clear homosexuality – so they become a giggle that serves only to confirm the audience's privileged point of view. In the film of *Sloane* the music performs the function of making the whole play a zany romp among the unwittingly vulgar. Whereas for Orton: 'A director who imagines that the only object is to get a laugh is not for me' (Lahr, 1978: 241).

The first appearance of Orton's work on stage, in however mangled a form, was countered by critical reviews which aimed to depoliticise the plays and to pigeon-hole them as perverse. 'Orton's terrible obsession with perversion, which is regarded as having brought his life to an end and choked his very high talent, poisons the atmosphere of the play' (Dollimore, 1983: 78). Of course Lahr's biography fits into the tradition of this sort of comment, and the tradition is sustained in the A-level edition of *Loot*. Here students are told about 'a coldly self-absorbed personality', 'predatory and promiscuous homosexua-lity' (pp.x-xi): not only is this the Orton mythology, but it's a classic version of '60s homophobia served up as '80s pedagogy. The heartlessness, we are told, affects the play where Hal and Dennis never feel 'a flow of genuine emotion', where although the characters may be funny 'spontaneous feeling is generally beyond their compass' (p.xxi) – as if these characters were real people, and as if this was the sort of play Orton was writing in the first place. This view of Orton and homosexuality also finds its way into plays about the pair. For example, Simon Moss' *Cock-Ups*, with its obligatory 'Ortonesque', or rather Lahresque, title, blurs together the plays and the life, encouraging a biographical reading of the plays and presenting the lovers stereotyped as the heartless one versus the neurotic.

The A-level *Loot* simply continues a process that has been a regular part of the Orton industry. Publication of the plays has always given an opportunity to contribute to the Orton myth, and in doing so to engineer the reader's response to the text. *Sloane* was first published by Penguin in 1964 as part of its New English Dramatists series. The volume's introduction by John Russell Taylor said: 'I think that all Mr Orton has set out to do is to provide an evening's light comic entertainment', and the bit Orton particularly hated: 'Theatre...needs the good commercial dramatist just as much as the original artist' (pp.12, 13). Orton angrily pointed out that the two were not separable. When *Funeral Games* appeared in 1970, Orton was dead, and Peter Willes supplied a commemorative introduction. This succeeded in trivialising the plays: 'he used to put in the most devastating remarks, generally made by nuns, just to see me take them out' (he is talking, for all the camp tone, of censorship); trivialising Orton: 'He did not have a heart – but I loved what was there instead, which was infinite kindness and good manners': and not one word about Halliwell. By 1976 Lahr had made himself into enough of a posthumous aficionado to write the introduction to the *Complete Plays*. Here the myth is authoritatively consolidated: 'Orton's plays are a flamboyant dance with the death he found in life... Hunger and how it disguises its craving was what amused him' (p.8). In a circle of self-proof, the plays mean what the biographer says they mean and thus in turn they demonstrate the truth of the biography.

The climactic flourish of the Orton industry, its single most expensive product, is the film of *Prick Up Your Ears*. But ironically this is the most dissenting product of the industry. Hitherto lone voices in a few radical and gay magazines had spoken of their objections to the myth around Orton. But the film's inclusion of a John Lahr figure aims to display, and to question, his role in constructing our image of Halliwell and Orton. In particular, his researches into the difficulties of Orton's 'marriage' are offset against the film's image of his own long-suffering and effectively silenced typist-wife. As a whole, the film seems unsure of what it is trying to say, and here is not the place to write an extended analysis. But it is usefully seen as a part of the Orton industry because it can't really free itself of the Lahr-viewpoint and because it popularises discussion of Orton's sexuality.

At one level, Alan Bennett's screenplay asks us to rethink the stereotyping of Halliwell and Orton, and the filming invites us to enjoy their good times together (there's a wonderful scene of cruising in a park). Unlike much of the Orton industry the film tries to be neither homophobic nor anti-feminist. But in its four main figures the film is, by contrast, caught in the assumptions of the industry. The central role allocated to Ramsay gives her a much larger, and more romantic, place in the pair's life than the diary would suggest was the case. Furthermore, the writing of this part, together with casting Vanessa Redgrave in it, gives the impression of a quite open-minded and independent woman, who in her own right could be 'shocking and Ortonesque'. But the picture of Ramsay both in the diary and in Lahr's biography suggests that she was bitchy about Halliwell and not always favourably regarded by Orton. A quotation from one of Orton's letters to Ramsay (received 1 March 1965) illustrates the tensions and the agent's paranoia: 'But if you dislike "LOOT" as well, perhaps it is the essential me as a writer you dislike... And we had both of us better think seriously of parting company.' Alongside the first sentence Ramsay has scribbled 'Who told Joe this? I'd told David I didn't want to discuss the play with him' and alongside the second: 'this, if it happened, would be due to *what you all said to Joe about me*' (her emphasis). So what was going on? It's certainly a bit of history that's vanished from the myth. The film casting, furthermore, tends to obscure Ramsay's economic role. As a theatrical agent, after all, she made her money out of the capitalist organisation of theatre; she made profits for, and out of, playwrights. By contrast Vanessa Redgrave's own political associations are known to be anti-capitalist. So the film is powerfully excluding from the myth the muckier aspects of this part of the industry, and is thus assisting the industry.

A crucial question about the film is to know why it was made, or, to put it in more general terms, why the Orton-Halliwell story has achieved this level of popularity in the '80s. To attempt an answer to my question, I shall analyse – as a text – a group of reviews of the diary. This choice of 'text' is partly dictated by convenience (it saves interviewing readers and film-goers, etc.), but I also want to show at work the language of journalism. This plays a part in formulating, if not in forming, a number of contemporary ideas.

3: Men Love It

The current appeal of the Orton-Halliwell story will inevitably derive from the way it connects with and reinforces both what may be called the 'mood' of our culture, and popular concerns and ideas. This reinforcement of current ideas may not be immediately perceivable, may indeed not be part of the superficial attraction of the story. Nevertheless the effect of the story's currency in our culture, I shall argue, is to perpetuate a set of ideas about society and sexuality.

My analysis is based, in the main, on two reviews, from the *Tatler* and the *Spectator*. Not only do they say a lot, but they are so vile that they need exposure to anger. Although tied down to these reviews, however, my arguments as a whole are formulated from a reading of all the Orton materials that have gone into this book.

A first reason for the appeal of the Orton-Halliwell story comes from the image of Orton as (in Lahr's words) 'aggressive clown'. The humour in the plays and especially in the diary can be made to correspond with a current trend for comedy which is supposedly sceptical of all values, which knocks any and all ideals. It's the comedy of some aspects of *Spitting Image* and some 'alternative' comedy. The street-wise 'mood' of the '80s acknowledges not simply the nastiness of the world, but the inevitability of that nastiness. The laughter is based on a combination of hard-headed knowingness and passive acceptance. While Orton's humour certainly had its political targets, he himself did not adopt the position of political radical. The prose of the diary presents him – to himself? to the world? — as unpolitical. In the *Tatler* Jonathan Meades admired the 'terminal humour': 'his brutality of sentiment allied to his felicity of expression, his contempt for the canons of propriety and taste, his super-sane single-mindedness are still thrilling' (*Tatler*, November 1986). 'How Orton could hate!' The hatred is always combined with poise and expertise. Meades contrasts this with the 'appalling Living Theatre': 'Avant-garde philistinism is a slingshot beside the Pershing of properly constructed work.' The reference to hi-tech weaponry is the give-away. The review enunciates a particular '80s admiration for hatred and for the expertise of individualism. It requires that we prefer efficiently destructive weaponry, recognise that hatred is the name of the game and pride ourselves on doing it well. The yuppie values are kitted out with '80s chic: 'he was not a politician, he was not a pop star; there was more to him than the mannerisms and vacuity of either. The man was a fully formed artist, an intransigent moralist, an enemy of the lies and hype that are presidential oxygen and pop-yob air.'

Orton here is constructed as a romantic myth. That he would now have been 53 is 'unthinkable really'. We fear that he might have gone off, so 'his death was apt'. The review text presents Orton's story as a type of snuff movie that confirms the romance of being a young, non-political, go-getting artist. Who never suffered from the yuppie disease of burn-out, because he was, efficiently, murdered.

Orton's image and humour, as constructed here, are used to express an '80s model of success. It is consequently no surprise to find that, while some of the objects of his hatred are listed, all mention of his distrust of class privilege is absent. The *Tatler* reviewer makes his own position plain: Orton was not only from the gutter, 'he was *of it* too and liked it there, a dandy in the crap'. The lower class as crap...hm! The appeal of this 'Orton' is that he can be seen, precisely, as an individualist who is very good at competition and hatred. The model on which this 'Orton' is constructed is that of the young privileged class of the '80s. Its Orton is hence not a hater of that class, but one who anticipated its outlook, if not lifestyle. Thus the Orton story gives chic status to the activities of the 'new industrialists'.

Lahr's introduction to the diary places the text not in a real history, but in a history that a certain element of the '80s is inventing for itself. The diary, he says, celebrates 'the cock-eyed liberty of the time – a time before the failure of radical politics, before mass unemployment, before AIDS' (p.14). Note that assumption about 'radical politics' (I suppose it's fairy dust that sent the nurses on strike and organised the mass opposition to Clause 28); note too the link with AIDS. Meades also makes the link: 'If Joe Orton was still alive he'd be dying of AIDS.' Both references encourage readers to understand that homo-sexual promiscuity leads to death. Lahr's pun on 'cock-eyed' concedes that Orton's promiscuity came before AIDS, but was still mistaken because it ignored his lover, and so led to his death. (For Meades AIDS is a convenience which provides a nice punchy opening to his review. It's stylistically necessary to assume Orton would not have heard of safer sex.)

The Lahr version of Orton is a tale which confirms the dangers of homosexual promiscuity. The reviewers regularly say that the accounts of Halliwell and Orton's sex in Tangier are the most distasteful part of the diary. Although the descriptions are said to be too explicit, they are little different from descriptions of the lovers' sex with each other. These sessions are *never* mentioned. Presumably the reason for this omission is that they don't fit the stereotype of Halliwell as jealous and Orton as adventuring. In the Lahr version the 'marriage' is unhappy; that means ignoring descriptions of its good sex sessions. In the myth the sexual descriptions are allocated a negative status: they are contributory factors to death. A more subtle version of anti-promiscuity suggests that it is dehumanising, and thus offensive to gays themselves. Writing in the *Irish Times* (13 December 1986) Maeve Binchy claims that 'The great majority of Gays must resent the presentation of these explicit memoirs, with their overtones of depravity.' 'The word "gay" was never so misapplied as to this life, and the many happy homosexuals glad to live in a climate of acceptance...must wish that Orton had not left such a damning document that implies...that this is the only life for a male homosexual.' Quite apart from the cosiness about 'acceptance' and the attempt to separate gays from their culture, this review gives value to gay monogamy and puts down the hedonist, raunchy sexual round that is a unique feature of the gay scene...and one in which many *happy and long-term partnered* gays participate. Binchy's review says what many others imply, that the only good homosexual partnership is one which most nearly approximates to naff marriage.

But the attack on gay sexuality contained in the Orton myth has its vilest expression in John Osborne's *Spectator* review. For Osborne the Orton story provides occasion to bash gays in the '80s: 'Jenny may indeed live with Eric and Martin but how would she and little Teddy have tucked up with Joe and Kenneth?' 'Joe's brains peeking out between Jenny and Teddy might have given even the most dim of Brent's social workers a bit of a turn' (*Spectator*, 29 November 1986). That does for positive images and social work. Now for safer sex: Orton had 'no time for bleeding hearts only those parts which, it is now exhorted, should not be reached without benefit of condom'. This is followed later by 'No one, in those pre-Terence {sic} Higgins days, loved a fairy when she's 40'.

Repeating the Binchy strategy of keeping promiscuity out of the gay image, Osborne denies Orton was 'Gay', 'rather a ferocious bum bandit'. He has already dealt with cottaging: 'The goings-on in these homo-heavens might seem grim rather than gay'. But the accounts are 'often hilarious'. So where's the 'grim' bit? (The public lavatory as 'homo-heaven' is some sort of fantasy of Osborne's, since those places are fraught with the dangers of police entrapment and queer-bashing.) As for Halliwell, he was 'the almost perfect type of that familiar social hazard, the homosexual "wife"... They are a nightmare to hostesses and frequently an embarrassment to their other halves, a perpetual *placement* problem'. A social hazard familiar to whom? To hostesses! My dear, how *awful*. Is this a joke? If so, where does it become clear? Halliwell is said to mouth 'the classic denunciations of a discarded mistress'. There is, of course, a great deal of hatred of women expressed through the myth's identification of Halliwell as wife. Osborne's is not the only review that tells us about the hang-ups of a hetero-, rather than homo-, sexual world. It could be said that the film, too, for all its pop feminism, expresses a hatred for women that is focussed on Halliwell: while Orton drags on jeans to go out, Halliwell puts on make-up; Halliwell is the one who is jealous, can't cope, bitchy, frigid (ignoring all the evidence in the diary about Orton's own display of these moods); Halliwell is emotional, domestic, while Orton is capable, public. Part of Halliwell's ugliness as partner to a successful man is his femaleness.

'Orton' in Osborne's review is used as a device to knock homosexual culture. Those people were wrong 'who linked him with Wilde or thought he might trail clouds of saintly buggery, an English Genet, both writers dismissed by Orton as flabby and preposterous'. In particular, the Orton story can show that positive images of gays are a fake. He would have laughed at 'little Jenny's Teddy'; he was, remember, a bum bandit, not gay.

Ironically, if we observe that the Orton industry attacks homosexuality we may not be explaining its actual *appeal*. What I take to be the genuine appeal may be seen in the reviews. The *Tatler* says Orton would not have faded as a writer: 'Joe would have kept it up.' The phrase invokes his sexual potency. Against Halliwell the wife, Joe is the male – with his 'easy, cherubic swagger' (Osborne).

Continually Orton's masculinity is stressed. As we know, the emphasis on it originates with Orton himself. He was attractive to those who fancied him because he was not the flaunting queer but the tight, controlled, bit of rough; or that was his role. His diary records the adventures of his prick. His sexuality celebrates the power of his penis; its size sustains his egotism: 'He had a heavy loutish body, large cock, but not so large as to make me envious or shy' (*Diaries*, p.160). Most often he liked to fuck those younger or less powerful than him. He notes the relationship between a big prick and a large bank balance. The penis is social as well as sexual power. To this power Orton was committed.

The diary relates many sexual adventures which have supposedly shocked both contemporaries and modern reviewers. The sexual scandal is part of the Orton industry hype. But what the hype ignores is how boring the sexual adventures were. In terms of cottaging, Orton was both a part-timer and very ordinary. He was not one of those who take their sandwich-box with them, to spend the day, nor could he cope with anything outside his own fairly straight interests. The diary records how a young biker in full leather gear and helmet tried to pick him up. Orton walked away. When Orton tells the story later, Halliwell remarks he was probaby a sado-masochist and Orton that he 'behaved in a very odd way' (*Diaries*, p.247). These sniffy responses confirm how little fetishism, fantasy and sexual experiment are recorded in the diary. In order for the film to make something shocking of this element in the myth it has Orton desiring people in awkward situations (at the funeral: but it's not in the diary) or while with Halliwell (not recorded as happening in England). And it has to film *the* Holloway Road cottage orgy (what, only one cottage orgy?) as if it was something out of Fassbinder's *Querelle*, in other words conjuring up associations of Genet and arty eroticism and the enigmatic Fassbinder in order to give the scene some sort of filmic pizzazz.

As gays go, Orton was a pretty straight gay, sexually speaking. He liked to fuck; the objects happened to be boys not girls. More importantly, he was very masculine. This connects with his contempt for the effeminate, and indeed for women. Not only was Orton the sort of queer most easily accommodated by straight society, his adventures celebrate the social and sexual power of the penis. The film offered its audience the picture of a masculine sexual outlaw, who was as successful in his sexiness as in his business. The casting of Gary Oldman as Orton helped this construction. Oldman had previously played Sid Vicious, which suggests the doomed 'outlaw' element and – *at the same time* – suggests, through Oldman himself, the up and coming star; and his image fixes in our minds a permanently young Orton, since Oldman looks prettier than the photos of Orton in his thirties. The film focusses our interest in a masculinity living on the edge: perilously successful and outlaw individualist. In this sense, without being *Rambo* or *Rocky*, the film is yet another cinematic exploration, even celebration, of '80s masculinity.

The narrative defines the masculinity: it continually sets up oppositions which suggest Orton's capability against Halliwell's hopelessness. So he copes better than Halliwell in dealing with the dust-jackets trial; it's supposedly him (not Halliwell) who prevents Halliwell going to the Drama Awards lunch; and it's him, the supreme fixer, who generously sets up sex for poor old Halliwell (and never the other way round). He's the gay who can get off with girls if he wants to and who can flirt with his female agent, whereas Halliwell is trapped as the dated older homo. Orton, says the myth, represents the 'free' sexual choice uniquely available to attractive men, but not available to older 'obvious' gays or women. And he displays the irresistible power of male attraction: Orton can pick up men anywhere, even at a funeral. In the film the manliness and attraction are combined with a falsified image of commercial success: it forgets the disasters of early productions of *Sloane* and *Loot*. The myth promotes a fantasy combination of attractive masculinity and instant commercial success.

'Orton' is the man murdered by Halliwell's 'female' jealousy, a man who can both swagger with confidence and yet be attractively innocent, a blameless macho. 'Orton' sex is always a hunt, always prick-centred, and always fun (audiences are persuaded to identify with Oldman in the film). The only pressure on the masculine 'freedom' comes from the partner, the failure, the womanly one. This is the source of danger to the sexy man, not the sex itself. The story makes it legitimate to be anti-female, anti-homosexual, where these are seen to be failures in a society that prizes success; where commercial success is part of being sexy. This 'Orton' offers a mixture of qualities that are so important to right-on straight men of the '80s.

By stressing Orton's charm and success the myth manages the apparently difficult task of extracting masculine affirmation out of a homosexual story. One reason why the Orton story is so popular is that 'Orton' is the sort of male that straights find fascinating, because his 'free' adventuring masculinity offers an image for fantasy identification. Yet his sexual availability to men makes that fascination taboo, so it is often expressed as revulsion. So often when straights get involved in the Orton industry, we hear the refrain about the lovely talent, the hateful sex. That hateful sex is always mentioned, returned to with the punctuality of obsession. And here we discover the convenience of Halliwell's role. So much of the anti-homosexual prejudice is transferred onto him, as an encumbrance, a failure, an irritant – someone who brought it on himself. Insofar as Orton's promiscuity damaged Halliwell, it is to be seen as tragic: but only tragic because of the marriage. Had Orton not been 'married', the promiscuity would have affected no one. Halliwell can be blamed for being there, for being the person who transformed the charming prick-hunter into tragic victim. And to the extent that hatred may be transferred onto Halliwell, 'Orton' is left free to play the role of successful pretty man, always *inevitably* making his conquests. Thus the Halliwell-Orton story is taken over for heterosexual male self-affirmation.

Insofar as Orton agreed, in the early stages, to allow himself to be marketed this way, he was agreeing to the process which would destroy both his lover and himself. We have been through this knot. Clearly, Orton did adopt the role of straight masculine queer because he found it a sexual turn-on. But that sexual pleasure could simultaneously be exploited socially. In the context of the '60s interest in the personal lives of rising stars, Ramsay saw commercial potential in a diary of his Tangier adventures. The power of closeted, and anti-liberation, homosexual men insisted that Orton would get on as a star while he played the role of masculine charmer. In one sense, Orton's personal sexual life was nothing to do with his death. The problem was what his society made of that sexual life. His private sex fantasy was taken over by their fantasy of success. He was constructed by the world around him, and although he was ripe for such construction they had the money and power. He had lived with Halliwell for 14 years before they started to take him over. It was when those entrepreneurs and theatre people started to work on him that the relationship began to disintegrate.

They were trying to make him into the product they wanted. The Orton industry continues to construct Orton and Halliwell into a product that serves the values of a privileged heterosexual society. Let us remember, in amongst the chic and sauciness, that the product created by the Orton industry amounted to more than a myth. It also produced two corpses. That was the real crime. And in this society it remains yet unpunished.

Works Consulted

ADAMS, Stephen, *The Homosexual as Hero in Contemporary Fiction* (Barnes and Noble, 1980).

ALTMAN, Dennis, *Homosexual: Oppression and Liberation* (Allen Lane, 1971).

ALTMAN, Dennis, *The Homosexualisation of America* (Beacon Press, Boston, 1983).

BALDWIN, James, *Giovanni's Room* (Corgi, 1957/1963).

BARR, James, *Quatrefoil* (Paperback Library, 1950/1965).

BAXT, George, *A Queer Kind of Death* (Pan, 1967).

BIGSBY, C. W. E., *Joe Orton* (Methuen, 1982).

BODY BEAUTIFUL: Studies in Masculine Art vol. 2: 2 (n.d.).

BOOKER, Christopher, *The Neophiliacs* (Collins, 1969).

BOONE, Bruce, 'Gay Language as Political Praxis', *Social Text* 1 (1979).

BRAKE, Mike, 'I May Be Queer, But at Least I Am a Man: Male Hegemony and Ascribed Versus Achieved Gender', *Sexual Divisions and Society*, ed. D. L. Barker and S. Allen (Tavistock, 1976).

BRITISH MEDICAL ASSOCIATION, *Homosexuality and Prostitution* (1955).

BRITTON, Andrew, *Cary Grant: Comedy and Male Desire* (Tyneside Cinema, 1983).

BRITTON, Andrew, 'For Interpretation – Notes Against Camp', *Gay Left* 7 (1978/79).

BRONSKI, Michael, *Culture Clash: The Making of Gay Sensibility* (South End Press, Boston, 1984).

BROPHY, Brigid, *Flesh* (Corgi, 1962).

BURGESS, Anthony, *A Clockwork Orange* (Penguin, 1962/1972).

BURROUGHS, William, *The Naked Lunch* (Corgi, 1959/1974).

BURTON, Peter, *Parallel Lives* (GMP, 1985).

CAMPBELL, Michael, *Lord Dismiss Us* (Heinemann, 1967).

CAMUS, Albert, *The Rebel*, trs. A. Bower (Penguin, 1962).

CHARNEY, Maurice, *Joe Orton* (Macmillan, 1984).

CHESSER, Eustace, *Live and Let Live: The Moral of the Wolfenden Report* (May Fair, 1958).

CLARKSON, Tom, *The Wounded* (Brilliance Books, 1983; orig. 1956).

COCKBURN, Alexander and BLACKBURN, Robin (eds), *Student Power* (Penguin, 1969).

COHEN, Stanley, *Folk Devils and Moral Panics* (Paladin, 1972).

COOPER, David (ed), *The Dialectics of Liberation* (Penguin, 1968).

CROWLEY, Mart, *The Boys in the Band* (French, 1968).

COWARD, Rosalind, *Female Desire* (Paladin, 1981).

DANNECKER, Martin, *Theories of Homosexuality* (GMP, 1981).

DELANEY, Shelagh, *A Taste of Honey* (Methuen, 1959).

DOLLIMORE, Jonathan, 'The Challenge of Sexuality', *Society and Literature 1945-1970*, ed. A. Sinfield (Methuen, 1983).

DYER, Charles, *Staircase* (Penguin, 1966).

DYER, Richard, *Stars* (BFI, 1979).

DYER, Richard, *Heavenly Bodies* (Macmillan, 1987).

FERNBACH, David, *The Spiral Path* (GMP, 1981).

FIRBANK, Ronald, *Valmouth* (Penguin, 1919/1982).

FLEMING, Ian, *Moonraker* (Pan, 1955/1962).

FLEMING, Ian, *From Russia with Love* (Pan, 1957/1964).

FLETCHER, Ronald, *The Family and Marriage in Britain* (Penguin, 1962/1970).

FORSTER, E. M., *Collected Short Stories* (Penguin, 1947/1984).

GAGNON, J. H. and SIMON, W. *Sexual Deviance* (Harper and Row, 1967).

GARLAND, Rodney, *The Troubled Midnight* (W. H. Allen, 1954).

GARLAND, Rodney, *Sorcerer's Broth* (W. H. Allen, 1966).

GAY LEFT COLLECTIVE, *Homosexuality: Power and Politics* (Allison and Busby, 1980).

GEORGE, ELIOT (Gillian Freeman), *The Leather Boys* (New English Library, 1961/1969).

GILBERT, Jay, *The Goose Girl* (Consul, 1963/1965).

GOFF, Martyn, *The Youngest Director* (Brilliance Books, 1983; orig. 1961).

GOSLING, Ray, 'Dream Boy', *New Left Review* 3 (1960).

GOSLING, Ray, *Lady Albermarle's Boys* (Young Fabian pamphlet, 1961).

GOSLING, Ray, *Sum Total* (Faber, 1962).

GOUGH, J. and MACNAIR, M., *Gay Liberation in the Eighties* (Pluto, 1985).

GUNN, T., *The Sense of Movement* (Faber, 1957).

GUNN, T., *My Sad Captains* (Faber, 1962).

HALL, Stuart et al. (eds), *Policing the Crisis* (Macmillan, 1978).

HALTRECHT, Montague, *Jonah and his Mother* (Mayflower-Dell, 1964).

HAMPTON, Christopher, *When Did You Last See My Mother?* (Faber, 1967).

HARPER, Leonard J., *Teddy Boy Ahoy* (Thames-side, 1963).

HAUSER, Richard., *The Homosexual Society* (Mayflower-Dell, 1962/1965).

HEATH, Stephen, *The Sexual Fix* (Macmillan, 1982).

HEBDIGE, Dick, *Subculture* (Methuen, 1979).

HOCQUENGHEM, Guy, *Homosexual Desire*, trs. D. Dangoor (Allison and Busby, 1978).

HOPKINS, John, *This Story of Yours* (Penguin, 1969).

HUMPHREYS, Laud, *Tearoom Trade* (Duckworth, 1970).

HUNT, Albert, 'What Joe Orton Saw,' *New Society* 32 (1975).

HYDE, H. Montgomery, *The Other Love* (Heinemann, 1970).

ISLINGTON LIBRARY, Joe Orton archive (mainly newspaper cuttings).

JACKSON, Neville, *No End to the Way* (Corgi, 1965/1985).

KEESINGS CONTEMPORARY ARCHIVES, 1964-1966.

JOHNSON, Pamela H., *Cork Street, Next to the Hatter's* (Macmillan, 1965).

JOHNSON, Pamela H., *On Iniquity* (Macmillan, 1967).

JEREMY vol. 1 (1969).

LAHR, John,*Prick Up Your Ears* (Allen Lane, 1978).

LAING, R. D., *The Divided Self* (Penguin, 1960/1965).

LASCH, Christopher, *The Culture of Narcissism* (Abacus, 1979/1982).

LAUDER, Stuart, *Winger's Landfall* (Eyre and Spottiswoode, 1962).

LE CARRE, John, *The Spy Who Came in From the Cold* (Pan, 1963).

LITTLE, Jay, *Somewhere Between the Two* (Paperback Library, 1965).

MACINNES, Colin, *Absolute Beginners* (Allison and Busby, 1980; orig. 1959).

MAGEE, Bryan, *One in Twenty* (Secker and Warburg, 1966/1968).

MARCUSE, Herbert, *One Dimensional Man* (Abacus, 1964/1972).

MARCUSE, Herbert, *Eros and Civilisation* (Routledge, 1956/1987).

MAROWITZ, Charles et al. (eds), *New Theatre Voices of the Fifties and Sixties* (Methuen, 1965/1981).

MARTIN, Kenneth, *Aubade* (Chapman and Hall, 1957).

MASTERS, R. E. L., *The Homosexual Revolution* (Belmont, 1964).

MAUGHAM, Robin, *The Man with Two Shadows* (Four Square, 1958/1967).

METCALF, A. and HUMPHRIES, M., *The Sexuality of Men* (Pluto, 1985).

MIELI, Mario, *Homosexuality and Liberation*, trans. D. Fernbach (GMP, 1980).

MITCHELL, Julian, *Imaginary Toys* (Four Square, 1961/1964).

MIZER, Robert, *Athletic Model Guild* (GMP, 1987).

MORSE, Benjamin, *Adolescent Sexual Behaviour* (Monarch, 1964).

MOSS, Simon, *Cock-ups* (Faber, 1984).

NATIONAL DEVIANCY CONFERENCE (eds), *Permissiveness and Control* (Macmillan, 1980).

NORMAN, Frank, *Fings Ain't Wot They Used t'Be* (Secker and Warburg, 1960).

NUTTALL, Jeff, *Bomb Culture* (Paladin, 1968/1970).

ONSTOTT, K. and HORNER, L., *Child of the Sun* (Pan, 1966).

ORTON, Joe, 'The Biter Bit', interview with Simon Trussler, *Plays and Players* (August 1965).

ORTON, Joe, *The Complete Plays* (Methuen, 1976).

ORTON, Joe, *Entertaining Mr Sloane* in *New English Dramatists 8* (Penguin, 1965).

ORTON, Joe, *The Erpingham Camp* (Methuen, 1967).

ORTON, Joe, *Funeral Games* (Methuen, 1970).

ORTON, Joe, *The Good and Faithful Servant* (Methuen, 1970).

ORTON, Joe, *Head to Toe* (Panther, 1971).

ORTON, Joe, *Loot* (Methuen, 1967).

ORTON, Joe, *Loot*, ed. Andrew Mayne (Methuen, 1985).

ORTON, Joe, *The Orton Diaries*, ed. John Lahr (Methuen, 1986).

ORTON, Joe, *The Ruffian on the Stair,* in *New Radio Drama* (BBC, 1966).

ORTON, Joe, *The Ruffian on the Stair* (Methuen, 1967).

ORTON, Joe, 'Until She Screams', *Evergreen Review* (May 1970).

ORTON, Joe, *Up Against It* (Methuen, 1979).

ORTON, Joe, unpublished papers exhibited in National Theatre (now in Boston?); unreferenced quotations in text are from this source.

OSBORNE, John, *Under Plain Cover* (Evans Bros. 1963).

OSBORNE, John, *A Patriot for Me* (Faber, 1966).

PEYREFITTE, Roger, *Diplomatic Diversions* (Panther, 1953/1968).

PEYREFITTE, Roger, *Special Friendships* (Panther, 1958/1964).

PHILLIPS, Thomas H., *The Bitterweed Path* (Brown, Watson, 1966).

PLUMMER, Douglas (pseud.), *Queer People* (W. H. Allen, 1963).

PLUMMER, Kenneth, *The Making of the Modern Homosexual* (Hutchinson, 1981).

PRAUNHEIM, Rosa von, *Army of Lovers* (GMP, 1980).

PURDY, James, *63: Dream Palace* (Panther, 1961).

PURDY, James, *Eustace Chisholm and the Works* (GMP, 1984; orig. 1967).

RAVEN, Simon, *The Feathers of Death* (Panther, 1959/1964).

RAVEN, Simon, 'Boys Will Be Boys', *Encounter* (November 1960).

RECHY, John, *City of Night* (Panther, 1964/1984).

RECHY, John, *The Sexual Outlaw* (Futura, 1978).

REES, Judge Tudor and USILL, H. (eds), *They Stand Apart* (Heinemann, 1955).

RENAULT, Mary, *The Charioteer*, (New English Library, 1953/1977).

ROBINSON, Paul, *The Sexual Radicals* (Paladin, 1972).

SCHOFIELD, Michael, *Sociological Aspects of Homosexuality* (Longmans, 1965).

SHEPHERD, Simon, 'Edna's Last Stand', *Renaissance and Modern Studies* 22 (1978).

SOPHOCLES, *The Theban Plays*, trs. E. F. Watling (Penguin, 1947/1983).

SOUTHERN, T. and HOFFENBERG, M., *Candy* (New English Library, 1958/1970).

STOREY, David, *Radcliffe* (Penguin, 1963).

THOMPSON, Denys (ed.), *Discrimination and Popular Culture* (Penguin, 1964).

TIMM, no. 1.

TYNAN, Kenneth, *A View of the English Stage* (Methuen, 1975/1984).

VIDAL, Gore, *The City and the Pillar* (Four Square, 1948/1965).

VIDAL, Gore, *A Thirsty Evil* (Granada, 1956/1974).

VIDAL, Gore, *Myra Breckinridge* (Granada, 1968/1983).

WEEKS, Jeffrey, *Coming Out* (Quartet, 1977).

WEEKS, Jeffrey, *Sex, Politics and Society* (Longmans, 1981).

WEST, D. J., *Homosexuality* (Penguin, 1955/1969).

WESTWOOD, Gordon, *A Minority* (Longmans, 1960).

WILDEBLOOD, Peter, *Against the Law* (Penguin, 1955/1959).

WILDEBLOOD, Peter, *A Way of Life* (Weidenfeld and Nicholson, 1956).

WILLIAMS, Raymond, 'Britain in the 1960s', *The Long Revolution* (Penguin, 1961/1965).

WILSON, Angus, *Hemlock and After* (Granada, 1952/1979).

WILSON, Colin, *Ritual in the Dark* (Pan, 1960/1962).

WILSON, Elizabeth, *Only Halfway to Paradise* (Tavistock, 1980).

WILSON, Elizabeth, *Mirror Writing* (Virago, 1982).

A Selection of non-fiction from
GMP - The Gay Men's Press

Michael Baker
Our Three Selves

The acclaimed biography of lesbian novelist Radclyffe Hall.
0-85449-042-6   400pp   £6.95

Paul Binding
Lorca: the Gay Imagination

An original study of the life and verse of Spain's greatest
modern poet, Frederico Garcia Lorca.
0-907040-36-5 pbk   208pp   £4.95
0-907040-37-3 cased   £12.50

Alan Bray
Homosexuality in Renaissance England

The author explores a crucial period in the evolution of
English society from a new and revealing angle. New revised
edition with index.
"An intelligent, scholarly work of social history" – Hugh
Trevor-Roper, *The Sunday Times*.
0-85449-095-7 cased 160pp £7.95

Michael Elliman & Frederick Roll
The Pink Plaque Guide to London

The delightful compendium of gay history with 100 famous
gays and lesbians – potted histories and illustrations
throughout.
0-85449-026-4 pbk   224pp   £6.95

Tobias Schneebaum
Keep the River on Your Right

A moving account of life among the Akaramas, a primitive
Peruvian tribe.
0-85449-061-2 pbk   192pp   £4.50

Joao S.Trevisan
Perverts in Paradise

This survey of gay culture and history vividly conveys the
exuberant and sensual texture of Brazilian society.
0-907040-78-0 pbk   208pp   £5.95

GMP books can be ordered from any bookshop in the UK, and from specialised bookshops overseas. If you prefer to order by mail, please send full retail price plus £1.00 for postage and packing to: GMP Publishers Ltd (M.O.), PO Box 247, London N17 9QR. (For Access/Eurocard/Mastercharge/Visa/American Express, give number and signature.) Comprehensive mail-order catalogue also available.

In North America order from Alyson
Publications Inc.
40 Plympton St, Boston MA 02118, USA.

NAME AND ADDRESS
IN BLOCK LETTERS PLEASE:

Name ....

Address ....

....

....

....